GUATEMALA
THE HUMAN RIGHTS RECORD

Amnesty International Publicatio

First published 1987 by Amnesty International Publications
1 Easton Street, London WC1X 8DJ, United Kingdom

Copyright Amnesty International Publications 1987

ISBN 0 86210 1182
AI Index: AMR 34/04/87
Original Language: English

Printed in England by Staples Printers Rochester Limited,
Love Lane, Rochester, Kent.

Contents

t, military and security officials including the
e and Chief of the Joint Chiefs of Staff,
or and Foreign Affairs, the Deputy Minister
ey General of the Republic, the President of
e Supreme Court, the Chief Medical Adviser
members of the Directive Committee of the
It met the commanders or directors of various
tallations and training schools throughout the
head of the Civil Affairs Unit of the Army,
ilitary Base No. 1 in Guatemala City, Military
ala, also in Guatemala City, and the military
go. Discussions were held with the head of the
n Sacatepéquez, the commanders and legal
al Police and the Director of the Intelligence
al Police, the *Departamento de Investigaciones*
partment of Technical Investigations. The del-
esentatives of non-government associations and

before the mission that their discussions would
s the safeguards against human rights violations
legal system and the application of standards
ce for the protection of human rights and the
abuse. Amnesty International had also indicated
ussing the programs for training members of
ry and police forces in internationally accepted
r law enforcement officials, and standards such
Conventions of 1949, on the protection of victims
cular Common Article 3, governing the conduct
ned conflict not of an international nature.
85 Amnesty International submitted a memor-
he findings of its mission, to both the out-going
t of General Mejía Víctores and the newly elected
sident Vinicio Cerezo Arévalo before it took office.
included a series of recommendations — concrete
mnesty International believes necessary to safe-
ts in the country.[1] Following a pattern established
tary governments the Cerezo administration did
memorandum.
n a letter to President Cerezo, Amnesty Interna-
t a dialogue with the new government. The organ-
its memorandum and once more urged that steps
ect human rights and to investigate past abuses.

ons are reproduced as Appendix I.

MAP OF GUATEMALA

■ Capital
● Capital of Departamento

MEXICO

BELIZE

● Flores

PETEN

CHIAPAS

Poptún ●

CARIBBEAN SEA

Puerto Barrios

San Mateo Ixtatán ●

ALTA VERAPAZ

IZABAL
Tenedores ●

Ixil
Triangle ● Chajul
● Cotzal
Nebaj

● Cobán

Lake Izabal

● Morales

Ixtahuacán ●
Aguacatán ●

Huehuetenango ●

EL QUICHÉ

BAJA VERAPAZ

Santa Cruz del Quiché ●

● Rabinal ● Salamá

Zacapa

San Marcos ●

Totonicapán ●
● Chichicastenango

● San José Poaquil

El Progreso

Chiquimula

Quezaltenango ●
Sacatepéquez ● ● Cantel

Sololá ●

● San Martín Jilotepeque
Comalapa ●
Patzún ● ● Chimaltenango

Jalapa

HONDURAS

San Pedro La Laguna ●
● San Lucas Tolimán

Antigua Guatemala
■ Guatemala City
● San José Pinula

Retalhuleu ●
Mazatenango ●

SACATEPEQUEZ ● Amatitlán

SUCHITEPEQUEZ

Escuintla ●

Cuilapa ●

Jutiapa ●

SANTA ROSA

Puerto San José ●

EL SALVADOR

PACIFIC OCEAN

Unless shown, departments have the same name as their capitals.

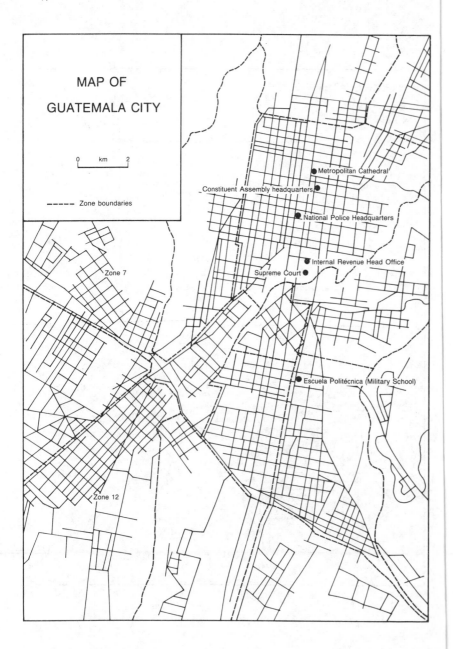

MAP OF

GUATEMALA CITY

0   km   2

- - - - - Zone boundaries

Metropolitan Cathedral

Constituent Assembly headquarters

National Police Headquarters

Internal Revenue Head Office

Supreme Court

Zone 7

Escuela Politécnica (Military School)

Zone 12

Pre

Amnesty International has recei
rights violations in Guatemala for
have come from a variety of sour
tions, government bodies, professi
Guatemalan and foreign journalis
tematically collected testimonies
survivors of torture or abduction
serving members of and defectors
forces about human rights violations
Amnesty International has also e
foreign delegations of inquiry.

Amnesty International has visited
of occasions and collected first-han
witnesses. In 1984, for example, it vis
in Mexico for this purpose and gat
within Guatemala and in the camp
border raids by the Guatemalan mili

Government officials have periodica
the effect that Guatemala had nothin
was open to visits from human rights i
Amnesty International. Despite such
had, for more than a decade, received
the authorities to its repeated submissi
of human rights violations. Nor did A
a direct invitation to visit the countr
Guatemalan Ambassador to France
mandated to negotiate the terms of re
visit. These were agreed and an Amn
visited the country in April 1985. It
organization last went to Guatemala
tigations into human rights violations.

The delegation was led by Rear Ad
President of the organization's Dutch S
members of the organization's Intern

Amnesty International also welcomed new legislation which was to be implemented, including improved procedures of *amparo* and *habeas corpus*.[2]

At the time of writing, November 1986, no response had been received to this letter.

In a series of detailed communications Amnesty International has called upon successive administrations to investigate reports of torture, "disappearance" and political killing and to take steps to end such abuses of human rights. These issues have also been raised in a number of publications. A *Special Briefing Paper on Guatemala* was published in 1976 following an Amnesty International mission to Guatemala that year. In 1979 Amnesty International again sent a mission to Guatemala and subsequently published a memorandum based on its findings, which was submitted to the government. In 1981 the organization restated its long-standing concerns in the country in *Guatemala: A Government Program of Political Murder,* a report which included a list of some 615 cases of "disappearance" between mid-1978 and November 1980. In 1982 the organization published *Massive extrajudicial executions in rural areas under President General Efraín Ríos Montt*, and listed a series of incidents in which over 2,000 Indian peasants were reported killed.

Amnesty International has also repeatedly raised the pattern of gross human rights violations in Guatemala with international organizations such as the United Nations (UN) and the Organization of American States (OAS).

In this book Amnesty International publishes an edited selection of the many reports and documents it has compiled from its long-term research work on the country. The book concentrates on events since March 1982 when a military coup brought General Efraín Ríos Montt to power. The book also includes previously unpublished material. Chapter I, for example, follows the lines of the memorandum which Amnesty International submitted in December 1985 to the present government before it took office and to the out-going military government of General Mejía Víctores. To that has been added eye-witness testimony collected by Amnesty International's mission to Guatemala, that year.

Chapter II, although drawn from an Amnesty International report of July 1982, contains material hitherto unpublished by the organization including detailed eye-witness testimony of massacres of entire villages during the Ríos Montt administration.

Chapter III is a brief account of human rights violations which occurred while Decree 46-82 of July 1982 was in force. This law

---

[2]   The text of this letter is published in Appendix II.

enabled General Ríos Montt to use military tribunals empowered to impose the death penalty to silence his opponents. This chapter also contains previously unpublished material.

Chapter IV examines "disappearances" between August 1983 and January 1986 under General Oscar Humberto Mejía Víctores. Although not a new phenomenon, the resurgence of "disappearances" in Guatemala became Amnesty International's major concern during the Mejía Víctores administration.

In Chapter V Amnesty International analyses the failure of the Guatemalan judicial system to protect basic human rights and traces the history of the *Grupo de Apoyo Mutuo por el Aparecimiento con Vida de Nuestros Hijos, Esposos, Padres y Hermanos* (GAM), the Mutual Support Group for the Appearance Alive of our Relatives. GAM was formed by relatives of the "disappeared" who have taken great risks to try and trace them. In 1985 two GAM leaders were killed in circumstances which strongly suggested official involvement. In this chapter Amnesty International presents the evidence it has collected indicating that their deaths were not accidental.

The tide of human rights violations has abated since President Cerezo, the first civilian to lead the country in 20 years, took office. But Amnesty International continues to receive reports of the finding of unidentified, tortured corpses, "disappearance", and individual "death squad" killings.[3]

---

[3] Appendix III gives a list of incidents reported to Amnesty International to have occurred between January and mid-May 1986. Amnesty International's information suggests the official security forces were involved in each of these incidents.

Introduction

In almost two decades of military rule in Guatemala deaths without number have followed flagrant breaches of fundamental human rights. Arbitrary arrest, torture, "disappearance" and political killings were everyday realities, affecting thousands of Guatemala's seven-and-a-half million people. Previous administrations refused to undertake serious investigations into reported abuses or to take steps to stop them. Instead they blamed the abuses on so-called "death squads" which they characterized as extremist groups "out of government control". Evidence that these "death squads" were government created and supported and drawn from the ranks of the army and the police force was disregarded. The killers, the torturers, the kidnappers — whether they operated as the uniformed forces of state security or in plain clothes in the guise of so-called "death squads" — have never been brought to justice.

Not only have the perpetrators escaped punishment, they have now been put beyond the reach of the law. Before handing over to the incoming government in January 1986, General Mejía Víctores warned in a statement widely quoted in the national and international press that "it would be a mistake to move against the army ... The army would not allow it".

And on the very eve of his departure he proclaimed an amnesty for "all people implicated in political crimes and related common crimes during the period from 23 March 1982 to 14 January 1986" in the form of Decree Law 08-86. This decree rules out any possibility of prosecuting the perpetrators of such crimes or their accomplices. Prosecution of anyone who concealed these crimes is also ruled out. According to the local and foreign press this and other decree laws passed in the final days of the Mejía Víctores administration, appear to have been drafted in agreement with the incoming civilian government of President Vinicio Cerezo Arévalo. During his presidential campaign he had made it clear that he would not sanction the prosecution of members of the military and security forces for past human rights violations. The *International Herald Tribune* quoted him on 4 November 1985 as saying that: "We are not going to be able to investigate the past. We would have to put the entire army in jail." He reinforced this principle after taking office by saying that: "Everyone was involved in violence. But this has to be left behind. If I start investigations and trials, I am only encouraging revenge".

Within Guatemala there have been efforts to persuade the new government to reverse this policy. Members of congress attempted to amend Decree Law 08-86, but abandoned their efforts when it became apparent that there would be insufficient votes for repeal. In February GAM presented President Cerezo with a list of 959 people who had "disappeared" between 1980 and 1985, and a list of some 100 police and military officers who they said were responsible. Although agreeing that past "disappearances" will be investigated, President Cerezo maintains that he cannot rescind Decree 08-86 and is therefore unable to prosecute those found responsible.

Amnesty International believes that unless and until past abuses are thoroughly investigated and justice is done, human rights remain at grave risk in Guatemala. The copious information presented in this book shows that there is enough evidence to investigate the crimes which have been committed in Guatemala for more than 20 years. The guilty must be brought to justice if the present government is to uphold its stated commitment to protect human rights.

The military in power

The counter-insurgency apparatus originally developed to combat Guatemala's guerrilla movement in the 1960s was later used to quell all real or perceived opposition to the government. It was reactivated in 1978 by General Romeo Lucas García in the face of the resurgence of armed opposition and continued throughout his four years in power. Once again, the victims were students, workers, politicians, Indian peasants from the Guatemalan highlands, priests, nuns, doctors, lawyers and others.

Since then the police, the army, and "death squads" acting with official sanction have been responsible for torture, "disappearance" and extrajudicial execution on a gross scale. People have been seized or gunned down in broad daylight by police and soldiers. Others have been abducted or murdered by heavily armed men in civilian clothes using weapons and vehicles issued to government agencies, while uniformed police or army units looked on and made no effort to intervene. Bodies have been found in the bottom of ravines, dumped at the roadside or buried in secret graves. Some could be identified as people who had been abducted by the security forces. Others were too badly mutilated for identification.

General Efraín Ríos Montt, who seized power in March 1982, continued his predecessor's counter-insurgency operations. Guatemalan troops penetrated deep into the countryside ostensibly to eliminate any logistic support the armed opposition might find among the rural indigenous Indian peasantry but in fact clearing these areas of their non-combatant civilian population in a concentrated spate of massacres.

Untold numbers died during the administrations of General Lucas García and General Ríos Montt. Estimates vary, but all put the victims in the tens of thousands. In March 1984 the Juvenile Division of the Guatemalan Supreme Court asked the country's mayors to draw up lists of how many children had lost parents since 1980 as a result of political violence. In September 1984 the Guatemalan press reported that the court's preliminary findings suggested that some 100,000 children (and perhaps as many as 200,000) had lost at least one parent and that some 20 per cent of them were orphans.

Other peasants in areas attacked by the Guatemalan army fled for their lives — to other parts of the country or across the border into crowded refugee camps in Mexico. Even there they were not safe. Guatemalan troops staged raids into camps on the other side of the border and either forced refugees back to the country at gunpoint or killed them on the spot. During an Amnesty International research trip to the Mexico-Guatemala border area in 1984, Mexican doctors showed the delegation death certificates of refugees killed on Mexican soil by Guatemalan troops. The victims were men, women, old people and children, some of them mutilated after death. One woman had been 36 weeks pregnant when she was killed. The body of an 11-year-old boy was found with the genitals sliced off.

The Guatemalan authorities have repeatedly claimed that the thousands of Indian peasants killed in rural Guatemala were in fact the victims of the guerrilla attacks, had died fighting in armed confrontations with government forces or had been caught in crossfire between the guerrillas and the army. In the context of the civil conflict which has emerged in recent years Amnesty International has received reports that guerrilla groups have carried out execution-style killings of people suspected of being government "spies". However, after studying the evidence in the cases reported to it Amnesty International has concluded that the great majority of killings were committed by government forces.

After General Mejía Víctores came to power in August 1983, human rights violations appeared to be more selective than had been the case under Generals Lucas García and Ríos Montt. However, although selective, such abuses continued to be both grave and widespread, and chief among them was the phenomenon of "disappearance".

The term "disappearance" first entered the international human rights vocabulary as a result of events in Guatemala, where it emerged as a dramatic problem in the 1960s. Amnesty International considers that people have "disapppeared" when there are reasonable grounds for believing they were taken into custody by the authorities or their agents, the authorities deny that the victim is in their custody or the custody of their agents and there are reasonable grounds to disbelieve that denial. In these circumstances the "disappeared" are likely to be tortured or killed, or detained for a long period, without any legal protection whatsoever. This is why "disappearances" are of major concern to Amnesty International.

In a report on Guatemala published in 1976 the organization pointed out that "the vast majority of the 'disappeared', when located are found to have been the victims of violent death. Many are found with signs of torture or mutilation along roadsides or in ravines, floating in plastic bags in lakes and rivers or buried in mass graves in the countryside . . ."

Since then successive military governments have claimed that those responsible for "disappearances" are organizations of both the left and right who are beyond their control. In fact, after studying thousands of cases over many years Amnesty International has concluded that most political abductions have been carried out by serving and reserve members of all branches of the Guatemalan military and security forces, operating in the guise of so-called "death squads" under the orders of their superior officers. The "death squads" were officially formed during the 1960s' counter-insurgency campaign. They have since provided a convenient fiction for successive administrations who could claim that waves of "disappearances" and extrajudicial executions of government opponents had been the work of "extremist groups" which were beyond their control.

A civilian government and a new constitution

On 14 January 1986 Christian Democrat Vinicio Cerezo Arévalo assumed the presidency in Guatemala. He heads the country's first civilian government elected since 1966. Throughout Guatemala the elections which brought him to power were greeted with fireworks and bonfires in traditional religious ceremonies symbolising "driving out the devil".

The new President himself publicly explained that "the devil" was Guatemala's past with its history of the suppression of fundamental freedoms. After the experience of some 20 years of military rule the election of a civilian government raised hopes that respect for human rights would be restored in Guatemala. President Cerezo had said that he came to the presidency in January 1986 with "the political will to respect the rights of man".

He is to govern under a new constitution which includes articles designed to protect human rights. For example, a Human Rights Commission to be made up of representatives from each of the political parties, and the office of Human Rights Attorney are to be established. The Human Rights Commission is mandated to improve understanding of human rights at all levels. It is also to investigate complaints of human rights violations and recommend to the government measures it should adopt to safeguard human rights.

However, it was only in November, some 10 months after President Cerezo had taken office, that legislation for the appointment of a Human Rights Attorney was finally approved. At the time of writing the attorney had not been appointed.

The new constitution further stipulates that, in future, international conventions to which Guatemala is a party will prevail in principle over the country's own laws. As an example of this, Guatemala's Foreign Minister announced to the UN Commission of Human Rights, during its February–March 1986 session, that Guatemala would no longer impose the death penalty for ordinary crimes related to political crimes. He also told the Commission that the new government had agreed to hold talks with the International Committee of the Red Cross (ICRC), in Guatemala. (The ICRC has been seeking entrance to Guatemala for many years.) Initial talks held in March were to deal with terms of reference for any future ICRC activity in the country. Reportedly, no agreement was reached.

In the weeks before President Cerezo came to office the Constituent Assembly also approved new *amparo* and *exhibición personal* (*habeas corpus*) procedures through Decree 1-86 of 8 January 1986. This act stipulates that *habeas corpus* may be applied for in writing, by telephone or verbally by the aggrieved party or by any other person. Article 95 of the act specifies that "disappeared" people should be sought in centres of detention, prisons or any other place where it is indicated, suggested or suspected that they might be found. The new act also specifies that a writ of *habeas corpus* cannot be suspended until all due legal steps have been taken in the interests of the person on whose behalf the writ was filed.

However, the outgoing military government left its own legacy in the form of a series of decree laws passed in its final days in office. These new measures dealt with such issues as the investigation and prosecution of past abuses and appeared intended to ensure that the army continued to control civilian matters, including refugee questions and regional development plans.

Investigation of past abuses

The new measure of most relevance to Amnesty International's human rights concerns was Decree 08-86, dated 10 January 1986. "In the interests of strengthening peace and social harmony", this decree promulgated an amnesty for "political crimes and related common crimes, for the period 23 March 1982 [when General Ríos Montt came to power] and 14 January 1986", the date of President Cerezo's inauguration. Under this law, it would not be possible to initiate or pursue prosecutions against the authors of such crimes, their accomplices, nor against anyone who had concealed such acts. The measure was similar to previous amnesty measures passed since the military coup of March 1982, all clearly intended to prevent the prosecution of military and police personnel for human rights abuses.

Upon taking power, President Cerezo declared that he intended to solve the problem of political violence and prevent future violations of human rights through improved legal structures and processes. He told the international press: "I am going to be really tough on violence from the right and from the left, within the boundaries of the law, even military officers will feel the full weight of the judicial system". But he had decided not to investigate past abuses, stating that the government intended to offer the guerrillas an amnesty and that he believed it would be "politically naive to prosecute or imprison officers while pardoning the insurgents". According to the *International Herald Tribune* he stated that he could not: "condemn one side of the confrontation, put the army in jail, and free the guerrillas". He further declared that even had he wished to initiate proceedings for past violations, the amnesty law would have prevented him from doing so, and maintained that any effort to amend or repeal the measure on the part of the executive would constitute interference with the judiciary.[1] Instead he suggested that injured parties pursue such matters through the courts. However, in widely reported press conferences he simultaneously expressed the opinion that because of

---

[1] Since the military coup in March 1982, and in accordance with the Fundamental Statute of Government of 28 April 1982, under which subsequent military administrations have governed, legislative powers were placed in the hands of the Executive (the Congress having been dissolved), which governed through such decree laws. These measures required only approval by the Cabinet and publication in the official record to attain the force of law. The new constitution under which President Cerezo is to govern recognizes in its Article 16 the validity in judicial terms of such decrees and of all administrative measures issued since March 1982. Nonetheless jurists who have commented on the judicial validity of these decree laws, including those issued just before President Cerezo took office, have declared that they need only remain valid until the sovereign constitutional organ (the congress) decides to derogate, annul, repeal or reform them.

the "silent" and "dirty war" in Guatemala in recent years, during which "the military committed excesses against the civilian population . . . it would in fact be very difficult for the judiciary to obtain the necessary evidence to prosecute crimes committed by previous governments".

Despite the President's announced intention of strengthening legal procedures to protect human rights, the judiciary has thus far declined to play a major role to this end. Towards the end of February 1986, the Supreme Court did announce that it intended to initiate an inquiry into the alleged existence of secret torture and detention centres throughout the country. However, Supreme Court President Edmundo Vásquez Martínez did not elaborate on the terms of reference or methods of such an inquiry for fear of "hindering the operation". He is also reported to have announced that he opposed the participation of the judiciary in any commission to investigate the whereabouts of the thousands of Guatemalans who have "disappeared" following arrest, and that he considered it "extremely difficult" for the "disappeared" to have remained alive, in view of the time which had elapsed. Meanwhile the Head of Public Relations of the Armed Forces, Captain Juan Fernando Cifuentes Herrera, declared that "there are no secret jails on any military base, since constitutional guidelines prohibit their existence". Simultaneously, however, the Guatemalan press quoted Minister of Defence General Jaime Hernández Méndez as acknowledging that captured opponents were generally held in unauthorized prisons at military barracks. In March President Cerezo announced that a special commission would be formed to investigate "disappearances" and that his aim was to provide responses to their families.[2] However he continued to maintain that he could not rescind Decree 08-86, and was therefore

---

[2]   Under the previous administration, two similar bodies, the *Comisión para la Paz* (Peace Commission) and the *Comisión Tripartita* (Tripartite Commission), had been formed in March 1984 and November 1984 respectively to inquire among other things into the fate of the "disappeared". The Peace Commission was directed, among other things, to secure the effective protection for all Guatemalans of the fundamental rights and freedoms established in law. It was also directed to ensure that violations of these rights would be investigated and punished. Representatives of the church, the press, USAC, business and professional associations were appointed to the Commission, as well as from the Ministries of Interior and Labour and the army. It dissolved itself in May 1984, when several of its prominent members withdrew on the grounds that the commission was effectively inoperative in the face of official violence. The Tripartite Commission, made up of representatives from the Public Ministry and the Ministries of the Interior and Defence, also disbanded itself, in June 1985, after reporting that it had been unable to clarify the whereabouts of a single one of the many hundreds of "disappearance" cases that had been denounced to it by relatives of the "disappeared" and local and international human rights groups.

unable to prosecute anyone found responsible for these abuses.

In May President Cerezo met representatives of GAM, following which the government announced that it would support a new joint commission to investigate "disappearances". The commission would be made up of representatives appointed by the government, others to be designated by GAM to represent the academic and trade union sectors, and international observers. GAM asked that the new body begin its work by 30 June and continue functioning for at least 10 months. GAM also asked for the resources to carry out its own investigations, announcing that it was ready to ask forensic scientists to exhume the hundreds of bodies buried in unmarked graves throughout the country.

However, it was later announced that the commission had been cancelled indefinitely on the grounds that it would interfere with the Supreme Court's examination of the writs of *habeas corpus* that have been presented to it, said to number 1,467.

In the meantime, the President has announced that relatives of "disappeared" people officially declared dead would be entitled to benefits. However, the basis on which such declarations would be made and the nature of the benefits have not been made clear.

Disbanding of the DIT — Guatemala's secret police

At apparent variance with President Cerezo's declaration that he did not intend to prosecute anyone for human rights violations, were reports that shortly after taking office he ordered a raid by the special operations unit of the National Police, the *Brigada de Operaciones Especiales* (BROE), Special Operations Brigade, on the headquarters of the intelligence division of the DIT. Initially it was reported that 600 DIT agents had been taken to the National Police Second Division headquarters for questioning and that charges were to be brought against some 115 of them.

The agency itself was reportedly to be disbanded, and a new "more professional" *Policía de Investigaciones Criminales*, Criminal Investigations Unit, established in its place. According to the Minister of the Interior, Juan José Rodil Peralta, this was intended to "dispel the fear and terror that people currently have of this corps and its members". Until the new agency was operational, President Cerezo announced that "in the interests of diminishing existing violence", army intelligence would give information directly to the Ministry of the Interior. DIT agents not charged with crimes were to be offered the opportunity for retraining and integration into regular uniformed units of the Guatemalan police. Two hundred agents reportedly took up this offer while a further 100 were reportedly dismissed from the police. Those dismissed were reportedly being disciplined because they had been involved in car theft, fraud and other ordinary crimes, and not because of human rights violations. It has also been reported that none of the leadership of the agency has been disciplined, while in the weeks leading up to the shake-up, several key agents were transferred from the DIT to G-2 army intelligence units. By June, only one DIT agent had been charged (with carrying the gun of a murdered policeman), and it was not clear whether even he remained in custody.

Following the announcement of the DIT's demise, several people reportedly came forward to denounce crimes allegedly committed by its operatives, but Amnesty International does not know of any government actions taken as a result.[3]

International reaction: the UN Commission on Human Rights

In a resolution passed at its February–March 1986 session, the UN Commission on Human Rights expressed its satisfaction at the new government's declared intention of promoting respect for human rights and the measures it had so far taken to secure this. Encouraging the new government to continue to take effective measures to ensure that all civilian and military authorities and agencies fully respect human rights and fundamental freedoms, the resolution substantially altered the terms of reference of the UN's monitoring of human rights in Guatemala.

The Commission's March 1986 resolution decided to terminate the mandate of the Special Rapporteur, previously appointed by the Commission to study the human rights situation in Guatemala. It decided instead to "to continue to observe the situation of human

---

[3]   The DIT itself was established — and its predecessor, the *Cuerpo de Detectivos* (Detective Corps, itself known by a series of names over the years, including the *Policía Judicial*, the Judicial Police) declared disbanded — during the administration of General Efraín Ríos Montt (March 1982 to August 1983) in what was at the time said to be a restructuring of security units frequently cited as being responsible for human rights violations. The current Minister of the Interior advised the Ríos Montt government in this restructuring, which saw the dismissal of some 200 *judiciales*. However, AI has received testimony from former security agents who have stated that, in fact, both under the administration of General Ríos Montt and his successor General Mejía Víctores, only the names of security agencies were changed. Those dismissed by General Ríos Montt were reincorporated into the newly named service by General Mejía Víctores, and the personnel employed by the police and their working methods remained essentially the same. DIT directors themselves had already told the Amnesty International delegation which visited Guatemala in April 1985 that the agency had by then taken measures to "cleanse itself" of agents who had committed crimes or misdemeanours.

rights in Guatemala" through a Special Representative charged with receiving and evaluating information from the government about the implementation of legislation to protect human rights as well as its efforts to guarantee fundamental freedoms. The previous requirement that an interim report on human rights be presented by the Special Rapporteur to the General Assembly has also been dropped. The Special Representative is asked only to submit a report to the next session of the Commission on Human Rights. The 1986 resolution also drops the request that the Commission on Human Rights consider further steps for securing effective respect for human rights and fundamental freedoms in the country.

Finally, the new resolution requests that the UN Secretary General provide whatever advice and assistance the government requests to help protect human rights and fundamental freedoms in Guatemala.

In their own addresses to the Commission during its February–March 1986 session, Guatemala's Foreign Minister and its Minister of Special Affairs vigorously declared their country's intention to return to respect for human rights and thanked the Commission for its previous vigilance which, they said, had helped make such progress possible. Both asked for the Commission's continued assistance.

Government response to international concern

There have been indications that the new government intends to be more responsive to concern from abroad about human rights violations in the country. A number of Guatemala's ambassadors have systematically begun to respond to expressions of concern about reported human rights violations by denying government involvement. Amnesty International has received several responses from the Presidential Palace to its own inquiries regarding reports of human rights abuses. On 22 May 1986, for example, the Public Relations Secretary of the Presidency responded to expressions of concern about reports of renewed threats and harassment directed at GAM, by declaring that the Guatemalan Government respected fundamental human rights and was therefore investigating the allegations. He stressed that organizations such as GAM "who opposed the government through the defence of human or constitutional rights . . . enjoyed the necessary security as provided by the government". He also stated that the administration itself was the most interested in clarifying the cases of Guatemalans who had "disappeared" under previous administrations. He said that the number of acts of political violence, including "disappearances" and killings, which had reached massive proportions under earlier governments had undoubtedly diminished since President Cerezo took office. However, his letter concluded in a manner reminiscent of previous administrations when he suggested that Amnesty International should not immediately think of the government when acts of violence were reported: "The truth is that armed groups operating secretly (of the right and like the guerrillas for example) were those carrying out the acts of violence, which in many cases had an irresponsible impact upon the civilian population."

Despite this new willingness on the part of the Guatemalan officials to respond to expressions of concern regarding human rights issues and the measures announced by the new government, Amnesty International remains concerned about certain aspects of the steps taken, and has noted that human rights violations continue to be reported in the country.

Amnesty International's continuing concerns in Guatemala

Since President Cerezo came to office there have been reports in the local and international press of the finding of unidentified corpses, and of individual "death squad"-style killings. The bi-monthly news review *Latin American Monitor* reported in its January–February 1986 edition, for example, that three tortured bodies were found on 23 January dumped in plastic bags with their hands and feet bound, while the following week, two bullet-riddled bodies were recovered from the beach at Puerto San José, Escuintla.

In the March/April edition, the same source reported that some 55 people had died as a result of violence in Guatemala during January, while opposition sources noted reports that 87 murders had occurred in Guatemala in the two weeks following the new President's inauguration and attributed 56 of these to the security forces and right-wing "death squads". On 8 February the local press and an international wire agency reported the President's acknowledgment that 76 people had died in violent circumstances in the first three weeks of his term of office.

These statistics are difficult to interpret, since there is often not enough detail to determine with any certainty the circumstances in which the victim died, nor is it always clear that those whose bodies were found had been killed since the new government came to office. For example, Amnesty International has noted that the figure of 87 murders reported by opposition sources to have occurred since President Cerezo took office included the finding, on 22 January, of the skeleton of 22-year-old agronomy student Emilio Yoc Serrano, who had "disappeared" on 10 August 1985.

Similarly, reports merely recording the finding of bodies of apparent victims of violence often do not give sufficient detail to establish conclusively that the victims died in political killings, nor to indicate who was responsible for their deaths. Observers have suggested, however, that the fact that many recent victims have been members or leaders of President Cerezo's own Christian Democrat Party may indicate that the killings were ordered either by military elements who opposed the electoral process or the accession to power of a civilian government, or by far-right political leaders opposed to Christian Democrat leadership of the country, as well as to the economic and social policies of President Cerezo's government.

In addition, several diplomats have said that they believed military officers were now ordering the killing of soldiers and police officers who had been involved in "death squads" and torture, in an effort to prevent evidence from emerging later. A number of bodies with their faces mutilated and hands cut off have appeared lately, and according to foreign press coverage there is speculation within the country as to whether some may have been members of military or security units.

In response to reports of killings and abductions, the Christian Democrat President of the National Congress Alfonso Cabrera Hidalgo promised that the new government would uphold its pledge to eradicate "death squads" regardless of whether the authorities were implicated. International observers, including prominent foreign journalists, have reported that the President's move to disband the DIT may have been a reaction to the "death squad"-style killings and abductions of Christian Democrats and others which followed his accession to office. It has been suggested that the DIT were responsible for these killings. President Cerezo told the Spanish newspaper *El País* in February that his information indicated that the DIT had been involved in acts of violence, both before and after he had taken office. He said that: "the appearance of bodies recently with signs of torture" had caused him to dissolve the agency because the secret police "were not carrying out the function for which they were created" and because they had "lost credibility with the public and had returned to attacks on human rights". It is also widely believed that President Cerezo suspects DIT agents were involved in past assassination attempts against him. At least three attempts have been made on his life and more than 340 leaders and members of his party have been assassinated in the last decade.

In all cases, however, and regardless of who is responsible, Amnesty International continues to believe that all reported abuses should be properly investigated by the new authorities and the perpetrators brought to justice.

CHAPTER I
The 1980s:
human rights violations continue

The victims testify

"I am the mother of three 'disappeared' people. One was 31, one 23 and the other 25 ... They were taken from our home, our other children told us this, at 9.30 at night. The local military commissioner[1] knocked on the door asking for some soft drinks, because we sell them, and my daughters, who knew him, opened the door. A group burst in — a group of armed men whom the military commissioner had brought with him. Then they tied up two of my sons with their arms behind them and searched the house. What could they find? Each one had his Catholic Bible which they read when they went to sleep. They didn't find anything, but they took them away ... Then they went and took my other son who lived about four kilometres from the house. They took all three away, leaving me with three small children to look after."

The speaker is an Indian woman from the Guatemalan countryside. She was one of many witnesses of human rights violations who testified to Amnesty International during the organization's mission in 1985.

During its visit to Guatemala in April 1985, Amnesty International's delegates collected scores of such eye-witness accounts of human rights violations. They were told of arbitrary seizure, torture, "disappearance" and political killing throughout Guatemala and particularly from the departments of Sololá, Sacatepéquez, Alta and Baja Verapaz, El Quiché, Huehuetenango, San Marcos, El Petén, Chimaltenango, Escuintla, Quetzaltenango and Retalhuleu.

Most witnesses and the relatives of the dead and the missing

---

[1] The military commissioners are civilian agents of the army, serving under army discipline. Many are former non-commissioned officers. They act as local representatives of the army and as intermediaries between the army and the local community. They are frequently in charge of organizing the civilian defence patrols, and have law enforcement functions. Military commissioners are stationed in every hamlet in Guatemala and one of their main tasks is to act as an intelligence branch to the army.

accused the police, army and paramilitary units such as the civil defence patrols of responsibility.[2]

The victims whose cases were presented to Amnesty International's delegation during its visit to Guatemala came from all sections of society. However, internal refugees, clergy and lay church workers working with them, trade unionists and university staff and students, particularly those at the state university, *Universidad de San Carlos* (USAC), University of San Carlos, appeared to have been singled out. People attempting to investigate human rights abuses, particularly members of GAM, Indian peasants in the areas of armed conflict in the countryside or those suspected of sympathizing with the armed opposition have also been persistent targets of human rights violations.

People told of entire families being executed by the army simply because they lived in areas where there was conflict between government troops and the armed opposition. Other victims had been abducted from their hospital beds, and had either "disappeared" or been murdered in circumstances which suggested that the security forces were responsible. One woman told Amnesty International that relatives had been killed and abducted when they attended her husband's wake: "My son was at a funeral parlour, keeping vigil over his father's body. Then they opened fire, they killed one son, a brother and a nephew, and took away my son-in-law and my son, who never reappeared."

The "disappeared"

Amnesty International collected testimony from over 150 people in just one day of its visit to Guatemala. All of them were relatives of people who had "disappeared". The youngest was a nine-year-old boy, who told Amnesty International's delegation that: ". . . as the oldest son, I have come to bear witness to the 'disappearance' of my father who 'disappeared' on 27 January 1984. At 9.30 at night he was taken off by 10 men. They surrounded the house and took him off in a car . . . We have looked for him at different detention centres, police stations, and with the military, but there is no trace. We never did anything except work hard earning our daily bread, trying to struggle to be a human being, and a good churchgoer. We never did anything except go from work to the house and from the house to church, just doing our duty."

---

[2] The *Patrullas de Autodefensa Civil* (PAC), civil defence patrols, are compulsorily recruited in the villages to act as an adjunct to the army. Their formation was ordered by the government of General Lucas García and stepped up under his successors, General Ríos Montt and General Mejía Víctores.

The people who came to ask if Amnesty International could help in the search for their relatives had travelled to the capital city from towns and villages throughout Guatemala. They brought with them whatever documentation they had — a photograph of the missing person, a *ficha* — a sheet of paper recording the essential details of the case[3] — or sometimes a thick file filled with copies of the *habeas corpus* writs, letters and telegrams to government authorities, and records of other initiatives they had taken in the search for their missing relatives.

One woman showed the delegation a testimonial she obtained from the mayor of the town in which her "disappeared" husband had lived. It read: "The undersigned, municipal mayor of the settlement of . . . , hereby declares that Mr . . . , identity card . . . registered at this registry, is an honest person of good habits, physically and mentally sound, that he devoted himself to his work, and lived in this municipality." "My husband was captured in Quiché," she said. "He was travelling up there to try and find some work, to earn a living, he looked for odd jobs everywhere. It was the army that captured him. I have all the information here. He was a good man. He was friends with everyone. He respected the authorities and he had his identity card with him."

Many were poor and barefoot, but had scraped together enough money to travel to the capital as a last hope in the struggle, which some had waged for years, to find out what had happened to their loved ones. Some had travelled great distances and had been mandated by their far-off villages to represent families who could not afford the fares: "I come on behalf of a family that couldn't come themselves, it is a village very far away . . . Maybe you can do something. I should have brought a photo, but I didn't have one . . ."

The delegation was presented with cases that spanned a period from 1980 through to "disappearances" which had occurred only days before it arrived in Guatemala. Most people could give no explanation as to why their relatives had been arrested, "disappeared" or murdered. Time and time again, when asked what association the missing person belonged to, the relatives replied "none" or "the Catholic Church" or "*la costumbre*", "the custom", meaning that they had practiced traditional Indian religious rites: "I have come to give you information about my son . . . I hope that you can find my son, because he didn't belong to any group, he was a student, he was a very obedient boy, the whole neighbourhood knew that."

Consistent throughout the testimonies given to the delegation was the plea that if a "disappeared" relative had broken the law, the

---

[3] These *fichas*, are data sheets prepared by the human rights group GAM.

charges against them should be made known and they should be brought to trial and judged according to the law: "We have hope in you, that you can help because our children are suffering unjustly, because they deny that they took them. We don't know if they are alive or dead. We also ask that you protect us from the threats we have received. We ask for the arrest of the military commissioner, so that it can be proved that innocent people were arrested, or if they are guilty of something that they be punished according to the law, and if not, that they be freed. We are waiting for them, hoping that they can return to their homes."

The wife of a community worker who "disappeared" shortly before the delegation arrived in the country declared "let them bring whoever is guilty of something to justice", and that if her husband had done something "let him be punished according to the law".

Another witness to recent "disappearances" had been held in unacknowledged detention and tortured by the army only days before he was interviewed by Amnesty International. He had this to say: "We all beg that if someone has done something . . . judge them, put them in for 20 years, but operate according to the law." Others simply begged that they be told the whereabouts of their missing relatives, and that if they were dead, the bodies be returned to the family for burial: "The government must explain what they did with her. If they killed her, let them return the body to me."[4]

Many said that they had repeatedly called on the authorities to investigate the death or "disappearance" of their relatives but had had no reply: "My father was kidnapped on 13 July 1984, and we just can't find a trace of him. We've looked in the military posts at Berlín, and at other military places, but they've never given us any reason for it . . . They say it wasn't them. It was a little blue car that took him away, with a spare tyre on the back. My father was wearing a light blue shirt and blue trousers. . . . We go on looking for him, but it's like talking to a stone. They just don't pay attention to you."

* * *

"I am the mother of X. He was in his sixth year of teacher training here in the capital . . . He was arrested by the National Police. I've sent telegrams to the President, but I've never had any reply."

---

[4] From testimony given to the Amnesty International delegation about a young woman who was arrested by the BROE along with three others, during the period when the Special Military Tribunals, empowered to pass the death sentence on civilians in secret courts, were in power (see Chapter III). Of the four detained, only two eventually appeared before the Special Tribunals. The other two, including this declarant's daughter, are now counted among the "disappeared".

* * *

"I have two kidnapped sons, one worked in the Bank of Industry, and was a trade union leader, and they kidnapped him on 17 December 1981. It's three and a half years [ago] and he hasn't appeared. We have looked for him everywhere, and we've filed writs of *habeas corpus*, and nothing [happens]. We've sent telegrams to the Chief of State, and he hasn't received us, the same with the Minister of the Interior. It's just about a year since the other "disappeared". He left the house to go to a class at the university. He never came back. We've looked for him everywhere. Perhaps you can do something for us."

* * *

"I am the mother of two young men, who were kidnapped on 22 February. I have all the information here. I received information that they were taken by the police . . . but when we went to the court to present a complaint, they denied it completely, and then some agents of BROE came to the house, but they are the ones who took them away, there is proof of that."

Relatives appeared to believe that if only they could give Amnesty International enough information about their relative's appearance and the circumstances in which they had "disappeared", then it might then be possible to find them: "I sent my son to . . . to bring back a few cents that my other son, X, sends me every month, something like around 10 *quetzales* for me and about 20 *quetzales* for his wife.[5] He was carrying a bag with cheese and four fish, he was wearing a navy blue shirt, with red cuffs and collar, brown trousers and black shoes, and he had his school ID card, but with no photo."

* * *

Some could neither read nor write. Their *fichas* had been filled in for them and were signed with their thumb prints. Others spoke only their Indian languages and had brought an interpreter — sometimes only a child with rudimentary Spanish — to translate their submissions. One old man was blind and lame, but was helped by his young grandson to make his way forward to lay his documentation before the delegation.

Many described how they had suffered since their relatives "disappeared", because of the uncertainty and sorrow of not knowing what had happened to them and also because of economic hardship

---

[5] The quetzal is the Guatemalan currency.

their "disappearance" had caused. Old and infirm men and women had been left to care for several grandchildren, after the parents had "disappeared": "I want to present a petition in the name of my son. He was taken away in 1983, it was 27 February. They took him to the military detachment at Mazatenango, and then to the post at Berlín. The same day they took his wife away — now there are four children without parents. My son was a hardworking man, a peasant, an honourable man, and he wasn't mixed up in anything. I know that because I knew him; he respected me so much, and all my neighbours said that he was an honourable and respectful man . . ."

Again and again it emerged in submissions to the delegation that the "disappeared" had been the families' sole breadwinners: "I am the mother of . . . He was a student of economics at the university. He was going to work, he left the house at two o'clock in the afternoon, but then he was taken by a group of heavily armed men. We know this from a boy who works waxing cars at the university. He was there, and he told us . . . Since then we have denounced this to the police, we've looked for him in hospitals, in all the detention centres. We even went to the morgue to look for him, but we've had no news of him . . . Yesterday, it was 11 months since my son 'disappeared', we've tried every means to try and locate him. He was the sole support of our house, he left a little one of nine months old. It's not possible that they just 'disappear' people like that. It's just as if the earth opened and swallowed them up. If he had been killed, he would have appeared already, but we can't find him anywhere."

A woman who was now the sole supporter of her family described how her peasant farmer husband had been abducted: "It was the lieutenant . . . from the military base who took my husband away. They took him out at two o'clock in the morning on 2 August, and they said they were going to kill him on the spot. They took him away from me, and left me abandoned, and badly beaten. I was gushing with blood. That's why I've come on behalf of my husband to give information . . . maybe through you . . ."

Another woman was left with two young children to support: "My husband . . . was taken away by a group of soldiers at four o'clock in the afternoon. He left two children, one of four years old and one two years old."

Many saw international human rights organizations as their last resort. They hoped that if world attention was drawn to events in Guatemala this might also help to prevent further human rights violations in the country: "I respectfully direct myself to you, thanking you for your presence in our country, for your interest in trying to investigate the whereabouts or establish the circumstances of the 'disappearance' of our family members. I hope that you can be effective in this, and that's why I'm addressing you, to see if through your resources you will be able to find out what happened to our loved ones, and demand that the government must now provide concrete information concerning the results of the investigations that have been carried out, because till now they have only given excuses (as if it is they who have captured and also 'disappeared' our relatives)." Some people were too overcome with emotion to give oral testimony but simply laid their *fichas* before the delegation, pointing to the attached photograph and saying only: "My son . . ." or "My husband . . ." or "My daughter. . ."

Displaced people

Those who fled before army sweeps through the Guatemalan countryside, particularly those who had sought refuge in Guatemala City, as well as the people who have assisted them, have been a prime target of killings and "disappearances" in recent years. Displaced people were apparently considered "subversive" because they came from areas where there had been armed conflict between the government and the armed opposition. Others are reported to have been killed or to have "disappeared" simply because they had witnessed army attacks on their communities resulting in the abduction or extrajudicial execution of non-combatant civilians — men, women, old people and children.

Some people told Amnesty International's delegation that they had fled their homes after army attacks, or had escaped from military custody, or had left after learning that the army was looking for them. They had sought safety for themselves and their families in the relative anonymity of the urban areas. However, according to their testimonies and to statements made by clergy who work with the displaced throughout Guatemala, their safety was jeopardized even in the cities. Witnesses stated that the army regularly brought government collaborators from areas believed to have been sympathetic to the armed opposition to urban centres where displaced people were known to congregate. The collaborators would then identify people from their areas believed to have been "subversives". Some local civil defence patrol members and others appear to have been brought to the capital under duress, and forced to accompany security forces seeking suspects among people who had fled to the capital. In some cases displaced people were taken back to their villages by the army and forced to point out "subversives". The delegation was told that sometimes those brought to identify "subversives" were hooded or masked and appeared to have burns on their hands, suggesting that they were tortured to force them to collaborate with the army. "Ten heavily armed people came with different types of weapons, one was wearing a hood. The neighbours saw how they took [the boy he identified] away, with his arms tied and a lasso around him as if he were a wild animal."

The delegation was told of a number of attacks on the displaced and those who helped them. In September 1984, three catechists (religious community workers) from the department of El Quiché, who had been working with displaced people in Guatemala City, were seized on a busy street in the capital. A well-known member of a civil defence patrol from their area was recognized by witnesses when he identified the catechists to their captors. Their bodies were later dumped on a street in the city, bound and showing marks of torture.

A woman from El Quiché told the delegation about her husband's "disappearance", also in September 1984. He was arrested by soldiers accompanied by civil defence patrol members because, she thought, of his work with a local community development committee. The committee was assisting people, many of them widows or orphans, who had been displaced by previous army attacks in the area. She said that her husband was beaten when he was arrested and that his captors stole his shirts, her child's shoes, a radio and some notebooks. She went to the local army base, but soldiers there denied that her husband had been detained. He remains "disappeared".

A priest interviewed by the delegation stated that between 16 July 1984 and January 1985, 11 displaced men and women from just one town in El Quiché had been detained and "disappeared" in Guatemala City. Amnesty International's sources reported that three of them were later found dead, near the Trébol intersection. Another witness working with displaced people in Guatemala City told the delegation that in the most recent case known to her, another displaced person from El Quiché had "disappeared" in the capital, on *Viernes de Dolores* (Good Friday), 5 April 1985, shortly before the delegation arrived in Guatemala.

Clergy, catechists and lay church workers

Clergy, catechists and lay church workers have long been targets of repression in Guatemala apparently because of their influence and leadership role within their communities. Between April 1980 and July 1981 Amnesty International had recorded the cases of nine Roman Catholic priests who it believed had either "disappeared" or been killed by the security forces. In the years 1981 to 1983, Amnesty International received detailed reports of the wholesale murder of catechists. Eye-witness accounts describe incidents in which up to 50 catechists were murdered during army attacks on their villages.

Some were garrotted, others were hanged from trees, chopped to pieces with machetes or locked into churches in groups and burned to death.

The last priest known to have been killed was Franciscan Father Augusto Ramírez Monasterio, who "disappeared" and was later found shot dead in November 1983. Two months earlier he had been detained and tortured by soldiers, who questioned him about alleged links with "subversives". The torture, "disappearance" and extrajudicial execution of catechists has continued, however, to be regularly reported to Amnesty International. During 1984, the organization received information about more than 20 catechists, from the department of El Quiché alone, who had either "disappeared" or been killed after being seized by the army.

In April 1985 Amnesty International's delegation was also told that religious workers who helped the displaced and the poor had recently been singled out as "sympathetic to subversion", and had subsequently "disappeared" or been extrajudicially executed. One such case was that of Felipe Balán Tomás, a Roman Catholic catechist and a member of the Missionaries of Charity. The Missionaries of Charity are dedicated to helping the poor and run a home in the parish of Las Escobas, in the municipality of San Martín Jilotepeque, Chimaltenango. According to Guatemalan church sources, Felipe Balán was seized on 9 February 1985 by armed men believed to be linked to the security forces, while attending a church service in Las Escobas. The Guatemalan Roman Catholic Church has condemned the "disappearance" of Felipe Balán and the Papal Nuncio, Monseñor Oriano Quillici has reportedly requested that the authorities clarify his whereabouts. However, Felipe Balán remains missing.

Another catechist, Partrocinio Gertrudis Pérez Ramírez, is also missing. He was seized by three heavily armed men accompanied by soldiers on 18 May 1985 from the settlement of Buenos Aires, Tenedores, Morales, Izabal. Rafael Yos Muxtay, a social worker from Patzún, Chimaltenango, who had helped widows, orphans and internal refugees in that department, has not been seen since he was abducted on 22 November 1985. His detention has not been acknowledged despite the fact that he was seized by members of the armed forces in front of witnesses. Luis Ché, a catechist from El Estor, Chimaltenango, was seized in the town market place in front of witnesses on 23 October 1985 by two soldiers in uniform. His body was found in Lake Izabal the following day.

Trade unionists

Efforts to organize workers in Guatemala have apparently been

26

considered "subversive" in recent years, and trade unionists have suffered systematic repression. In 1979 Amnesty International visited the country specifically to inquire into reports of human rights violations suffered by trade unionists and concluded that: "To be a trade unionist in Guatemala is to risk one's life". In the years since then Amnesty International has received repeated reports of the extrajudicial execution or "disappearance" of hundreds of trade unionists.[6]

During its visit to Guatemala in April 1985 Amnesty International's delegation collected scores of such reports. Among them was the case of Celita Floridalma Lucero Lucero, a member of the *Consejo Disciplinario del Sindicato de Trabajadores de la Fábrica Productos Adams,* Disciplinary Council of the Adams Products Factory Workers Union. Celita Floridalma Lucero, 26 years old, was reportedly seized along with a friend on 12 April 1985 as she was leaving her home in Zone 19 of the capital. Her friend was reported released but there has been no further news of Celita Floridalma Lucero.

Amnesty International has continued to receive similar reports of human rights violations since its visit to Guatemala in April. The cases include that of Julio Celso de León Flores, a former Christian Democrat congressman and a leading trade unionist. He was reportedly seized by armed men in the centre of the capital on 11 September 1985. Julio Celso de León was drugged and dumped in the centre of Guatemala City four days later; he had been beaten while in the custody of the Guatemalan army, and threatened that his family would be brought in for interrogation and he would be killed.[7]

University staff and students

For many years university staff, students and workers have been singled out for torture, "disappearance" and extrajudicial execution, apparently because, like trade unionists, they are regarded as "subversives". The state university, USAC, has carried out a number of studies critical of government economic and development policies, and has often been publicly described by the authorities as a centre of "subversion". In March 1984, Amnesty International compiled a partial list of "disappearances" under the administrations of General Romeo Lucas García (July 1978–March 1982) and General Efraín Ríos Montt (March 1982–August 1983). Of 14 staff members of USAC who had "disappeared", only the bodies of two were found

---

[6] A detailed account of recent cases of the "disappearance" and killing of Guatemalan trade unionists is given in Chapter IV.

[7] See Chapter IV.

later and identified, reclaimed and buried by the families. In the case of a third, Benfeldt Zachrisson, Professor of Architecture when he "disappeared" on 1 September 1981, Amnesty International was told by the Guatemalan Ambassador to Washington in 1983: "From information unofficially revealed by an official of the previous administration, it could be concluded that Zachrisson died shortly after his disappearance." In this same period — July 1978 to August 1983 — six USAC staff members were shot dead in the streets of Guatemala City in circumstances suggesting security force involvement.[8]

Indian peasants

For many years, Amnesty International has received detailed reports about the arbitrary arrest, torture, "disappearance" and extrajudicial execution of Indian peasants by the army. Such abuses are most usually reported in those parts of the country where the army is engaged in armed conflict or in areas where the local population is believed to be sympathetic to the armed opposition.[9] During its visit to Guatemala in April 1985 Amnesty International's delegation was able to visit one such area, Patzún in Chimaltenango. The systematic abuses suffered by civilians in the Patzún area were by no means unique, but are representative of the abuses suffered by rural villagers at the hands of the Guatemalan military.

Large-scale abuses in Chimaltenango were first reported to Amnesty International in the early 1980s, shortly after a military base was established in the area. During its April 1985 mission to Guatemala, Amnesty International's delegation was given eye-witness accounts of wholesale extrajudicial executions of civilians in Chimaltenango — men, women, children and old people — by army counter-insurgency forces. These accounts confirmed information Amnesty International had received at the time of the incident. They included killings attributed to the army in the hamlets of Papchalá, Patzal and Panimac in the municipality of Comalapa during the first week of February 1981. Missionaries and aid workers in the area had at that time estimated that 168 peasants died in these operations. They reported that in the same week approximately 85 men, women and children were killed when soldiers opened fire on villagers in Las

---

[8] A detailed account of the "disappearances" and extrajudicial executions which staff, students and workers at USAC suffered during the administration of General Mejía Víctores is given in Chapter IV.

[9] An account of the massive extrajudicial executions in the countryside under General Ríos Montt is given in Chapter II.

Lomas, municipality of San Martín Jilotepeque. They also reported that 171 people from Chimaltenango had been extrajudicially executed by the army during two weeks in March 1981 and that 23 others, including a five-year-old child, were killed by security forces in the village of Chuabajito in April. Similar reports from Chimaltenango continued to be received throughout 1982 and 1983.

Amnesty International's delegation also collected detailed information about a new wave of "disappearances" and political killings which began in Chimaltenango in mid-November 1984, after the army had claimed that guerrilla groups were again active in the area. Local residents, however, told Amnesty International's delegation that there had not been significant insurgent activity in the area for some years, and that the victims of most "disappearances" and extrajudicial executions were non-combatant civilians, including men, women, children and old people. Eight peasants were reported to have been killed and others abducted at the end of January 1985 when the army attacked the hamlet of Xeatzán-Bajo, also in the Patzún area. The following account of this incident was given to Amnesty International by eye-witnesses both before and during the organization's visit to Guatemala in April 1985.

Some 200 to 300 regular army troops, accompanied by 20 *kaibiles*,[10] arrived at the hamlet at 8am on 21 January 1985. With them were two local farm labourers who had been badly tortured with a knife, but were later released, and another person, whose face was covered and who was apparently there to identify suspected "subversives". Once in the hamlet, the soldiers grabbed a 10-year-old boy, Antonio Jocholá, and began torturing him, demanding that he tell them who in the village was collaborating with the guerrillas. To make the soldiers stop torturing him, the boy finally agreed that there could be some guerrilla sympathizers in the village. That afternoon they slit his throat.

The soldiers then seized two peasants, Santos Cuy, aged 38, and a 16-year-old boy, Toribio Yos, and tortured them in the village school with ropes, knives and hatchets. That evening, a hole three metres deep was dug. The local military commissioner and his assistant were then forced to bring other suspected local peasants to the school house on the following day, 22 January. They were Lázaro Sicaján, 25, Rosalio Yos, 45, whose daughter Leonora had "disappeared" after being kidnapped in April 1984, Marcelo Jocholá, 55, Justo Morales Canú, 16, and Tiburcio Jocholá, 30. According to the testimony of five witnesses, some of those held in the school house

---

[10] The *kaibiles* are elite army counter-insurgency units named after a Mayan god of war.

were killed and their bodies burned and thrown in the hole dug the previous day. The army took the others with them when they withdrew at 6am on 23 January. Their bodies were found in a nearby hamlet, five days later. They had apparently been tortured, and two of them had been decapitated.

Although the army blamed the guerrillas for these acts, eye-witnesses stated over and again that they were certain that soldiers were responsible. In a testimony about the January killings in Xeatzán-Bajo one peasant stated: "I saw how the army took the four people and tortured them. And the army says it was unknown people who did it. No, it was the army. We saw it because the army came during the day-time to call the people together. It is not the guerrillas, it is the army."

In a written statement about the same incident, the witness remarked that it was clear who was responsible because: "These were not night kidnappings as has happened in other places. This time it was as clear as daylight that it was the army that came to kill those *campesinos*." Another witness stated: "The people they took away, they took them to throw them somewhere, and then the army says that they have found a secret cemetery; but it's not a secret cemetery, it's them that made the cemetery. It's our brothers that they have grabbed, and that's where they bury them; it's them, the army that does this, but they say it's the guerrillas."

The killings at Xeatzán-Bajo were reported by both the national and international news media. Apparently in reaction to the international interest expressed in establishing exactly what had happened, the local commander at the Patzún military base later summoned the military commissioners from the nearby hamlets, including Xeatzán-Bajo, and asked them why they had been so careless as to allow international journalists into their villages, as it was nobody else's business what was happening in Guatemala. According to eye-witness accounts, the Patzún commander was holding cuttings from the international press about the incident. He declared that he already had the names of those who had talked to journalists about the killings and "disappearances" and warned civil defence patrollers to be more careful how they dealt with journalists, telling them "you have to double your watch". Army personnel reportedly went to the Guatemala City offices to question staff on one of the newspapers that had published the reports. Amnesty International has the detailed testimony of a foreign journalist who attempted to visit Patzún after the commander's warning, in order to investigate what had happened, and, with another journalist, was prevented from entering the village and was detained by the civil defence patrol. The two were held for several hours by the patrol, which confiscated their papers and forced them to drive to the local army base in Patzún, where they were eventually released.

Amnesty International's delegation was also told that shortly after the incident at Xeatzán-Bajo, approximately 15 peasants from the village were presented on Guatemalan television as supposed guerrillas who had recently turned themselves in to the army. They appeared to be in a poor physical condition. One, asked by the journalists how he had turned himself in to the army, said: "No, I was arrested". When asked which armed organization he had been a member of, what arms he had carried, and in which combats he had fought, he stated that he belonged to no organization, that he had no arms, and that he hadn't been in combat. The present whereabouts of the 15 are unknown.

Similar incidents to that at Xeatzán-Bajo were reported to have occurred in the area around Patzún in the same week. Three members of the Calel family were reported killed and decapitated in Chisanic, a small hamlet; two others, brothers Marcelino and Juan Cocón, aged 33 and 35, were reported to have been killed by soldiers. People who reported these killings stated that the brothers were slashed in the neck with machetes and then hung by a rope passed through the wounds. Subsequent to these incidents, on 30 January 1985, Eduardo Puluc Cum was reportedly killed in the area; on 3 February, 27-year-old Juan Batzin was reportedly found dead with marks of torture one night after he had been seized and "disappeared". On 6 February, Mario Sincal Coyote, from Patzún, was reportedly seized by armed men in plain clothes who took him from a bus at the Chimaltenango terminal. He remains "disappeared".

According to the reports received by Amnesty International 28 people were "disappeared" or extrajudicially executed by the army in the municipality of Patzún between the end of December 1984 and the beginning of February 1985. A number of sources independently interviewed by the Amnesty International delegation said that many of the victims were people who had taken advantage of an amnesty decreed in August 1983, which invited people who had belonged to or supported opposition groups to "reincorporate themselves into society".

The Guatemalan authorities have made statements about a number of the incidents which occurred in February 1985. In a submission to the UN Assistant Secretary General in February 1985, the Mejía Víctores administration attributed such abuses to the armed opposition. However, other sources claimed that although the killers had been in plain clothes, vehicles used by them had later been seen at the military base or at the local headquarters of the *Guardia de Hacienda,* Treasury Police, suggesting that even if the army had not directly ordered the killings and "disappearances", it was nevertheless involved in their execution.

There had been other such incidents in March and April, shortly before Amnesty International's visit. Witnesses subsequently interviewed by the delegation insisted that those responsible had been uniformed Guatemalan soldiers. Three peasants who were collecting wood in the Chuinimachicaj area, near Patzún, were reported to have been arrested on 18 March by the army. According to accounts of the affair received by Amnesty International, some of the soldiers were dressed in camouflage gear and carried Israeli-manufactured Galil rifles. Others were in regular uniform. The soldiers asked the peasants for their papers: one could not produce his, and was taken away. The other two were released, but were told that they should go back to the village and not say anything or the same thing would happen to them. They could hear the third man screaming as they returned down the mountain. Since then, according to testimony taken in Mexico in April 1985 by Amnesty International from a peasant who had recently fled the area, there had been no further news of the man who "disappeared".

On 11 March, Agustín Batz Taquira, 30, Miguel Angel Motta, 28, and Pedro Sindo, were reportedly detained. The last was said to have been "put into a sack" in Patzún. In the same month, Abel Queche, from the northern district of Sabalpop was reportedly killed two days after he had formally requested a reduction of civil defence patrol duty. On 9 April, a local man protested about the detention and "disappearance" of his wife, and the burning of his home and possessions.

Amnesty International's delegation received reports of other incidents which occurred in the area in April. Ramón Ravaric Gipac was seized on 6 April. Lucas Jocholá and his four sons, one of them said to be mentally handicapped, were abducted at around midnight on 9 April. All were civil defence patrollers. Amnesty International was told that the men may have been abducted because they were suspected of dereliction of duty. Another six people were reported abducted in the same area between 12 and 14 April. Amnesty International has their names and those of others who "disappeared" around this time.

Only the family names are known of other young men who reportedly "disappeared" in the area in April. They are: Zepún (also reported to Amnesty International as Tepún, although this could in fact be another person), and Aroba.

Reports in the Guatemalan press in April also carried a statement by Florencia Matzuel, saying that her husband Benito Salvador

Ajuchán had been kidnapped on 15 April 1985 from the western district of Patzún. Amnesty International's delegation was told that she had appeared on Guatemalan television, and had stated that she knew the army was responsible for her husband's "disappearance", and was not afraid to say so, for unless her husband was returned to her, she could not support her children, and she and they might as well be dead. At the beginning of May, seven civil defence patrollers were allegedly kidnapped by the army from the hamlet of Chuiquel and taken to the military base at Patzún. Another five local residents, four men and a woman, were seized from the hamlet of Xeatzán-Bajo on 6 May.

In June, it was reported that the commander of the Patzún base had called together all male inhabitants of the town, and warned them that he believed that one or more of them was responsible for the recent killing of an army collaborator, and that unless they came forward there would be reprisals. Some days later, a number of people from the Patzún hamlets of Popabaj and Chuikel were reported to have been seized by troops. On 17 June a 17-year-old girl was seized in Xeatzán-Bajo and remains missing. The following day, in another hamlet nearby, Saquilla, soldiers dressed in plain clothes were reported to have seized eight people, one of them an 11-year-old girl, from their homes on orders from the Patzún base commander. Initial reports suggested that they were taken to the military base at Patzún, but the army and local authorities denied that they were detained. Also in June, 20 people, most of them women, were reported to have been kidnapped in the town of Patzún, as were another 15 to 20 people in the nearby hamlet of San Jacinto, Boca de Oro. On 2 July the bodies of three people whose throats had been slit were found at the municipal water pump in Patzún.

At the end of July, the *New York Times* reported that at least 60 Indian peasants had been killed or had "disappeared" in the area over the past seven months, and that according to local residents almost all of them had been victims of the Guatemalan army. Archbishop Próspero Penados del Barrio also considered that the army was responsible. The government-directed violence had, according to the newspaper, left a total of over 140 orphans and 45 widows.

In August, church workers reported that soldiers had killed three civil defence patrollers in the area and hanged them from trees. Although the army blamed the deaths on the guerrillas, "all of the villagers know it was the army". On 16 September, another five civil defence patrol members were kidnapped during the night from the village of Xepatán, Patzún. The abduction was witnessed by other patrollers who managed to escape. They, too, said it was the army.

The government-run Highland Residents Aid Program[11] had found that over one third of the population of Chimaltenango had been displaced from their homes for between several weeks to several months and that about 10 per cent of them were still displaced in March 1985. In 1980 Chimaltenango had a population of 230,000. A Supreme Court study conducted during 1984 and 1985 reported that some 6,500 children in the department had lost at least one parent in recent political violence.

An independent church-based study made available to Amnesty International's delegation provided information on 362 widows and 716 orphans counted in 16 small hamlets in Chimaltenango. A number of the incidents referred to in this study in which the women and children concerned had lost their husbands and fathers have been studied by Amnesty International. The evidence suggests that they were killed by the army.

Difficulties of investigation in a climate of fear

In April 1985 Amnesty International attempted to visit the hamlet of Xeatzán-Bajo to investigate the reports of killings and "disappearances" it had received. This experience illustrated the difficulties of undertaking such research in a climate of fear and when access to certain areas can only be obtained under military escort. When the delegation reached Xeatzán-Bajo they found the entrance to the hamlet blocked by a wooden pole and guarded by members of the civil defence patrol armed with machetes, who would not permit them to enter. Several Guatemalan officials later reiterated earlier official statements and said that the delegation could visit any site it wished and the delegation asked that it be taken to Xeatzán-Bajo. This time the delegation travelled in two armoured cars provided by the government, accompanied by military personnel and two carloads of army intelligence personnel. Upon arrival at Xeatzán-Bajo, the highest ranking officer in the escort was heard to tell an individual described as the civil defence patrol commander that the delegation should be permitted to enter the hamlet as "you have already received your instructions". The delegation asked to be allowed to circulate and talk freely with villagers, but were told by the man introduced as the hamlet's civil defence patrol commander that this would not

---

[11] *Programa de Ayuda a los Vecinos del Altiplano* (PAVA), previously *Programa de Ayuda a las Víctimas del Altiplano*, Highland Victims Aid Program, the name given by the government to an advanced stage of its counter-insurgency program which was implemented after the army had gained supremacy in the conflict with the armed opposition and turned its attention to the pacification of the non-combatant civilian population through obligatory labour and resettlement programs.

be possible, because "then we would not know what people were telling you". Instead, the entire hamlet and people from outlying settlements were called together and the delegates were allowed to address them. The address was translated into Cachiquel, one of the local languages, by a member of the civil defence patrol but as the delegation did not have a Cachiquel interpreter, it did not know whether the translation was accurate.[12]

Villagers were then invited to ask the delegation questions. The entire exchange took place in the presence of the military escort, and so the delegation did not expect, nor did it obtain, testimonies about human rights violations in the area. In the crowd were people who had earlier given the delegation information about recent abductions of their relatives by the army but they were understandably unwilling to repeat their accusations with the army present. In fact, one of them had previously told the delegation that: "If you come back, even tomorrow, on an official visit then nobody is going to talk to you because they will be watched. People won't give taped testimonies either, because if the tapes fall into the hands of the authorities, they will be used as evidence against them". The villagers did protest that they could not speak freely because a member of the military escort was seen to be surreptitiously tape-recording the exchange. One member of the civil defence patrol declared to the delegation: "You, Amnesty International, cannot bring us what the army can. Do you bring us food?" Later the delegation received reports that prior to its pre-arranged visit to Xeatzán-Bajo with the army, the hamlet had been visited by troops who had distributed food and alcohol, and warned the villagers not to talk to any visiting foreigners. As one villager who fled the area had previously told Amnesty International: "They go and kill, and then they come back another time and give us things."

Much of the testimony in this chapter is unattributed because people feared reprisals should they be known to have spoken about abuses they had witnessed or suffered. Amnesty International considers these fears to be entirely justified. The delegation was often asked not to cite specific cases or names or even areas when reproducing testimony they were given. Certain names and identifying

---

[12] Other human rights delegations have in the past been assigned official interpreters. On one occasion, it is known that the interpreter provided was a high-ranking member of army intelligence (G-2). On another occasion, a civil defence patrol member who offered to translate a peasant woman's denunciation of recent killings in her area told a foreign delegation of inquiry that the woman had said the guerrillas were responsible. Later independent anthropologists and linguists who viewed the video-recorded testimony stated that in fact, the peasant woman had actually said the army was responsible for the killings. This incident is described in Appendix IV. It occurred on 11 June 1982.

details have therefore been withheld. These precautions have been taken for the protection of those who spoke to Amnesty International's delegation as they clearly did so in fear of their lives: "I've got here three information sheets about my three family members that were taken away by the military commissioner in my village. The truth is that we know what will happen to us, they will kill us or make us disappear." In another instance, a woman giving testimony about the "disappearance" of her husband stated that local people who had inquired about him had been told they should go to the military base, and that when she herself had gone there, she had been threatened with death.

Others who had sought to discover the whereabouts of their missing relatives were themselves later the victims of "disappearance" or apparent extrajudicial execution.[13]

Witnesses and victims of human rights violations were particularly reluctant to discuss even widely reported abuses if they thought government representatives might be present. On one occasion villagers, knowing that government escorts were accompanying a foreign delegation of inquiry, declared that there had been no recent human rights violations in their area. However, a foreigner living in the village approached the delegates and whispered in English: "They are killing them, these poor peasants, they are killing them, so many of them." When asked who was killing them, the person whispered: "The army, it is the army." Warned that an English-speaking member of the delegation's escort was approaching, the same person then raised his voice and declared in Spanish: "These poor people. They are caught in the middle. They are being killed by both sides."

Even when government representatives were not known to be in the area, Amnesty International found that people were reluctant to speak within hearing or view of even the most casual-looking passer-by. Interviews could only be held in places such as hotels, diplomats' homes or religious institutions which offered a greater measure of protection than could normally be expected. Even then, many declarants were initially reluctant to accuse the army of the "disappearance" or killing they were describing and would only indicate this indirectly. Only when spoken to in her own language, for example, did the wife of a community worker who had just "disappeared" reveal that witnesses had seen the army take her husband away. She told the delegation "it is clear it was them" as neighbours had seen the local military commissioner in a store with

---

[13] A full account of the attempts by GAM to discover the whereabouts of the "disappeared" and of the abduction and killing of GAM members is given in Chapter V.

the same soldiers who, shortly afterwards, followed her husband in a car, then seized him, threw him into the car, turned off the headlights and left the area. She continued: "All entrances to the hamlet are controlled by the civil patrol. Who else would enter? And if it wasn't [the army], they should investigate. No, I'm 100 per cent sure it was the army."

Frequently, informants explicitly stated how dangerous it was for them to give testimony or denounce violations to authorities or to local or international human rights groups. A young member of a civil defence patrol in Sololá told the delegation: "The people know perfectly well that if anything happens, it is done by the army. They know this, but if anyone talks he is taken away in the night." This was echoed by a member of the clergy who works with the displaced: "The displaced people say they would like to speak over the radio about how they have suffered, but they know they wouldn't come out of the broadcasting station alive." A man whose daughter had "disappeared" told the delegation: "Others are afraid to come because of fear of repression or 'disappearing' themselves for having asked the authorities to clarify the whereabouts of our children. This has happened many times in the past." For this reason a woman from Chimaltenango who testified to the delegation was reluctant to have her case put to the authorities: "We must protect our families. Our children need us, and if we 'disappear' . . . You can no longer count on living because of this terror. We all run this risk. If the father goes, the mother has to continue trying to find a way to support the children. If you mention my husband's case to the authorities, then definitely they'll come looking for me, because I'd be the obvious one that would have given information, so I'd run much more risk."

"You must watch their eyes. No one will talk. You must try and see what they may be trying to tell you with their eyes.", said a priest, and a nun told the delegation that: "You won't get a sound out of them, because they are terrified. I think that if you try and go to the Ixil Triangle on an official trip for example, the thing that will move you most will be the silence. They will not talk to you because to talk would mean risking their very lives, and the people are already terrorized and prefer not to talk. What you'll really notice is that the people will do one of two things. Either they will say that the army is very good, or they will not say anything. They are never going to tell you that it's the army that attacks them."[14]

---

[14]The Ixil Triangle is the region between Nebaj, Chajul and Cotzal in the department of El Quiché with a predominantly Ixil Indian population. It was once an area of armed conflict between the army and the guerrillas and large-scale extrajudicial

The Ambassador to Guatemala of a European country which was occupied during World War II described the climate of fear in the country as: "... an occupation mentality. People will tell you what they think will protect themselves."

"To go beyond this would mean death", said students explaining why the USAC students' council operates in virtual clandestinity.

Amnesty International's 1985 delegation to Guatemala was repeatedly told by radio, television and newspaper journalists that any journalist who writes or broadcasts on human rights issues "takes his life in his hands". As one journalist put it: "The government buys off the press so that it will run certain stories and pays for other stories not to run. Any mistakes could mean death for a journalist. Violence against journalists really began in 1980. Since then many have been killed. They have sacrificed their lives to defend the freedom of the press." Amnesty International's delegation to Guatemala in 1979 had been given details of two journalists who had been killed and one who had "disappeared" between June 1978 and May 1979, in each case after they had written articles critical of the government, and of the arbitrary arrest or short-term abduction of 10 other journalists in the same period. After this visit Amnesty International was told that a further 13 radio and newspaper journalists who had criticized the government had been killed, apparently by government agents, between 1 January and 27 August 1980.

Other declarants described specific techniques which they said had been used to terrorize victims or witnesses of human rights violations into remaining silent. A member of GAM showed the delegation the death threats she had received, along with copies of the advertisement she had placed in the press appealing for information about her "disappeared" husband. The threats warned her that "he that lives by the sword shall die by the sword", and that "he who has done nothing, has nothing to fear". A nun told the delegation that: "X— was released on the understanding that he would return to his home and then he should come to a certain restaurant every day to

---

executions have been attributed to the army in recent years. The army has since controlled the region, and many people displaced by earlier army sweeps have been resettled in "model villages" under army supervision. Foreign delegations of inquiry are often invited to visit the Ixil Triangle and interview the Indian peasants resettled there, as was the Amnesty International delegation. However, as this nun pointed out, the strong army presence in the Triangle inhibits efforts to gather information about human rights violations. It is also reported that many of those settled in the "model villages" in the Triangle were brought by the army from other areas of Guatemala and given land formerly farmed by Ixil Indian communities so that they are both unwilling and unable to give information about past events in the region. The same is said about other areas in Guatemala where the army has established other "model villages".

give information. They told him that if they released him and he tried to leave the country that they would kill him the next time they could get to him. I am afraid to tell you any more about the specific tortures he suffered because then they could identify him, and it could be dangerous for him or his family."

Another church worker testified: "Two years ago a foreign voluntary agency was given letters that had been circulated to families who had lost relatives saying that if they gave any information to the international agency currently visiting the area to inquire into the human rights situation, they would lose someone else.

"Last year, a foreign nun began to denounce human rights violations. She did a report to her own embassy. The press came, and interviewed people in the presence of the military. She later received a letter from them saying they had been threatened and had had to say certain things during these interviews. Then the G-2 came and told the nun they couldn't guarantee her safety and she had to leave the area."

A woman whose son had "disappeared" described her attempt to tell a member of an earlier international human rights delegation about his "disappearance": "The security at the hotel was so heavy that I was the only person who actually got to talk to him during his visit because no one else dared to go and see him."

Clandestine cemeteries and secret detention centres

During its visit to Guatemala, Amnesty International's delegation was urged by relatives of the "disappeared" to visit a number of places, including army bases, which were said to have secret cells, "pits" or wells where "disappeared" prisoners were held and tortured. The delegation also received detailed reports of places used as secret cemeteries where the bodies of people extrajudicially executed were said to have been dumped.

One "dumping ground" described in great detail to the delegation was said to be located on a state-run forestry project near San José Pinula in the department of Guatemala. According to one source some 80 bodies had been found on the site since 1978. The bodies had been seen by local peasants, including the informant's family and friends, who collected wood in the forest. He said that bodies had been found on this site as recently as January and April 1985. In January the naked bodies of four unidentified women, and a young girl dressed in what appeared to be a school uniform were found there. In the same month, witnesses saw armed men holding a captive drive into the forest in a pick-up truck. The captive was killed, the body burned, and the pick-up set on fire. The destruction of clothing and documents and, in the last case, burning the body, appeared to have been intended to make identification of the victims impossible.

The same source said that two bodies had been found at the site eight days before he testified to the Amnesty International delegation. He stated that a woman looking for fire-wood had seen the bodies of two young men wearing what appeared to be factory overalls. Their arms were hand-cuffed behind their backs and then strapped to their bound ankles. They appeared to have been kicked and beaten. Men at the scene carrying army-issue machine-guns told the woman they would kill her if she talked.

This man told the delegation that the local people believed members of G-2 operating in plain clothes were responsible for the killings. He further stated that the property was patrolled by the *Guardia de Honor*, the Honour Guard,[15] and that it would have been impossible for anyone to have entered the property without their knowledge.

He declared that for some time he had wanted to expose the situation, but had not known to whom he could present his testimony without endangering himself; he had already been told by people in the area that he was in danger, and he was living clandestinely, only occasionally visiting his family. He said he had done nothing to warrant this. Although visibly distraught, and obviously concerned that he might be seen talking to Amnesty International, he begged the delegation to try and enter the forestry project. He gave precise instructions as to where the secret cemetery could be found, describing in great detail the topography of the area. The delegation was also told by foreign journalists that peasants from that area had entreated them to travel to the site and confirm that it was being used as a body dump, but that the *Guardia* patrols made it impossible to enter the area.

Other witnesses told the delegation that secret cemeteries were sited on a number of private estates guarded by the police, and on sites adjacent to army bases or close to villages which were patrolled by the army or civil defence patrols.

The delegation was also told that there were secret torture and detention centres at army and security force buildings in the capital and other towns and army bases in the country. A priest said that members of the civil defence patrol had been punished for not

---

[15] The *Guardia de Honor*, Honour Guard, was described by a military spokesman as a brigade responsible for supplying reinforcements in areas of conflict, and for carrying out counter-insurgency operations as well as regular warfare.

patrolling by being put in covered wells in his parish in the department of El Quiché. They were put practically nude in 12 wells, up to two metres deep, and kept in water up to their knees. One of them had died later. A nun said that people who protested about being forced to join the civil defence patrols had been detained in secret cells at an army base in Huehuetenango. Other secret detention centres were said to be situated in the departments of Sololá, Sacatepéquez, Retalhuleu, Quetzaltenango, Alta Verapaz, El Petén, and Chimaltenango.

Amnesty International's delegation attempted to visit the Patzún army base in Chimaltenango, in order to conduct an on-the-spot investigation into reports that the base was being used as a secret detention and torture centre and had a clandestine site where the bodies of those who died in custody were disposed of. When eventually permitted to enter the base, the delegation found evidence consistent with details given in the allegations it had received.

Amnesty International had previously received testimonies stating that in Chimaltenango victims had sometimes been taken to the Patzún base, where they were held and tortured in what was described to the delegation as a hole or "pit". Bodies were also said to have been thrown into the pit, before being buried in a cemetery adjoining the base.

Amnesty International's delegation had travelled to Chimaltenango with its official escort to discuss with local army officers any steps they were taking to ensure that troops under their command were abiding by human rights legislation governing the conduct of hostilities and the treatment of prisoners. The delegation also wished to discuss official investigations of allegations that the army was responsible for human rights violations in the region. Amnesty International had already been repeatedly assured by a series of senior officials, including the Deputy Head of State, that its delegation would have complete freedom to visit government offices and military installations.

When the delegation requested permission to visit the Patzún base it was told that authorization was required from the regional army commander at Chimaltenango. The delegation was also told that authorization could not be obtained by radio as radio transmissions were not secure, despite previous assurances that radio communication with the field was excellent, so that commanders at their bases and officials in Guatemala City could be kept up to date with reports of human rights violations and investigate them immediately. The delegation had also been told that local military posts were in contact with the base at Chimaltenango on a regular basis, half-hourly in some cases. Accompanied by its escort, the delegation duly travelled to the regional base at Chimaltenango where it received permission from the commander to enter the base at Patzún. Over two hours elapsed between the time the delegation requested permission to visit the Patzún base and the time it gained entrance to the base.

Once in the Patzún base the delegation did find a pit in the ground, exactly as described by peasants from the area. The pit was underneath a hut-like structure with a corrugated-iron roof at the rear of the base. It measured approximately 1.6 metres by 1.6 metres by 1.5 metres and was covered by a lid of wooden boards. One of the delegates entered the pit, and found a tin tray, fresh rice, mouldy *tortillas* and bits of rope and paper, which suggested that the pit was indeed used to hold captives.

The delegates also discovered an underground hole in a wall at the rear of the soldiers' barracks. On passing through this they found a cemetery. Soldiers ordered by the base commander to accompany the delegates into the cemetery prevented them from inspecting it in its entirety. However, the delegates were able to observe that the cemetery adjoined the encampment in such a way (it was surrounded by guard towers and was also the site of an obstacle course apparently used in training exercises) that it appeared to be an integral part of the base. The delegation also noticed fresh, unmarked graves in the cemetery. The base commander said that they were those of local peasants, too poor to afford tombstones.

When questioned about the pit, the base commander said it was used to punish drunk or disobedient soldiers, and that two had been released from it only that morning. The delegation then asked to interview those soldiers concerned and two were summoned. The delegation asked the base commander for the opportunity to interview the soldiers without the presence of the other troops, and the commander complied by ordering his men to withdraw from the positions they had assumed surrounding the delegation with their rifles cocked.

The two soldiers said that they had been confined to the pit for disciplinary offences, but stated that they had been released four days earlier. When asked whether other soldiers had been in the pit after them they said, "No". When the delegation drew this discrepancy to the commander's attention he stated that in fact it was not those soldiers who had been released that morning but two others. He refused, however, to give the names of the other soldiers and said they were not available for interview. According to the commander they had been involved in the more serious abuse of "attacks on the civilian population" and had been sent to the base at Chimaltenango to be disciplined before Amnesty International's delegation arrived at Patzún. The commander at Chimaltenango, however, had told the delegation that he was not holding any prisoners.

The delegation considered its findings with respect to the pit and the cemetery at the military base at Patzún to be consistent with details it had received in testimonies about the detention, torture and extrajudicial execution of prisoners there. It also had grave misgivings about events at the base immediately before its arrival and particularly about what might have happened to any prisoners held there before it was finally granted access to the base.

Forces responsible for human rights violations

Witness after witness was certain that the police or army, sometimes assisted by the civil defence patrols, had been responsible for the abuses which they had seen or suffered. Among the forces they accused were the DIT and the BROE as well as the regular army, its intelligence division, and the *kaibiles*.

Sometimes abductions and killings were carried out by soldiers in uniform in front of witnesses. One such case was the abduction of a six-year-old girl in Chichicastenango, El Quiché, in full view of her parents: "The soldiers came to capture us, the parents, but we fled with the other children. The oldest one was 15 years old but the littlest one was asleep in the house. From our hiding place we, the parents and the brothers and sisters, could see the soldiers when they captured the little girl." The child has "disappeared".

Amnesty International's delegation heard many similar testimonies, of which the following are examples: "I am the son of . . . he was travelling in a bus, coming to the house, and he was detained by the army. They were searching everyone, and they took him off the bus with some other people and those others have never come back either . . ."

* * *

"On 18 November, at two in the morning, armed troops from the Lynx Battalion, from the brigade based at Poptún, came and arrested [10 people] when they were doing their civil defence patrol duty. They killed . . . in the doorway of his house and burned three houses. On the 25th, they returned at 11 o'clock at night and captured [three people] leaving the brother of one of them dead in the doorway of his house . . . We blame the military. On 28 November, the army came, and called everyone together, and sent for the military commissioner. He said that he had already given a list of 27 names to the brigade at Poptún."

* * *

"I am from the city of . . . On 13 April, they kidnapped my boys, they were young boys. We have looked for them everywhere. We are sure it was the army who took them away . . . I have brought you the report that gives all the details . . . It is them, the army, that has sown this unhappiness."

* * *

"Up to 100 soldiers arrived; the whole town witnessed the event. Later they denied that they were holding him."

* * *

One woman told the delegation that a Guatemalan newspaper had actually carried a photograph of her son being arrested by uniformed traffic police. Despite this evidence the authorities denied that he was detained and he has "disappeared".

On several occasions would-be kidnappers were overpowered by their intended victims, and found to be carrying identification credentials issued by the army General Staff and the National Police. In other incidents, assailants or captors were known by witnesses or victims to be members of specific army or police units, even though they had carried out the torture, "disappearance" or killing in question while in plain clothes. A young girl, testifying to the delegation about the "disappearance" of her father and brother, said: "We were selling in the central square when some armed men arrived dressed in plain clothes, but we knew they were members of the army, and they took away my father, and at the same time, also one of my brothers." A young civil defence patroller in Sololá told Amnesty International's delegation that: "We know who the soldiers are in the area. We recognize them when they come and do these things." Similarly, a witness from Alta Verapaz told the delegation: "He was arrested by military commissioners who came with their faces covered. But in spite of this I recognized them, and I called out their names; then they uncovered their faces and it was them."

A woman whose son and nephew "disappeared" also knew the army was responsible because: "They were arrested by members of the G-2 in plain clothes. A boy who was playing with them took down the numbers of the licence plates. He knew that the kidnappers were from the army because he played football at the military base football field." The witness she referred to "disappeared" the next day when the same cars came and took him away.

And in one case the wife of a man who had "disappeared" recognized some of his captors when she went to file a complaint with the DIT. The man's sister told the delegation that: "They kidnapped him at 6.20 in the morning. He asked them to identify themselves, but they wouldn't. They just carried him off in front of my mother and his wife and his two children. One of the children tried to hang onto his legs but the soldiers just threw the child aside. There were a lot of witnesses. The next day, no, the day after that, my sister-in-law went to file a complaint at the DIT, and she recognized there some of the men who had taken him off."

On other occasions, the equipment, including vehicles, communications apparatus or armaments used by the perpetrators, identified them as members of the security forces. A priest from Chimaltenango gave the delegation the following testimony: "A company of soldiers came to Chimaltenango and put a woman and her brother into a truck and started to rape her. The brother tried to get some peasants who were around to help. There were 16 of them. The soldiers took them all. The parish priest asked us to intervene. I went to the base and talked to the commander, who denied that the incident had taken place. It could not have been the 'subversives', as the commander tried to suggest, as they do not have trucks." Another witness described the abduction of a surgeon from the municipality of Cantel in the department of Quetzaltenango. "He was kidnapped [by men] in two military vehicles from the military zone in Quetzaltenango on 28 March last year."

Similarly, agronomist Jorge Alberto Rosal Paz was forced into a jeep from an army base near his home in Zacapa, eastern Guatemala, on 12 August 1983 in the presence of witnesses, but military and government officials have consistently denied that he was detained, and he remains missing.

Other evidence from witnesses attesting to the involvement of the security forces in specific incidents included the dress, the military manner in which members of a group addressed each other, and the information to which they had access in order to carry out an abduction or killing. One witness reported that while held in unacknowledged detention she had seen files on herself and her brother. Her brother had been killed earlier, apparently in a motor-cycle accident but in circumstances which suggested this was not the cause of death. Both files carried photographs, which she recognized as those from her and her brother's government-issued *cédula*, identity cards. She believed that her captors could only have obtained these photos from official files.

Witnesses often said that the army or the police had tried to blame "subversives" for incidents which, they were convinced, had been the work of those very units. For example, a priest told the Amnesty International delegation that: "Three people were arrested last week in ... They were people who had formed committees to receive food aid. Two were freed after being badly beaten. I myself spoke to the person who arranged to get them out of the military hospital at the base in Chimaltenango. The military announced that the army had freed them from the subversives, but they remember that they had been arrested by soldiers and badly beaten by them." And a foreign church worker, describing killings in the town of San Pedro La Laguna, Sololá, said: "They killed the military commissioner and some of his relatives at the beginning of February 1985. The first reports indicated that the widow said she recognized the leader of the group who killed her husband. He had his kerchief down, and she recognized him as an army captain. She addressed him by his name and rank, and he put his kerchief back up. She told the army she had recognized him, but they said that was impossible. Then army officials came to town, and got together with town officials and the captain, and then they put out the story that she was wrong and hadn't recognized him."

Another witness testified to having lost 19 members of her family since 1980. They had either "disappeared" or been extrajudicially executed by the security forces. In 1981, following a bazooka attack on her home, some of her relatives, including a six-year-old child, had been taken away by the National Police. The photographs of several of the adults subsequently appeared in newspapers and on television; they were described as guerrillas who had died fighting the army in a region far from their home in Guatemala City. Photographs of another relative seized in the raid later appeared in the Guatemalan newspaper *Sucesos*, as an unidentified person whose body had been found near Escuintla, again some distance from the place where he had been seized by the police. This newspaper regularly prints photographs of the mutilated, unidentified bodies which are found throughout Guatemala. While this undoubtedly helps people establish the fate of missing relatives and friends, it also has the effect of terrorizing the population by graphically portraying the fate of many of Guatemala's "disappeared".

Security force involvement in kidnappings and killings has also been established when the cars or belongings of the victims were later seen in the possession of the police units or army units accused of responsibility. A woman, whose son had "disappeared" in 1983, told Amnesty International's delegation that he had actually been driven away in his own car. She then saw the car at the local army base: "They came to the house at two in the morning. It was the army. I am absolutely sure of that, because they left in our car with my son, and I followed them. They stopped the car outside the army post, and then went in with the soldier who was there ... The next

46

day they went out on foot and went and kicked down the door of another house. They took away another boy and stole another car, and then delivered the boy to the army command. It was the *pintos*."[16]

As well as the testimony Amnesty International's delegation collected from victims and witnesses, information about human rights violations was often published in the Guatemalan press and the delegation collected scores of such reports during its visit. These included newspaper advertisements paid for by people seeking information about relatives who had recently been seized and "disappeared" in seven of Guatemala's 22 departments. Details given in the advertisements, such as the type of arms carried by the abductors, the fact that the "disappeared" had been seized with impunity in full view of soldiers or police officers or close to police or army installations, and the fact that the advertisements called on the government to account for the missing people indicated that their relatives believed they had been kidnapped by the security forces.

There were also a number of press reports about attacks on civilians, apparently carried out with official sanction. For example, *El Imparcial* reported on 17 April 1985 that inquiries were being made to determine how an armed and hooded group had been able to enter a hospital in Escuintla on 15 April and kill a patient in his bed despite the presence of police and security guards. The patient had been taken to the hospital after being shot and left for dead. Amnesty International knows of a number of incidents in which patients have been shot and killed in their hospital beds or taken from hospitals despite heavy police guards, and subsequently murdered.

Often accounts of incidents such as abductions and killings were independently corroborated by several different witnesses. For example, displaced people in both Guatemala City and Antigua Guatemala, Sacatepéquez, who had fled their homes following attacks upon themselves or their families, gave testimony to the delegation which was consistent with testimony from people independently interviewed by Amnesty International who were still living in the area where the attacks were said to have occurred. In one such case the delegation was given information about three men, who were detained together by the army and badly beaten, by people who saw one of the men arrested in Chimaltenango, and by a local priest who interviewed two of the men after their release. An army statement declared that the military had freed the two released men from the "subversives". The third man remains missing. Amnesty International's delegation later interviewed one of the released men in

---

[16] "The spotted ones" — a colloquial term for soldiers in camouflage uniform.

Guatemala City, where he had fled. He and another displaced person interviewed by the delegation had fresh wounds and heavy bruising. The delegation photographed these but since it did not include a doctor it could not conduct a medical examination. However, the delegation considered that the wounds sustained by both men were consistent with their description of how they had been treated in custody. Both said they had been arrested and tortured by the army, one of them in Huehuetenango, the other in Chimaltenango, only days before they were interviewed. Both had left their homes, declaring that once having been arrested and tortured, there was nothing for them to do but flee for their lives, for the army would wish to kill them to prevent them testifying about their experiences in detention.

The man from Chimaltenango told the delegation that he was arrested on 21 February 1985 by six soldiers, whom he identified as *kaibiles*. They had arrived in his village accompanied by a man whom he believed had denounced him as a "subversive". His hands were tied behind his back and he was taken to any army post at San José Poaquil, where he was held for seven days, two of them in a well three metres deep, partially filled with water. He said he was tortured five times with electric shocks, and showed the delegation wounds he said had been caused when he was slashed with a knife on three separate occasions. Soldiers had threatened him with death, saying: "We're going to cut you up, piece by piece". He said that he was not fed for three days and that he had found it difficult to breathe as he was hooded the whole time. He said other detainees received the same treatment. He was eventually released after his employer intervened, but is now in hiding.

The other man who had fresh wounds apparently sustained under torture was a civil defence patrol member who had served one year as chief of the regional patrol but nevertheless had been arrested and tortured by the army only two days before he was interviewed by Amnesty International's delegation. He said he was arrested with his brother-in-law and a friend in the central market place of Aguacatán, Huehuetenango on a Sunday evening between 10.30pm and 11pm. They were tightly bound at the ankles and wrists, with the ropes then passed around their necks, and thrown onto the patio of the local military commissioner's house. At 3am the soldiers came to take the three to the local military post, but he escaped by throwing himself down a mountain-side. The soldiers fired at him, and a civil defence patrol nearby returned their fire, but he was not hit in the exchange. However, he had wounds consistent with his claim that he had been hit in the mouth with the butt of a gun, kicked in the back, and bound tightly at the wrists and ankles. He said that the following day, while he was still in hiding, he saw the two other men, who had also been badly beaten, brought blindfold to his house by three soldiers who set fire to his house and crops. He knew nothing about what had happened to the other two, and said that he would have to go into exile, for his own security. He had also warned his family that they were now in danger and should immediately join him in the capital and then flee the country. When Amnesty International's delegation spoke to him, he had not heard from them; he feared that his warning had been too late and that the army had already come for them.

He was proud of both his military and civil defence patrol service and said: "I've never had problems with anyone . . . I've never done anything, never been in jail for any reason, any crime. No, I've never had anything like that, thank God . . . I've never been against the army, on the contrary, I've served it, and I have held my country in high esteem." He had no idea why he had been arrested: "I asked them why they were taking us. What was the reason? They didn't say anything, they just said get going, and that's how they grabbed us, kicking us, they took us away. You don't discuss anything with soldiers. You just have to do what they say."

This man also gave the delegation information about his military service and the period during which he had served as chief of his region's civil defence patrol. He stated that civil defence patrols had sometimes killed suspected guerrillas on the spot or else had turned captured suspects over to the soldiers at the regional army base and then had heard nothing further of them.

Human rights education for the police and army

Before it visited Guatemala, Amnesty International had expressed its interest in methods used to train the security forces in international and national legal standards for the protection of human rights. During its visits to a number of army installations, Amnesty International's delegation was shown a great deal of material, such as text books and training manuals, said to be used for training in human rights issues. The material included the rules of Guatemala's legal system, according to which, the delegation was told, anyone who was arrested or captured had to be taken before a judge within 24 hours.

The delegation was impressed by the understanding shown by the officers it met of the rules and standards laid down in Common Article 3 of the four Geneva Conventions of 1949, which govern the conduct of parties to a conflict not of an international nature. However, the delegation found they had little familiarity with other international standards of relevance to military conduct, such as the UN Code of Conduct for Law Enforcement Officials or Articles 4.1 and 4.2 of the UN International Covenant on Civil and Political Rights (1966) concerning the non-derogability of certain rights, including the right to life and to be protected from torture, even during times of public emergency.

Nor did basic human rights standards appear to be systematically incorporated into the curriculum of elite units such as the *kaibiles*, which are most frequently deployed in counter-insurgency operations. The *kaibiles* have often been accused of responsibility for human rights violations, particularly the large-scale extrajudicial execution of non-combatant civilians.

However, of most concern to the delegation was the evident discrepancy between the principles espoused in the training material shown to it, and information it had received attesting to the gross violation of human rights practised by the Guatemalan army in the field. There was also a marked contrast between the human rights educational materials which the delegation was shown and the tone and content of news media coverage of army and police operations, army publicity materials directed at children and the general public, slogans prominently displayed at the various police and army head-quarters which the delegation visited, and the literature directed at the average soldier, including the official magazine *Soldado* (Soldier). These materials encouraged a concept of "total warfare", whereby both the enemy as well as anyone suspected of sympathy for it, must be "implacably destroyed" (*Soldado* No. 12, 31 March 1984).

Soldado was first published on 15 June 1983. It is circulated to all military zones as well as to all army schools and installations and its expressed intention is to improve communication between officers and the ranks of the army, to discuss tactics against "subversion" and to make each reader a "better combatant". The magazine warns over and again that the enemy has infiltrated the churches, schools, trade unions, the university, the press and even the government, and that it is the army's duty to "overcome any repugnance it may feel" when called upon to kill, cut and burn this "satanic" enemy, and "fight it to the death" (Issue 1, June 1983). Soldiers are constantly reminded that the guerrillas infiltrate the local population and are exhorted to "implacably destroy" the enemy and "all its supporters", these "satanic revolutionaries" (Issue 12, 31 March 1984).

Only one of the nine issues of *Soldado* which Amnesty International's delegation examined referred to how captives should be treated. It called on soldiers to be magnanimous to those who surrendered but this fell among a series of exhortations to "annihilate" the enemy, and to "destroy" or "exterminate" the enemy (Issue 14, 31 July 1984). Each issue of the magazine carried graphic photographs of grotesquely mutilated corpses said to be those of people who had died in combat with the army; the units responsible were fulsomely praised.

When Amnesty International's delegation attempted to discuss international standards on the treatment of prisoners they were repeatedly told by officials that the Guatemalan army had not taken a single prisoner from its guerrilla opponents. Explanations given for this varied. Some officials claimed that the guerrillas always "fought to the death". Others maintained that the opposition was invariably able to remove its dead and wounded from the battlefield even when decisively defeated. Still others maintained that the military held no prisoners, since any captured opponent was amnestied and released within 24 hours, even if taken with a gun in their hands. In contrast Amnesty International noted that each issue of *Soldado* concluded with *Noticias de Combate* (Combat News) which gave the human and equipment losses of both sides in recent engagements and the number of captives taken by army units after victorious encounters. Amnesty International remained concerned about the fate of those whose capture was noted in *Noticias de Combate*. The policy of automatic amnesty was hard to credit, given that Guatemalan officials have never admitted to taking prisoners and considering the repeated exhortations to kill the enemy in army literature.

The National Police responded to Amnesty International's request for information about human rights education by presenting the delegation with a volume said to include all the directives issued to its departmental headquarters during 1984. However, Amnesty International found that in urging its personnel not to commit certain acts, these directives in effect repeatedly indicated that such acts were commonplace. On several occasions, the directives explicitly declared that practices common under previous administrations were now to cease. These included dealing with the deaths of citizens and detainees at the hands of the police by simple reference to the *ley de fuga* (law of escape), whereby police or security agents justify the killing of detainees on the grounds that they had attempted to escape; imprisoning people for the sole purpose of extorting payment in exchange for their release; arresting obviously innocent people during drag-net operations for the same purpose; assigning men in plain clothes to carry out police actions; using police equipment and identity cards while ostensibly off-duty; using out-of-date identity cards; using army weapons for police work; ignoring the law stipulating that detainees must be brought before a judge within 24 hours of arrest; falsifying police records.

Constraints encountered by Amnesty International's delegation

In December 1985, when Amnesty International submitted its memorandum to the Government of General Mejía Víctores, the organization expressed its appreciation for the opportunity to investigate reports of human rights violations in Guatemala and to meet many government officials. However, Amnesty International also expressed its objections to constraints and obstacles it had encountered during its visit to Guatemala.

The organization observed, for example, that the authorities had invited the news media to attend meetings between the Amnesty International delegation and the National Police commanders and their legal adviser and Amnesty International's meeting with the Executive Committee of the Constituent Assembly. It is Amnesty International's general practice not to make public statements to the news media during a mission, other than a written statement explaining that practice.[17] This was made clear to Guatemalan government representatives with whom the terms of reference of the visit were arranged, and to the escorts assigned by the Ministry of Foreign Affairs and the Guatemalan army to accompany the delegation during its talks with governmental and military authorities. Following the meetings at which the news media had been present, the newspaper and television coverage the delegation was able to monitor quoted only what officials had said to the delegation. This gave a one-sided and inaccurate representation of the discussions.

Amnesty International's delegation was also disturbed by the press statement distributed during its visit in the name of the press officer of the Office of the Chief of State. Although Amnesty International had been officially invited to visit Guatemala, the statement denounced the delegation for infringing freedom of the press and for being "latter day inquisitors". While the delegation was in Guatemala, advertisements appeared in the press hostile to Amnesty International and its delegation, which were attributed to various private groups.

Both prior to the visit and on repeated occasions during its discussions with senior government officials, including Deputy Chief of State General Rodolfo Lobos Zamora, Amnesty International's delegation was assured that it could travel wherever it wished and

---

[17] This practice is followed in order that observations and information collected in the course of a mission are carefully analysed and cross checked against other sources of information, including Amnesty International's extensive archives, before the organization makes any public assessment of a country's human rights practices.

see whatever it wanted to see. Human rights violations frequently occur in areas impossible to visit without official permission and escort — on private estates or army posts, for example. In such circumstances witnesses are often unable to give testimony. The difficulties encountered by the delegation during its initial attempt to visit the Patzún military base in Chimaltenango and when it attempted to visit the hamlet of Xeatzán-Bajo near Patzún have already been described.

On the grounds of security, armed guards were posted at the doors of two of the delegation's hotel rooms, and two armoured cars accompanied by another two cars carrying armed soldiers in plain clothes accompanied the delegation whenever it left its hotel for scheduled meetings with officials.

The delegation appeared to be under constant surveillance by a number of people, particularly when it attempted to conduct interviews or hold meetings in its hotel. On one occasion, the delegation was photographed repeatedly in the course of such a conversation by a person posing as a freelance photographer. The same person had earlier been observed near the delegation, dressed as a hotel bellboy. He was later seen in the same hotel in army uniform.

Private individuals told the delegation on a number of occasions that people would not give information to the delegation as those who did were clearly being closely observed. Others who gave testimony said they had not risked speaking to previous international human rights delegations because they were afraid of being seen by security agents who had the delegations under close surveillance, or because they had received threats of the consequences should they do so.

The delegation itself had observed that many of the victims and witnesses interviewed were extremely frightened. They would only speak if they were certain that the conversation could not be overheard and on at least one occasion the delegation observed that the appearance of its official escort caused people to refrain from giving frank testimony to the delegates.

CHAPTER II

Massacres in the countryside under General Ríos Montt

Introduction

In 1982 many thousands of non-combatant civilians, most of them Indian peasants, were massacred in the Guatemalan countryside. They were the victims of the counter-insurgency strategy of a military government led by General Efraín Ríos Montt which seized power in March 1982; killed by the army in a drive to crush growing rural guerrilla opposition. The exact number of dead is not known, but all estimates put the toll in the tens of thousands.

Three months after the coup which brought General Ríos Montt to power, on 27 May 1982, the Guatemalan bishops issued a statement denouncing the massacre of "numerous peasants and Indian families". "With profound sorrow", the bishops said, "we have learned and verified the suffering of our people by these massacres ... Numerous families have perished, vilely murdered. Not even the lives of old people, pregnant women, or innocent children were respected. Never in our national history has it come to such grave extremes."

The mass killings, the wholesale destruction of villages and crops, instilled terror in the countryside. The strategy which resulted in human rights violations on a gross scale was frequently described as the "scorched earth" policy.

Amnesty International had followed reports of the massacres with grave concern and in July 1982 published a "Special Briefing" on Guatemala. Entitled *Massive Extrajudicial Executions in Rural Areas under the Government of General Efraín Ríos Montt*, the report was based on a wide range of evidence, including eye-witness testimony, given directly to Amnesty International. It also drew on information from Guatemalan and foreign journalists, health, refugee, assistance and religious workers, working in or visiting both Guatemala and Mexico, and from independent foreign missions of inquiry. A list of incidents between March and June 1982 in which over 2,000 people were reported to have been killed was appended to the report.[1]

---

[1] See Appendix IV.

In the report Amnesty International pointed out that it was unable to verify in each instance who was actually responsible for specific massacres. However, the various incidents reported formed a pattern consistent with the military counter-insurgency strategy being pursued by General Ríos Montt, and described in statements by a series of public officials, including General Ríos Montt himself and the military commanders responsible for its implementation.

Amnesty International concluded its 1982 report with the following assessment: "There have been consistent reports of massive extrajudicial executions in Guatemala since General Efraín Ríos Montt took power in March 1982. Following a pattern not significantly different from that implemented under previous governments, Guatemalan security services continue to attempt to control opposition, both violent and non-violent, through widespread killings including the extrajudicial execution of large numbers of rural non-combatants, including entire families as well as people suspected of sympathy with violent or non-violent groups ... The majority of extrajudicial executions have been reported from isolated rural areas, particularly those in which guerrilla groups have been active. Information available to Amnesty International including press reports, testimonies of witnesses and official government pronouncements, repeatedly identifies the regular army and civilian army auxiliaries organized as civil defence units under the Ríos Montt government."

No direct response to this report was ever received from the government. Instead it informed the Guatemalan and international news media that Amnesty International was engaged in a campaign of defamation against Guatemala. After the report was published Amnesty International continued to receive evidence from a wide range of sources that the security forces were involved in widespread killings of non-combatant civilians throughout 1982.

The March 1982 coup and its aftermath

The three-man *junta* which had assumed power in Guatemala in an almost bloodless coup was led by General Ríos Montt. His fellow *junta* members were General Horacio Maldonado Schaad and Colonel Francisco Luís Gordillo.

The new *junta* immediately annulled the results of elections held earlier that month. In those elections, as in earlier ones, the victor, General Anibal Guevara, was the handpicked successor of the outgoing President, General Lucas García, under whom he had served as Minister of Defence. The elections had been immediately and widely denounced as fraudulent as was also customary in Guatemala.

Upon taking power the *junta* declared that it would respect human rights in Guatemala and put a stop to "death squad" killings. It called for all guns held by private citizens to be handed in. It announced the formation of a body to receive complaints and to investigate past "disappearances". It ordered the arrest of some civilian officials who had been involved in repression during the previous government and disbanded the *judiciales* (the common term for the Detective Corps of the National Police) who, over the years, had been repeatedly cited as responsible for "disappearances" and killings.

In the immediate aftermath of the coup, "death squad" killings and abductions in the urban areas of Guatemala appeared to decrease and the distinctive, unmarked cars of the *judiciales* vanished from the streets of the capital city. However in the weeks that followed there was little indication of any efforts to investigate past "disappearances", renewed instances of which were once again reported from the major urban centres. And on the day that the *junta* formally disbanded the *judiciales*, the National Police announced the formation of a new group, the *Comando de Operaciones Especiales* (COE), Special Operations Command, to support counter-insurgency actions. The DIT was formed at the same time and took over many of the functions of the *judiciales*.

At the time this was described as a restructuring of the security unit most frequently cited as responsible for human rights violations. However Amnesty International subsequently received testimony from former security agents stating that only the names of the agencies had been changed. The personnel and their working methods remained essentially the same.

On 9 June General Ríos Montt dissolved the *junta* and assumed sole control of the government as president and commander of the armed forces. He also replaced the country's 324 elected mayors with his own appointees. A 30-day amnesty was offered to the guerrillas in June, with the proviso that they lay down their arms and abstain from violence. General Ríos Montt announced that as of 30 June, the last day of the amnesty, he intended to declare a "state of siege" in the departments of El Quiché, Huehuetenango, San Marcos and Quezaltenango, areas where the guerrilla forces were strongest.

Throughout June Guatemalan newspapers carried articles about "subversives" who had turned themselves in under the amnesty. Other sources suggested, however, that many of those said to be amnestied were actually people suspected of opposition to the government who had been abducted from their homes and severely tortured until they agreed to appear before the press and state that they had accepted the amnesty offer of their own free will.

On 1 July, the day the amnesty expired, a "state of siege" was declared throughout the country and a series of decree laws introduced. Many of these laws reduced legal and political constraints on the military and police forces, who were empowered to arrest and detain people without charge, and without the right of *habeas corpus,* and to requisition private houses and vehicles. The police and the army were given the right to break into houses and offices at night. Under Decree Law 46-82 special military tribunals were established with the power to impose the death penalty for an extended range of political offences.[2]

All political activity was declared illegal. Official control of the news media was ensured by making it a criminal offence to publish any information about guerrilla activity other than that which had been officially issued to the press through the President's public relations office. The "state of siege" remained in force until the anniversary of the coup which had brought General Ríos Montt to power, when he replaced it with a "state of alarm".

The massacres

The massacres that were being carried out in the Guatemalan countryside were first brought to public attention in May when a group of peasants occupied the Brazilian Embassy in Guatemala City to demand an official investigation into killings in the countryside. They claimed that there had been a series of massacres in over 20 villages in the departments of El Quiché, Chimaltenango, Huehuetenango and Sololá. They stated that almost 800 people had been killed in these regions between 2 April and 8 May and that peasant livestock and property had been destroyed. They stated that although some of the killings had been carried out by men in plain clothes in fact the army were responsible for most of them. A United States (US) congressional fact-finding mission which visited Guatemala in the same month concurred. They reported that "army massacres of civilians are continuing in some parts of the country despite a sharp drop in security-attributed violence in other areas."

Until the "state of siege" was declared and press censorship imposed, the Guatemalan news media reported at least 30 massacres which had taken place since the coup, with a death toll of 584. The newspaper *Diario El Gráfico* carried editorials, signed for the first time in many years, in which the newspaper's director denounced the massacres. "It would be difficult," he wrote on 17 May, "for any person in his right mind to imagine this kind of extermination. How

---

[2] Amnesty International's concerns about Decree 46-82 are described in Chapter III.

is it possible to behead an eight or nine year old child? How is it possible for a human adult to murder in cold blood a baby of less than a year and a half? ... In war ... one cannot hope for mercy on the battlefield ... that is understandable, but not someone who kills defenceless non-combatants, children and old people who are not involved in anything. Nor is it acceptable to murder pregnant women."

One of the massacres described by the peasants had taken place in the villages of Chocorales and Semejá I in El Quiché. They said that 29 people had been burned alive in their homes. In another village, in northern Quiché, they said that the army had forced everyone into the courthouse, raped the women, beheaded the men and battered the children to death against the rocks in a nearby river.

Peasant, religious and human rights organizations, journalists and foreign delegates, reported further massacres of peasants in rural Guatemala since General Ríos Montt took power. The killings reported were brutal. The army was said to be burning people alive, garotting them, hacking them to death with machetes and killing whole families with a blast of machine-gun fire.

Many of the reports came from eye-witnesses; Indian peasants who had fled across the border into Mexico, where they gave accounts of what was happening to religious and refugee workers. The diocese of San Cristóbal de las Casas in Chiapas issued a statement which declared that, according to numerous refugees, "They [Guatemalan soldiers] have cut open the stomachs of children of nursing age, and left them to die in agony in front of their mothers. They kill other people with machetes, or by hanging, or they drown them in rivers or break all their bones and leave them to die. None of this is fantasy or exaggeration. There are abundant testimonies to document this. It is dreadful to see the faces of those who survived."

A nun working with refugees gave the following account to a Swedish mission of inquiry. "A case I have here is of an 18-year-old girl who recently married. Two months after the wedding she was pregnant. Then the soldiers came to the house to arrest the husband. He was only 17. They cut him to pieces.

"In another village, all the catechists were gathered for a meeting. Soldiers came and surrounded the house so that nobody could get away. They took them all and cut their feet with machetes and then forced them to walk, and they followed them and killed them with the machetes. We have their relatives here.

"One of the women who is here now lost her brother on 26 May. The soldiers surrounded the village and arrested everybody in the church and locked them up there. The brother, a 14-year-old boy, had just returned from the maize field and was sorting the cobs, as they always do. He was arrested because they believed he was a guerrilla. He was hung from a tree. Then they forced the people from the village to whip him. The soldiers were standing behind those who pulled the rope and those who had the whips and they pushed them with their bayonets and forced them to continue. So the women whipped him to death. And one of them was his sister."

One of the witnesses of such killings was a 17-year-old Kekchi Indian, from the hamlet of Chirrenquiché, Cobán, Alta Verapaz which was attacked by the army on 7 April. The girl was hacked with machetes and wounded in the neck, head and foot. One of her hands was almost amputated. Her brother, a child of 13, was also seized and wounded by the army. Of their entire family, only the two of them remained alive.

The girl went into hiding, but gave foreign journalists the following testimony about the attack: "The soldiers came; we went to the mountains; there we found tree trunks and stones where we hid. A group of soldiers came from behind, they came in behind us. They seized three of us; they took them to the mountains; they tied them up in the mountains and killed them with machetes and knives. There they died.

"Then they asked me which ones were the guerrillas, and I didn't tell them, so they slashed me with the machete; they raped me; they threw me on the ground and slashed my head with the machete, my breasts, my entire hand. When dawn came, I tried to get home. By then I could hardly walk. I came across a girl from our village, and she was carrying some water. She gave me some and took me to her house.

"The army also seized my 13-year-old brother Ramos and dragged him away, and shot him in the foot and left him thrown on the ground. My brother and my parents and my other brothers and sisters had been in the house. The soldiers said: 'They are guerrillas, and they must be killed'. My brother saw how they killed my parents, my brothers and sisters and my little one-year-old brother; the soldiers machine-gunned them to death when they arrived in the village. Only my brother, Ramos, and I are alive. Our friends are giving us injections and medicines. We can't go to the hospital at Cobán. I think they would kill us there." Amnesty International has a video tape recording of her testimony, which shows the girl displaying wounds consistent with her statement about the injuries inflicted on her.

A 10-year-old boy from the San Ildefonso region of Huehuetenango, also interviewed in Mexico, described the killing in his village as follows: "I saw the massacre which they committed in my village.

I was there one night when a group of men came. First, we heard the trucks. Then the men came, they carried arms. They came to take everyone out of their houses and I heard in the night how the people were screaming. They passed behind the house where I was lying. I heard when the people screamed and everything. They asked for help, that someone help them. But no one could for fear. Then in the morning we went to see the road. They were all thrown there, already shot dead. There was blood all over the road. Later when we were going in a bus to San Ildefonso we saw naked women strewn there, already killed by the soldiers. There were a lot of them. I don't know how many, maybe more than 30. Later in the afternoon, we saw about 25 more dead people. They were being buried without any coffins. They just made a hole and put everyone in it without a coffin or clothes. We were afraid that they were going to kill us too. That is why we came to Mexico."

In July, about two weeks after the "state of siege" had been declared, almost the entire population of the village of San Francisco, Nentón, in the department of Huehuetenango were killed. The massacre at San Francisco, Nentón was among the best documented incidents of large-scale extrajudicial executions of non-combatant civilians in rural Guatemala. Much of the initial documentation was carried out by priests in Mexico working under the auspices of the Guatemalan Justice and Peace Committee. Their findings have been confirmed by numerous independent missions of inquiry and visiting journalists and television teams who either interviewed the survivors in Mexico, or spoke to residents and foreign clerics in villages near San Francisco. The priests who collected testimony in Mexico stated that they had investigated this, one among many massacre reports, in depth in order to make clear to those abroad who were unable to believe such reports, that large-scale massacres of non-combatant civilians at the hands of the Guatemalan military were, indeed, occurring. Their study was also intended to go beyond recounting of figures of those killed, in an attempt to give an idea of the people who were daily the victims of such abuses and how they had died.

The few survivors of the massacre at San Francisco gave the following account of how the villagers were killed. At 11am on Saturday 17 July the army arrived in San Francisco having passed through the nearby villages of Bulej and Yalambojoch. The army had previously visited the village on 24 June and had told the inhabitants that they would be killed if they were found not to be peacefully working in their homes and fields. Soldiers had also said, however, that the villagers should not run away from the army, as it was there to defend them. On 17 July some 600 soldiers arrived on foot. A helicopter circled nearby and eventually landed. The military were accompanied by an ex-guerrilla, now in military uniform, who was apparently acting as the army's informer. (According to a US priest, resident in the area, this same man had denounced other villagers from nearby hamlets both before and after the San Francisco massacre.)

The people were told to assemble for a discussion with the colonel. It was the first day on which the village's new civil defence patrol was to have begun its duties. Some of the survivors said that the patrol, of 21, was taken away shortly after the arrival of the army and had not been seen since. They are presumed dead.

According to the testimonies collected by the priests, the villagers first sensed that they were in danger when a man whom survivors said had been "tied up like a pig" was brought before them by the soldiers. They knew he had not been involved in anything, and yet saw that he was being "punished". They also saw how "angry" the commander appeared to be and began to fear for themselves. They were first asked to unload the soldiers' food supplies from the helicopter, which they did. The men were then shut up in the courthouse, and the people were told that they must provide two of their own cattle for the soldiers to eat. A team was sent out to get the cattle. The women were then shut up in the church, many of them carrying young children tied to their backs. The catechists told the men in the courthouse to begin praying "to make their peace with God", as they were about to suffer. A survivor described how: "We pray, 11 o'clock, 12 o'clock passes. By now, everyone has come into town and been shut up. And then, at 1 o'clock, it begins: a blast of gunfire at the women, there in the church. It makes so much noise. All the little children are crying."

This witness went on to tell how the women who survived the initial gunfire were then taken off in small groups to different houses by soldiers where they were killed, many apparently with machetes. After they had been killed, the houses were set on fire. This witness and the others interviewed, described a particularly atrocious killing they had seen, the murder of a child of about three. The child was disembowelled, as were several others, but kept screaming, until a soldier smashed his head with a pole, then swung him by his feet and threw him into a burning house. "Yes", said the witness, "yes, I saw it. Yes, I saw how they threw him in, how they beat him hard on the head, then threw him away, threw him into the house."

This witness continued: "At 3 o'clock, they began with the men. They ordered them out of the courthouse in small groups, and then blasted them with gun-fire. It went on and on. They tied up the men's hands and then 'bang, bang'. We couldn't see, we could only hear the noise of the guns. The killing took place in the courtyard outside the courthouse, then they'd throw the bodies into the church. They killed the three old people with a blunt machete, the way you would kill sheep. They cut their throats."

Another witness described how the old were killed: "The old people said, 'What have we done, no, we are tired and old. We're not thinking of doing anything. We're not strong. We can't do anything anymore.' But they said, 'You're not worth anything anymore, even if you're tired. Get out of there'. They dragged them out, and knifed them. They stabbed and cut them as if they were animals and they were laughing when they killed them. They killed them with a machete that had no teeth. They put one old man on a table, and cut open his chest, the poor man, and he was still alive, and so they started to cut his throat. They cut his throat slowly. He was suffering a lot. They were cutting people under the ribs, and blood came rushing out and they were laughing." Another survivor continued: "When they got to the end, they killed six people in the courthouse. One was a military commissioner. They didn't care. They killed him there at his table with his three policemen.

"By now it was about 6.30pm. It was getting dark outside. They threw a bomb into the corner of the courthouse. It was bloody, two were killed. How the blood ran! It ran all over me. Then they fired at the remaining people in the courthouse. Then they threw all the bodies in a heap. They dragged people by the feet, as if they were animals. They threw me on top of the dead bodies."

This witness went on to describe how he fled, by climbing out of the courthouse through an open window and then crawling away. Four tried to escape this way, but one was shot and killed. On the road, this witness met another man who had also escaped through the window and together, after passing through villages nearby, deserted after their inhabitants heard what had happened in San Francisco, the two arrived in Mexico the following day. People from nearby villages, also interviewed in Mexico, told of coming across these survivors, covered in blood, as they made their way to the border.

One witness ended his testimony: "Father, my heart is so heavy with pain for the dead, because of what I have seen. I saw how my brothers died. All of them: friends, godparents, everyone, as we are all brothers. My heart will cry for them for the rest of my life. But they had committed no crime. Nobody said: 'This is your crime. Here is the proof.' They just killed them, that's all. That's how death came." According to the priests to whom this account was given all the survivors seemed to be genuinely bewildered about why this should have happened to them. Some could only interpret it as a punishment from God for some sin they must have committed.

Besides the men who escaped from the courthouse, other survivors who reached Mexico included people who were at work in the fields when the army came and stayed outside the town when they heard gun-fire: three villagers, one of them a young girl, whom the soldiers had left for dead, and a man who was one of the team sent to bring cattle for the soldiers' meal, but decided not to return to the village. He said: "I was sure we were going to be killed and I decided to hide." His companions did return and were killed, as were his wife and nine children.

The priests also interviewed refugees from nearby hamlets who had fled largely as a result of the terror caused by the San Francisco massacre. Some of them had heard the gun-fire or seen the smoke. Others were warned by word of mouth. Some had gone to San Francisco to investigate, after hearing of the massacre, or had passed through the village on their way to Mexico and were able to confirm that the buildings where survivors said the village's inhabitants had been confined before being killed had indeed been burnt to the ground, and that they had seen bodies which had their hands tied behind their backs, with clear signs of having been tortured. One of these witnesses stated: "Many had been burned and others had their heads cut off. They had torn the intestines out of some of them. The bodies were piled up in the courthouse and in some of the houses. The dogs had begun to eat the bodies that hadn't been burned. It smelt awful ... They left a 13-year-old girl alive who was without a foot. She was alone in a house, one of the few that didn't burn. She told me that members of her family had been killed."

A US priest, resident in the area, was told by a man from a nearby village that he had seen the smoke rising from San Francisco and had realized that the army was burning the village. In the evening, the man went to San Francisco to see what had happened. When he came near he saw "corpses everywhere, children without heads or with their arms cut off, women with their bellies cut open and the intestines torn out. They had done the same to many older children." The same priest later reported that the people from Bulej, a village in the vicinity, were ordered to go to San Francisco to bury the remains of those killed.

A list of the dead at San Francisco was compiled in Mexico on 5 September by a young Indian and two or three older men, who called the survivors to name their dead relatives, so that the names could be read out at a mass to be held at La Gloria, Chiapas. The list compiled included 302 names. Ninety-one of them were children under the age of 12. The youngest victim of the massacre, André Paíz Garcia, was less than two months old. Each person who named relatives killed in San Francisco was asked who had killed them.

Each replied that it was the army.

Other refugees told of smaller scale massacres in nearby hamlets, both before and after the San Francisco incident, suggesting that the area had been subjected to an army "sweep" in mid-July. On 19 July, testimonies indicate that the army went to Yalambojoch and killed villagers there, passing through Yaltoyas first, where 30 people were killed. Fifteen women and 15 children were also killed by the army on the road from Yalambojoch. The women were peasants from Aguacate who were fleeing to Mexico after hearing of the San Francisco massacres and encountered the army on the road. Their husbands had sent them on ahead. One of the husbands found the women's bodies as he hurried to catch up with them. Among the dead were Maria Domingo, Magdalena Gomez, Petrona Domingo and Juana Catarina Domingo. One was a child of eight months, Catarina Domingo.

Another well-documented massacre was the reported killing of 89 people in the village of Petanac, San Mateo Ixtatán, also in Hue-huetenango, on 14 July. Here too, the villagers were divided into groups of men, women and children and killed in different houses which were then burned. A list of the dead was also compiled, this time in Guatemala itself, by the priest in whose parish the killings had occurred. Testimony received from within Guatemala concurred with accounts given to investigators in Mexico, including a US doctor and a French ethnographer, by survivors who had taken refuge there. The list of victims included 37 children.

In the words of an American priest who wrote abroad to denounce the massacre: "The local military commander sent word for all the people of the hamlet to be assembled for his 11am arrival. One man had gone to work in his corn field, so was not present. At 4pm, all of the men, with their hands tied behind their backs, were escorted by the soldiers to one house, shot, stabbed, piled on top of each other and covered with burnable items of the very house, which were sprinkled with gasoline and set on fire. The women were treated the same as the men, differing only in that some had live babies on their backs when they were stacked for burning. The other children were tied, one to another, and pulled alive into the flames of a third house by some soldiers. The two houses of the women and children were completely gutted; the fire designed to consume the men went out without burning the house or even the ropes binding their hands. Since the soldiers had left, they were unaware that one of their three pyres was ill-prepared."

A survivor testified that: "I didn't realise that the army was there and I went into the village. The army began to shoot at me, to chase me, and I ran. I didn't realize that a bullet had hit my hand. I got away to the hills, and that's why they didn't kill me. I didn't see how many they killed. I was going to go to the hospital, but many people said to come here [Mexico]. The army goes to the hospital and if anyone goes to the hospital with a bullet wound, they say you are a guerrilla. The army is killing many peasants in the areas near the frontier. In that area the army has moved in."

Another witness, who was working in the fields at the time of the attack and saw the smoke, stated that: "When I came near, I saw the army. They shut up the men, the women and the children in different houses. They decapitated the people from the civil patrol, there were 12 of them. They burned the houses where the people were. They were pillaging all of the homes."

In another incident reported to Amnesty International, some 50 soldiers and a civil defence patrol of 150 entered the village of Agua Fria, Rabinal in the department of Alta Verapaz on 13 September. Witnesses said that the civil defence patrol was ordered to surround the dwellings and the paths while the soldiers gathered the families together. Women and children were separated from the men. The soldiers then poured gasoline on both groups and ignited them, burning them alive and machine-gunning those who tried to escape.

A number of foreign delegations investigated reports of killings in the department of Chimaltenango in October 1982. The army was reported to have promised peasants who had fled into the hills following earlier military attacks that they could safely return to their homes. However the delegations found that returning peasants who were suspected to have been in any way involved with opposition forces had been summarily executed.

By the end of 1982 it was reported that some 30,000 Indian peasants fleeing the massacres had sought refuge in Mexico. Even then they were not safe. During 1982, Amnesty International received reports that large groups of refugees had been forcibly repatriated to Guatemala by local officials in southern Mexico. There were reports that some of these refugees who had been sent back to Guatemala had suffered further abuses there, and that some had been killed. Amnesty International also received detailed accounts of the incursion into Mexican territory of Guatemalan troops. Some of these accounts were collected by Amnesty International during a visit to the Mexican refugee camps. Eye-witnesses told how Guatemalan soldiers had, in 1983, killed Guatemalans on Mexican territory and abducted others and taken them back across the border, where they were summarily executed.

In March 1983 a nominee proposed by the Chairman of the UN Commission on Human Rights to act as the Commission's Special Rapporteur on the human rights situation in Guatemala was accepted by the Guatemalan Government; the Commission had first sought to make such an appointment in 1981. Following on-site investigations, the Special Rapporteur reported to the UN General Assembly in November 1983. He said that for a number of reasons, such as limited time and the difficulties of travelling in areas of conflict between the army and the guerrilla opposition, he had been unable to verify all the allegations he had received concerning human rights violations. He stated, however, that he had found no reason to doubt that the Guatemalan military had been responsible for at least some of the massacres attributed to it, including the extrajudicial execution of more than 300 men, women and children at San Francisco, Nentón, Huehuetenango in July 1982.

The counter-insurgency strategy of General Ríos Montt

General Ríos Montt pursued a counter-insurgency strategy similar to that of his predecessors. However, during his administration army operations in the countryside intensified.

Within one week of the March coup the members of the *junta* which had seized power flew by helicopter to visit strategic local counter-insurgency bases in the areas where the guerrillas were strongest.

A formal indication of the *junta's* counter-insurgency strategy was given the following month in a confidential four-page document circulated by the Guatemalan military.[3] The document, entitled "National Security and Development Plan" stated: "The manpower, armaments and equipment of the Guatemalan army are not adequate to cover the different fronts presented by armed subversion". It declared that "changes in the basic structure of the State" would therefore be necessary, and called for a public campaign of "psychological action at all levels" to win popular support while the *junta* privately "increased the legal and functional capacity of anti-subversive organisms" and created "at the highest political level, an organism for the direction of anti-subversive functions".

In the following months massacres by the army of non-combatant civilians in the countryside increased. The killings appeared to be concentrated in very specific areas: those where guerrilla activity was strongest. So although there was less killing in some provinces after the coup, in the departments where the guerrilla forces had made the most advances — El Quiché, Chimaltenango, Sololá, Sacatepéquez, Huehuetenango and Alta and Baja Verapaz — reports of the

---

[3] A copy of this document was made available to Amnesty International.

raiding and burning of villages and the murder of large numbers of Indian peasants continued.

Information about the strategy implemented by his predecessors and continued by General Ríos Montt had been given by high-ranking officials of former administrations who testified that both the military and the police had been behind such killings while they had served in government. Two such officials were General Lucas García's vice-presidential running mate, Francisco Villagrán Kramer, who eventually left the country and went into exile in protest at the continuing violence under General Lucas García, and the dismissed former head of the *judiciales,* Jesús Valiente Téllez, also in exile after an internecine police feud during which several members of his family were killed. Both men unequivocally stated that past killings were carried out on orders from the highest level of the government and then officially attributed to "extremist groups of the left and right". Jesús Valiente told a foreign journalist he wanted to return to Guatemala to, "denounce those assassins who subjected our country to a bloodbath, and tried to make governments around the world believe that the guerrillas were responsible". After the March coup he offered to return to give evidence concerning attacks in which he had participated or of which he had been the victim, but the *junta* publicly announced that he would be arrested if he tried to enter Guatemala.

Similar testimony was given by Elías Barahona y Barahona, who had worked in the press office of the Ministry of the Interior until his defection in September 1980. He confirmed that the steps being taken by General Ríos Montt were consistent with the Lucas García administration's National Security and Development Plan, to which he had had access. According to Elías Barahona the full plan envisaged a strategy based on the destruction of hamlets, burning of forests and the extermination of the civilian population in an attempt to stop the guerrillas. The plan also contained a blue-print for a counter-information campaign, necessary in order to confuse public opinion on both a national and international level about who had actually been responsible for the massacres which were to be carried out by paramilitary units, the police and the army in rural areas of the country. Elías Barahona further stated, in a declaration made available to the UN Working Group on Disappearances in September 1982, that the full plan outlined the formation of civil defence patrols, specified that soldiers should use civilian clothing to pose as guerrillas, and that after they had attacked, were to return in helicopters to collect bodies and aid the victims.

A North American pastor, who spent three years in Guatemala, said, in a report to his church's central body[4] that the army was continuing to carry out intact policies initially instituted under former President Lucas García. He wrote that under this "scorched earth strategy", officers determined or alleged that a certain village was "cooperating" with the guerrillas. Once that judgment had been made, according to the pastor, "nothing stops the ensuing process. First people received threats or were simply picked up for interrogation or "disappeared". Later key village people were murdered. Finally, the entire village would be wiped out, with large numbers of people killed, while the survivors fled into the mountains or to nearby cities or villages." He stated: "I have seen the results of this action in Chimaltenango. I have talked often with villagers from that area and from Huehuetenango, San Marcos and Quezaltenango. Only occasionally had the people known of the guerrillas. But the army policy knew no nuances. The policy was to destroy, with the result that today there are large sections of the altiplano to the north of the Pan American highway that are virtual wastelands. Villagers blamed the army and had only the question 'Why?' ".

Blaming the guerrillas

The *junta* publicly denied that the massacres were being carried out by the army and repeatedly maintained either that those killed were guerrillas or else had been killed by guerrillas. However Guatemalan peasant organizations, foreign religious workers, Indian groups, Christian groups and foreign missions of inquiry accused the government of responsibility for the massacres and produced reports which documented them in detail. They believed the killings to be a deliberate tactic in the government's counter-insurgency program, designed to clear the civilian population from areas of conflict and thus remove any possible logistic support for the guerrillas. Some areas were cleared of their inhabitants, who were either killed or fled, across the border to Mexico, to larger cities in the area or into the mountains or jungles surrounding threatened villages.

On a number of occasions well-documented evidence, including testimonies from surviving relatives of murdered Guatemalans, indicated that the uniformed military had been responsible for specific killings: press reports, however, gave the official version — that guerrilla groups had been responsible.

In other instances, opposition groups have alleged that government troops or paramilitary units carried out massacres in plain clothes,

---

[4] The report was made available to Amnesty International on condition that not even the church's denomination be named.

Indian peasants, Guatemala © *Jerome Liebling*

Guatemalan soldier. The inscription on the truck reads: "The army of Guatemala at the service of the people".

© *fotografia mercadini*

In almost two decades of military rule in Guatemala arbitrary arrest, torture, "disappearance" and political killings were everyday realities for thousands of Guatemalans. (*Top*) Grave of the victim of a political killing. (*Above*) The sole survivors of a family of 23. All the others "disappeared" in recent years.

© *Jean-Marie Simon*

Guatemalan children in a refugee camp in Mexico. Thousands of Indian peasants in areas attacked by the Guatemalan army fled for their lives across the border into Mexico. Even there they were not safe. Guatemalan troops staged cross-border raids into the camps and either forced the refugees back at gunpoint or killed them on the spot.

People came from all over Guatemala to present evidence of human rights violations to Amnesty International during the organization's visit to the country in 1985.

© *Jean-Marie Simon*

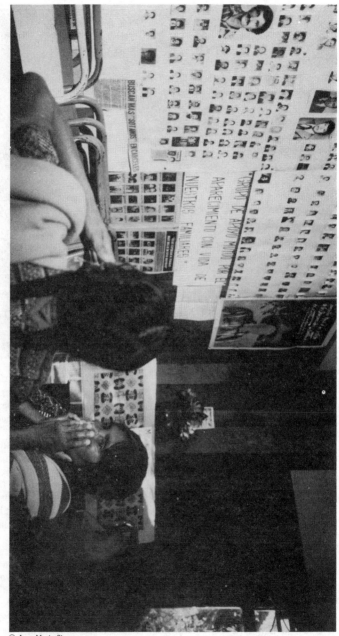

The walls of the Guatemala City offices of GAM, the Mutual Support Group for those whose relatives have "disappeared", are lined with photographs of the missing. GAM was formed in June 1984 by people trying to trace their relatives.

© Jean-Marie Simon

74

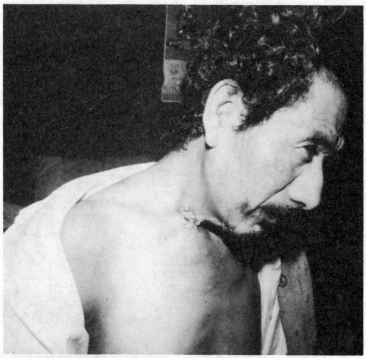

© Jean-Marie Simon

Clergy, catechists and lay church workers have long been targets of repression in Guatemala, apparently because of their influence and leadership within their communities. Between 1980 and 1981 nine Roman Catholic priests were reported to have "disappeared" or been killed by the security forces.

Rogelio Cruz (*above*), a catechist, escaped after being tortured by the army in Santa Ana and sought refuge in Mexico.

Rafael Yos Muxtay (*left*), also a catechist, has not been seen since he was abducted in November 1985. His detention has not been acknowledged despite the fact that he was seized by members of the armed forces in front of witnesses.

Security force involvement in kidnappings and killings has often been established by the equipment used, such as vehicles, when the person was abducted or killed in front of witnesses. Such a case is that of agronomist Jorge Alberto Rosal Paz (*right, with his baby daughter*) who "disappeared in August 1983. He was forced into a jeep from an army base near his home in Zacapa, eastern Guatemala in front of witnesses. However army and government officials have consistently denied that he was detained. (*Above*) His wife Blanca Rosal, with their two children. His son was born after he "disappeared". Blanca Rosal left Guatemala with the children after she had received death threats. The family is now living in the United States.

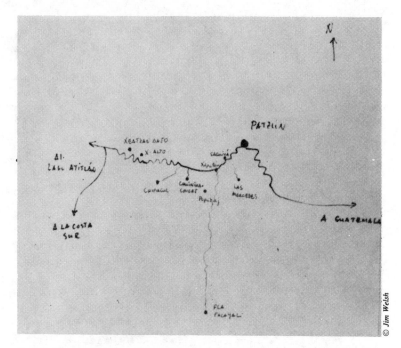

© Jim Welsh

Having received detailed information about "disappearances" and killings in the area, Amnesty International's delegation visited the Patzún military base in Chimaltenango to investigate reports that it was used as a secret detention and torture centre and had a clandestine burial site. (*Above*) Map of the Patzún area drawn for Amnesty International's delegation by local people. (*Left*) Testimony given to the delegation stating that people are taken to the military base, killed and buried there. (*Opposite, above*) Civil defence patrol member at the barrier blocking the entrance to the hamlet of Xeatzán, near Patzún. (*Opposite, below*) Entrance to the Patzún military base. The sign over the entrance says "Welcome to the military base".

In 1982 many thousands of rural Indian peasants were massacred by the Guatemalan army in a drive to crush growing guerrilla opposition. The exact number of dead is not known but all estimates put the toll in the tens of thousands. These drawings, by a young girl, depict what happened when the army attacked her village.

This 17-year-old Keckhi Indian is from a hamlet in Alta Verapaz which was attacked by the army in April 1982. She was hacked with machetes and wounded in the neck, head and foot. One of her hands was almost cut off. Her brother, a child of 13, was also wounded by the army. All the rest of their family were killed in the attack. © *Jean-Marie Simon*

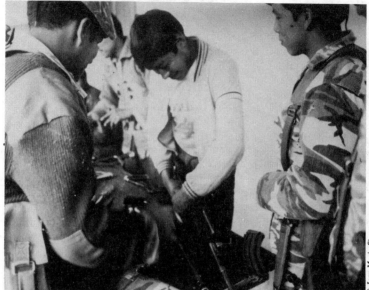

© Jean-Marie Simon

© Jean-Marie Simon

Members of civil defence patrols (*above*) receiving weapons training from the Guatemalan army and (*left*) on duty. These patrols were introduced during the Lucas García administration and were intended to further its counter-insurgency strategy. They were greatly extended by General Ríos Montt. Although the authorities claimed that the patrols were voluntarily formed by villagers to defend themselves against guerrilla attacks, Amnesty International has concluded that villagers were forced to join the patrols under military orders and that they acted under military supervision as adjuncts to the regular army. Peasant organizations reported, for example, that peasants were told that they would be killed and all their property burned if they refused to join the patrols.

(*Top*) Members of the *kaibiles*, the elite counter-insurgency units, addressing the inhabitants of the village of Chajul, El Quiché, in May 1982. The unit is named after a Mayan war god. (*Above*) Army helicopter landing in Nebaj, El Quiché, April 1982.

82

The town of Chiché, in the department of El Quiché, in April 1982, deserted after its inhabitants fled from the army.

These files, supposedly of people targetted for assassination, were found in the house of Donaldo Alvarez Ruiz, who was Minister of the Interior during the Lucas García administration. GAM believes he was responsible for "disappearances" between 1978 and 1982.

© Jean-Marie Simon

(*Above*) **La Verbena Cemetery in Guatemala City. People come here to see whether a missing relative or friend is among the many unidentified bodies brought to the cemetery and buried in unmarked graves as "XX".** (*Opposite*) **A woman and her child at a demonstration on behalf of the "disappeared".**

Trade unionists and their leaders have frequently been victims of human rights violations. In 1980 trade unionism in Guatemala was dealt a heavy blow when 25 leaders of the CNT (the National Workers Congress) were abducted by the security forces. They have never been seen again. (*Above, right*) Irma Candelaria Pérez Osorio, one of the CNT leaders, was only 19 when she "disappeared". (*Above, left*) America Yolanda Urízar, a labour lawyer and adviser to the CNT, "disappeared" in 1983 after being arrested near the Mexican border.

Ileana del Rosario Solares Castillo (*left*) was last seen alive in August 1983 in the Guatemala City women's prison. Amnesty International fears that she is among the many "disappeared" who have been secretly and summarily executed.

In 1984 the EGSA factory, which bottled for Coca-Cola and other soft drink companies, was occupied to prevent its closure. Amnesty International was concerned because in the past security forces had invaded the plant and killed or abducted the workers. (*Top*) The delivery van is loaded with food sent by other trade unionists to support the occupation. (*Above*) The canteen during the occupation. On the walls are pictures of past leaders of the plant union who were killed or abducted by the security forces.

Hugo de León Palacios (*left*), a primary school teacher and law student, was abducted in March 1984 by four heavily armed men in plain clothes. His wife and two daughters (*above*) have neither seen nor heard of him since. Luis Fernando de la Roca Elías (*right*), a 25-year-old USAC engineering student, was abducted in Guatemala City on 9 September 1985. Three days later armed men in plain clothes searched his house and told his mother he was being held by the National Police. However, the authorities deny that he was detained and he is still missing.

CARTA ABIERTA
A QUIENES TENGAN EN SU PODER A MI PAPITO
EDGAR FERNANDO GARCIA

El mundo está lleno de padres extraordinarios. Padres que dan todo por sus hijos, incluso la vida. Yo quisiera hoy realzar a un padre que sobresale entre los demás. Por lo que es y por quien es, ocupa un lugar de excepción en mi vida. Ese padre, es el mío; EDGAR FERNANDO GARCIA. Yo amo a mi papito, por su vida noble y llena de amor. Sin lugar a dudas, su virtud máxima es el amor. Un amor que da todo por los demás.

¿Dónde está él? El es indispensable para mí, sin lugar a dudas ni vacilaciones.

PUEDEN IMAGINAR LA TRISTEZA DE UNA NIÑA QUE NO HA VISTO A SU PAPITO DESDE HACE TANTO TIEMPO? O su desconsuelo por las noches cuando no le ve volver? O su angustia inexpresable, de que con su amor al que tanto ama está sucediendo algo que ella no comprende.

¿Dónde está mi papito? El ser más querido por mí, mi ángel.

El constantemente piensa en nosotros, pero nunca en sí mismo. ¡Cuánto te amo papá! A mi adorado papito, estoy segura que te veré pronto. Cuánto agradezco a Dios por ser tu hija. Eres una persona sensible a los sentimientos de los demás. Me siento orgullosa de ti, y solamente viviré para el día cuando te vea otra vez y no nos separemos nunca más.

The above is an example of an advertisement placed in the newspapers by relatives of the "disappeared", begging for them to be returned alive. This advertisement, placed on behalf of USAC student and trade unionist Edgar Fernando García (*inset, right*) and accompanied by a photograph of his 18-month-old daughter, is headed "Open letter to those who are holding my daddy", and continues "I love my daddy . . . Where is he? . . ."

90

(*Top*) Demonstration in support of human rights in 1985. The banner calls on the governmental Tripartite Commission to investigate the fate of the "disappeared". The commission disbanded itself in June 1985, after reporting that it had been unable to find out what had happened to a single one of the missing people whose cases had been submitted to it. (*Above*) GAM member Isabel Castañon taking information from Indian women about their "disappeared" husbands. Her husband, trade union and USAC student leader Gustavo Adolfo Castañon Fuentes, has also "disappeared".

91

(Top) GAM organized this demonstration by relatives of the "disappeared". White carnations are the symbol of mourning in Guatemala. *(Above)* Rosario Godoy de Cuevas, GAM leader and founder member, addressing a GAM rally. She was killed in 1985 (see following pages).

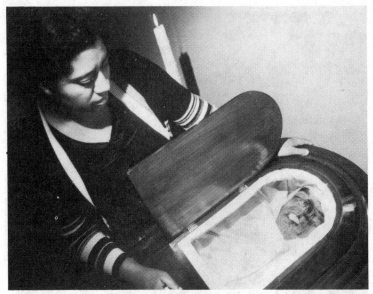

In 1985 GAM leaders Héctor Gómez Calito and Rosario Godoy de Cuevas were killed in circumstances which suggested security force responsibility for the deaths. (*Top*) Mercedes Gómez at her husband's wake and (*above*) at a demonstration called in protest at his murder. He was abducted on 30 March 1985, a few days after GAM had notified the international community of its plans for future public activities. His tortured and mutilated body was found the next morning.   © *Jean-Marie Simon*

Rosario Godoy de Cuevas with her husband, Carlos Ernesto Cuevas Molina. A USAC student and trade union leader, he "disappeared" in May 1984. Witnesses saw him shot and forced into a car by four heavily armed men believed to be members of the security forces. The following month Rosario Godoy de Cuevas helped found GAM. She was killed four days after Hector Gómez' body was found, along with her brother and three-year-old son, victims, according to the authorities, of a car accident.

or while wearing indigenous clothing, in order to make it appear that guerrilla groups were responsible. This corresponded to testimony received by Amnesty International. Before the March coup, survivors of attacks on villages who had fled to Mexico told of fellow villagers being killed by men in plain clothes who later changed into uniform.

Other testimony made available to Amnesty International also tells of the army carrying out raids on villages while dressed in the olive-green garb of the guerrilla forces or in plain clothes. Official communiques subsequently attributed the raids and their consequences to the guerrillas. Often soldiers returned to "investigate" abuses they had themselves carried out. Amnesty International's 1981 report on Guatemala contained the testimony of a former soldier who told of being instructed to attack villages, and then of having returned in uniform to "investigate" and look for whoever had killed the people. "But", he said, "how are we supposed to find them if it was us who did it in the first place. It is an *idea mágica* [fantastic idea]."

In one testimony received by Amnesty International a peasant described the use of similar tactics during the Ríos Montt administration: "In some cases, the soldiers go disguised as guerrillas when they massacre people, so others will think it is the guerrillas who are responsible. This is just something they have been doing recently. When they massacred the people in a village near ours, first they passed by our community dressed as guerrillas. Six hours later, they conducted a massacre nearby, dressed in their military uniforms. On the highway that goes to Monjieto they killed one of our neighbours. Our neighbour was carrying some boxes when the army passed by. We found him there, with his eyes cut out, his face torn up and his arms cut off."

Amnesty International has also received testimony on a number of occasions from relatives who spoke of a variant of this tactic, whereby young men who had been kidnapped were later found dead dressed in combat fatigues which were not their own, in order to support government statements that the dead men were guerrillas with Galil rifles.

Again and again, testimonies stated that the army could be readily distinguished from the guerrillas, even when in disguise, by the type of equipment and arms they had. It is said that the guerrillas tend to be armed mainly with M-16 rifles and other US-produced arms, bought on the open market, whereas the army is generally equipped with Galil rifles.

The arrival of men in the type of heavy transport, double traction vehicles normally used by government agencies (such as the agrarian reform body or the forestry service) is another sign that, even if they are in plain clothes, they are actually the regular army. Witness after witness insisted that only the military have armoured vehicles and that it is only in such vehicles that certain of the hamlets which have been attacked could have been reached by heavily armed men travelling in convoy.

The use of helicopters was also taken by most observers as a convincing indication that an action was carried out by the military, as it is generally agreed that the guerrillas have not got any helicopters. And, as a *Miami Herald* article of 23 August 1982 pointed out, after a series of interviews with survivors of attacks on villages, Guatemalan peasants may be unsure what uniform they saw on their assailants, but it is impossible to disbelieve them when they describe being strafed from attacking helicopters. Military commanders interviewed by foreign journalists themselves repeatedly pointed out the strategic advantage the army gained by using helicopters, as this enabled troops to surround villages or hamlets during the night, for morning attacks. In addition some of the villages where large-scale killings of non-combatant civilians occurred could only have been reached by helicopter.

In testimony about the massacres refugees frequently stated that they could easily distinguish the army from the guerrillas, even when the former were dressed in plain clothes or guerrilla uniforms. They said that the behaviour and appearance of the army was totally different to that of the guerrillas. Soldiers' hair was cut in a readily recognizable and standard way. Even when posing as guerrillas or trying to secure the trust of the people, the general behaviour of the soldiers was repeatedly said to have made it clear who they were.

One Indian woman, whose testimony was credible in all other respects, told Amnesty International that it was not only the boots worn by the army, or their haircuts, that had enabled her to recognize them when they invaded her village in plain clothes. It was their whole comportment and posture that was different: "It's the way they walk, the way they strut", she said. Another witness said that even when the soldiers who came to villages were Indians, like themselves, the soldiers were noticeably better fed. Soldiers also said, in testimony given to foreign journalists, that they were better fed in the army than they would otherwise have been, citing as advantages of having joined or been conscripted that they now had eggs regularly and enough food to send some to their families.

On a number of occasions Indian villagers did appear at government-organized press conferences or on television to tell of guerrilla responsibility for large-scale killings. However, in no case known to Amnesty International has an Indian peasant who succeeded in reaching comparative safety abroad supported claims that the guerrillas were responsible for massive extrajudicial executions. On the contrary, most declared that the atrocities they had witnessed were the work of the army.

The civilian as 'subversive'

During an interview with General Ríos Montt foreign journalists had questioned him about a report produced by Amnesty International in 1981. This report had implicated the former President, General Lucas García and the official security forces in massacres of non-combatant civilians.[5] General Ríos Montt denied that any Guatemalan general could order the death of an innocent person. However, when pressed further about reported massacres of civilians, including women and children, since the coup which brought him to power, Guatemala's military leader replied: "The problem of war is not just a question of who is shooting. For each one who is shooting there are 10 working behind him." His Press Secretary, Francisco Bianchi, continued: "The guerrillas won over many Indian collaborators. Therefore the Indians were subversives. And how do you fight subversion? Clearly you had to kill Indians because they were collaborating with subversion. And then it would be said that you were killing innocent people. But they weren't innocent. They had sold out to subversion."

The "official" view that Indian peasants were "subversive" and collaborating with the guerrilla opposition appeared to be commonly held in the ranks of the army, apparently reflecting official training courses where officers and conscripts were warned to beware of the penetration of communism and subversion in many areas of Guatemalan life, including the countryside. This emerged in many interviews foreign journalists conducted with regular soldiers, most of them illiterate conscripts, often Indian peasants themselves. Soldiers frequently insisted in interviews that the fact that villagers fled when the army came meant they must be "subversives". In an interview in La Perla, El Quiché an army sergeant said that because children carried guns even three-year-olds who fled from the army were collaborating with the guerrillas. A US priest confirmed that an army commander had told him that because a peasant had fled after being stopped at a roadblock and interrogated, he must be a guerrilla. The priest knew the man in question and considered this accusation ridiculous. Another priest described the killing of a couple

---

[5] *Guatemala: a government program of political murder.*

and their children, aged 15, 10, eight and one, in Huehuetenango. "Their offence", he said, "was being afraid of the soldiers and running from them".

People who had business which took them out of their villages, such as having to travel to administrative centres in connection with settling land disputes, reported that the army regarded them as suspicious. One soldier told his interviewer in El Quiché that the mere fact that someone was travelling along a mountain road indicated that they must be a "subversive" and should be shot. Amnesty International received numerous reports of people being shot and killed as they moved along roads, sometimes leaving villages which had been attacked by the army, sometimes going about their normal business.

Peasants, resident foreign missionary and relief workers have testified that, in an effort to prevent food or supplies reaching the guerrillas, the army forbid people to go to the towns where they usually did their shopping, or had limited the amounts of food or medicine they could buy at any one time to such small quantities that it was impossible for peasants to provision their families or their small stores without repeated trips to town. The mere fact of travelling so frequently then made them suspicious to troops who carried out constant road checks and took the names of all passengers on buses. A British journalist described to Amnesty International an incident in which he was stopped at one such roadblock in north-western Guatemala. A young soldier, he said, seemed anxious to deal on the spot with a man he had hauled off the bus and taken to one side. His commanding officer, apparently not aware that he was being overheard or understood, told the soldier to: "Wait until these foreigners have gone. Then we can finish him off. Just wait 15 minutes, can't you?"

In interviews with journalists, military commanders and soldiers in Chimaltenango and El Quiché admitted that they had summarily executed villagers on the mere suspicion of involvement with opposition forces, or simply because they lived in hamlets believed to have been sympathetic to the opposition.

One foreign journalist obtained training manuals designed to teach officers and soldiers to identify "subversives". These manuals suggested a number of specific techniques which could be used to determine which inhabitants of a hamlet might be guerrillas. One suggestion was that the army should circulate rumours that a certain hamlet was about to be invaded. It could then be noted which of the inhabitants fled and photographs could be taken of those who remained. Any whose photographs were not taken, but who were found in the village when the army returned, could be considered likely "subversives". Soldiers were also urged to look out for those who did not take steps to protect themselves from being kidnapped as this would suggest they had links with the guerrillas. On the other hand those who did change their habits and schedules should also be considered suspect.

Rank and file soldiers also spoke openly to foreign journalists about interrogation techniques used by the army to discover the whereabouts of the opposition forces. Young conscripts in El Quiché told foreign journalists in a video-taped interview made available to Amnesty International of garrotting, of hanging people from trees and houses by their necks and of hacking off pieces of people's bodies with machetes during the interrogation and torture of suspected "subversives". Soldiers in Nebaj, department of El Quiché, described in another interview how they used a garrotte to extract information from prisoners under interrogation. They said they would put a noose around the prisoner's neck and use a stick to tighten it, as though it was a tourniquet. "When the person is dying you loosen it [the noose] and question him and if he doesn't talk you give it to him again until he talks." The soldiers said they had been instructed in the use of this and other techniques by their officers. In another videoed interview in the same region soldiers admitted that they had cut off people's hands in order to make them talk.

The civil defence patrols

Members of *Patrullas de Autodefensa Civil (PAC)* local civil defence patrols were also accused of the killing of Indian villagers.

These civil defence patrols had been formed during the Lucas García administration's counter-insurgency strategy. They were greatly extended during the administration of General Ríos Montt and when General Mejía Víctores succeeded the latter he stated that his government intended to "strengthen the organization of the people in various ways, including civilian defence."

The authorities maintained that these patrols were voluntarily formed by local villagers to defend themselves against guerrilla attacks. However Amnesty International concluded, after studying the available information, that villagers were forced to form these patrols under military orders and acted under military supervision as adjuncts to the regular army. Peasant organizations reported, for example, that peasants were told that they would be killed and all their property burned if they refused to join the patrols. They also said that the army was offering those who joined the patrols the land, harvest, women and property of the massacred peasants.

Amnesty International also received detailed testimony about killings of individuals who refused to join such squads. Even when carrying out their assigned duties, civil patrollers have on some occasions been summarily executed by regular Guatemalan soldiers. The organization also received reports that many of the massacres which the government blamed on the guerrillas had in fact been carried out by the civil defence patrols. In April 1982 a foreign journalist interviewed civil defence patrol members from Baja Verapaz, who admitted that they had been involved in such killings. They stated that they acted on the orders of army commanders who had instructed them to seize and kill anyone over the age of 12 in areas or houses which the commanders considered "suspicious". Even younger children considered to be "involved" with the guerrillas were to be summarily executed. They said that although women used to be left in the house when the men were taken away, women were now being routinely raped, even when they were pregnant. One member of the patrol described the rape of a woman who had given birth five days earlier. He also said that he had seen people drowned and mutilated, some by having their ears cut off. His brother-in-law had told him that he had witnessed people being garrotted. The soldiers who led these civil patrols were, according to this man, also young Indians obliged by their commanders to order the patrols to commit such atrocities.

Another member of the patrol described the recapture of a man who had tried to escape. All his muscles were cut and gunpowder was placed in his navel and set alight. His eyes were gouged out, and his skin cut off. The soldiers jokingly described this as a barbecue. The civil patrol members said that they had been told they should denounce any family or relatives they suspected of involvement with the guerrillas. They described an incident in which the soldiers who had committed atrocities in one village returned to hand out toys to the local children as part of a "civil action" program intended to win support for the government. The soldiers then rounded up all the men who had gathered to watch the toys being distributed and took them to the village clinic. Later, six bloody ears were found in the clinic.

In another interview, a civil patrol member questioned about the killing of children had this to say: "We have to go finishing them off house by house because the parents pass on the poison [of subversion] to their children. You have to kill the parents and the children of 10, eight, five years, you have to finish them off because they've already heard the things their father says, and the children will do it."

100

Conclusion

In December 1982, during a visit to Washington DC, General Ríos Montt was asked at a news conference about reports that a "scorched earth" policy was being followed, in areas where guerrillas had been active, by destroying villages suspected of harbouring them. Giving his own interpretation of the strategy the army was pursuing, he replied: "We have no scorched earth policy. We have a policy of scorched communists." Privately he was said to have acknowledged the massacres and on one occasion to have admitted, during a meeting held with representatives of legal political parties that, "We are killing people, we are slaughtering women and children. The problem is, everyone is a guerrilla there."

The same month the US magazine *Newsweek* published the following description of the effect of the Ríos Montt counter-insurgency program: "In the far west and far north of the country, large stretches of once green farmland lie ash-black and deserted. And along the Mexico border, refugees huddled in crowded, muddy camps tell harrowing stories of army guerrilla-hunters beheading babies, setting fire to sick old men and driving stakes through the bellies of pregnant women . . ."

CHAPTER III

Death penalty by decree: Decree 46-82

Decree 46-82 represented an attempt by the Ríos Montt administration to give a veneer of legality to its effort to crush all real and imagined opposition. The Guatemalan Human Rights Commission described the decree as a "judicial monstrosity". It was crucially flawed and illustrated the *junta's* lack of understanding as to what constituted fair trial procedures or just treatment of political detainees suspected of ordinary crimes.

The decree was issued on 1 July 1982, the day on which General Ríos Montt declared a "state of siege" in Guatemala. It established *tribunales de fuero especial*, special military tribunals, with the power to impose the death penalty for an extended range of political and politically related offences after summary proceedings which severely restricted the legal safeguards of defendants. The 11th Judicial Congress of the Guatemalan Bar Association stated that it was "totally opposed" to the decree, saying that it was "anti-judicial and unjust". The decree remained in force until September 1983.

The list of offences punishable by death under this decree was lengthy: kidnapping or abduction; aggravated arson; disabling or rendering useless defence material or operations; manufacture or possession of explosives; causing a railway disaster; assault on the safety of any means of transport; causing a maritime, river or air disaster; offences against the safety of public utility services; piracy/air piracy; poisoning of water supplies or foodstuffs; treason; acts against the integrity or independence of the state; genocide; terrorism; storage of weapons or munitions and traffic in explosives. Those not sentenced to death by the military tribunals could, under Decree 46-82, be sentenced to double the penalties established by the Guatemalan Penal Code.

The death penalty had been infrequently imposed in Guatemala in recent history. The last execution known by Amnesty International to have been carried out before Decree 46-82 was issued took place in 1975, when four executions for ordinary crimes were reported. A political element was apparent in two of these. Two former agents of the National Police, Lauro Alvarado y Alvarado and Marco Tulio Osorio, were detained and prosecuted for a shooting in September

1972. Facing a possible death sentence, Lauro Alvarado smuggled a declaration out of prison stating that he had arrested, on "superior orders", a number of opposition personalities who had been turned over to higher authorities and were subsequently found dead. He also reportedly prepared a tape recording in which he detailed police involvement in the "disappearance" of further named individuals, and threatened to name the agents responsible. Although opposition leaders appealed for a stay of execution until the allegations could be investigated, both men were executed by firing-squad on 16 April 1975.

Guatemala's 1965 constitution, suspended under the July 1982 "state of siege" stated that "the death penalty shall be considered extraordinary" and imposed only for aggravated or premeditated murder.

Following the imposition of the decree, Amnesty International wrote to General Ríos Montt in August 1982 to express its concern that aspects of Decree 46-82 fell far short of international standards of fair trial. No response was received.

In all, 15 people were known to have been executed between September 1982 and March 1983 under Decree 46-82. Some of those executed had neither attended nor been legally represented during the proceedings, if indeed there had been any proceedings. In the cases of those who were tried and executed under the decree, Amnesty International's information indicates that when legal representation was permitted, it was only permitted after sentence of death had been passed. Even then, lawyers were not informed of where or to whom they should make depositions on their clients' behalf. Others were allowed legal representation but their lawyers reported being threatened with violence by heavily armed groups of men who turned up at their homes in unmarked cars and appeared to be members of the official security forces.

The first executions under Decree 46-82 were carried out at dawn on Friday, 17 September when four prisoners were shot by a firing-squad in a cemetery in Guatemala City. The four, Jaime de la Rosa Rodríguez, Julio Hernández Perdomo, Marcelino Marroquín and Julio César Vásquez Juarez, had been charged with membership of the *Ejército Guerrillero de los Pobres* (EGP), the Guerrilla Army of the Poor, which they denied. Officials of the opposition forces grouped under the *Comité Guatemalteco de Unidad Patriotica* (CGUP), Guatemalan Committee of Patriotic Unity, stated that they had no record that any of the four men were militants and other sources reported that three of the four were known to be Christian activists, but that there was no information to suggest that any of them had joined the guerrillas. They were reportedly convicted on the basis of having EGP literature in their homes, but the proceedings were held in secrecy.

The executions had been announced only 12 hours before they were carried out and it was only when they heard the announcement that the men's families learned of their whereabouts. They had "disappeared" some time earlier. Following an international outcry that the executed men had not had an adequate defence or the right of appeal, a *pro forma* appeals mechanism was later established.

The next executions under Decree 46-82 took place on 3 March 1983, shortly before Pope John Paul II arrived in Guatemala, despite worldwide appeals for clemency — two of them from the Vatican. The six victims were Héctor Haraldo Morales López, two brothers, Walter Vinicio and Sergio Marroquín González, Marco Antonio González, a Honduran national, and two Indian peasants — Carlos Subuyug Cuc and Pedro Raxon Tebet. All six were convicted on 19 January 1983. Héctor Morales was charged with kidnapping for ransom in the name of an armed opposition group, possession of firearms, possession of US$40,000 and the rape of the alleged kidnap victim.

Héctor Morales was arrested on 9 September at the bank where he worked: there is documentary evidence that he had been at work that day — cheques and receipts that he had signed, for example. Eye-witnesses said they saw him seized in the bank by armed men in plain clothes, who grabbed him by the neck, threw him into a car and told him not to say a word or he would die on the spot.

However, the official indictment against Héctor Morales stated that he and another two of the men executed with him had been arrested on 4 September as they arrived to collect the ransom they had demanded from the parents of the woman they were charged with kidnapping and raping. Similar evidence exists indicating that the other two had been arrested separately on different days in early September.

Not one of the six was legally represented at the proceedings which found them guilty and condemned them to death. Even the alleged victim's parents filed a formal protest saying that they did not think the proceedings under which the men were convicted had been just or in accordance with the law, and that they had never seen any of the case documentation or other evidence on which the conviction was supposedly based.

Amnesty International repeatedly expressed concern to the authorities about the judicial proceedings which led to the executions. The organization was particularly concerned by reports that the six were convicted on the basis of "confessions" extracted under torture. Eye-witnesses reported, for example, that the six were subjected to constant rounds of "Russian Roulette" by prison guards who joked that the men were going to die in any case. While awaiting execution the men were held in a cell which one of them described as "sub-human". The walls were wet and damp and the only light came from a small barred window. There were no sanitary facilities.

On 2 February, the men were taken to a cemetery. There they passed by coffins which they were told were for them. They were blindfolded and lined up against a wall. At that moment they were told that they had been granted a last-minute stay of execution because their lawyers had filed a writ of *habeas corpus* on their behalf. Héctor Morales' family only learned of the stay of execution when they went to the cemetery to collect his body.

The lawyer for Marco González, the Honduran, only saw his client after the last minute reprieve. Marco González had been condemned on general charges of "subversion" and was not accused of any specific offence. He told the lawyer he had been forced to sign a document which he was not allowed to read. His nose had been broken when he was beaten with a fire-iron.

The six men were executed at the same cemetery one month later.

Torture of political detainees

Several of those executed under Decree 46-82 were reported to have been convicted solely on the basis of "confessions" extracted under torture, such as beatings, burning with cigarettes, and the *capucha*, a rubber hood impregnated with noxious chemicals including game-san, a powerful insecticide. Amnesty International has received detailed testimonies from the victims and from those who witnessed their torture.

Relatives who visited Héctor Morales in prison before his execution say that he had been tortured. They described him as pale and thin. He said that he had been beaten. There were red marks and bruises on his chest and stripes on his neck. He said that the latter had been caused by the *capucha* impregnated with lime, which had been put over his head. When the hood was on his interrogators had punched him in the stomach, winding him. When he tried to get his breath, he inhaled the lime.

A friend who also saw him before he died said that his hands were black and blue from electric shocks. He had marks on his chest too, but tried to conceal them so that his friend would not see how badly he had been treated.

The Marroquín brothers both told a visitor that they had been given electric shocks on the testicles and beaten. A former detainee, held with them, testified to seeing the *capucha* used on Sergio

Marroquín. He also said that the interrogators had stretched Sergio Marroquín out between two beds and jumped up and down on him repeatedly.

An evangelical pastor arrested under Decree 46-82 and held in G-2 barracks with Héctor Morales and the Marroquín brothers was himself beaten until he lost consciousness. After his release, reportedly following the payment of a large bribe collected on his behalf abroad, he gave Amnesty International the following description of the tortures he saw others suffering: "They hit some of them with a kind of long hosepipe. Others had a hood put over their heads. The hood consists of part of the inner tube of a tyre sewn at one end. They put this over their heads. Then handcuffed they are thrown on the floor. As they can't breathe they suffocate. If they are willing to talk they have to nod their heads.

"Others they hit in the stomach. There were three who were covered by weapons all the time, so that no one could [help] them. I was very saddened to see two of the men covered in blood. One of these crawled up to his torturer and said: 'Forgive me, *papito*.' (A term of endearment meaning 'little father'.) The torturer kneed him in the mouth and I saw one of his teeth fly out. It was very sad to hear the screams and groans of those being tortured. Everything they did had a great psychological impact on me. I was terrified and tried not to think about it.

"One day our captors came to the door and told us we were to leave early the next morning. We were very surprised to find ourselves taken to the main prison where they hold those who are to appear before the 'special courts'. There we realized that our situation had changed. On arrival they kept us apart for 13 or 16 days. We were taken to the torture sessions but they didn't hit us. With the rest it was very different. Some even lost their arms, or their feet, or were blinded through being hooded for so long. The hoods had been filled with *gamesan* ... a chemical which disfigures the face and damages the eyes. Altogether we were about 250 prisoners."

Another former Decree 46-82 detainee left Guatemala in 1984 with the help of a US citizen, who had helped raise the large sum of money his captors had demanded for his release. In a taped testimony to Amnesty International she related his description of the torture he suffered in detention: "One of the things he told me was that he was kept for at least 50 per cent of the time in a kind of coffin box where he couldn't stand and he couldn't even lie down. He could barely kneel and for most of the time his hands and feet were tied and he was blindfold. He had no access to a bathroom and had to urinate and defecate in this box ... He was severely beaten many, many times and interrogated verbally to the point where he would pass out ... They made him eat nails — he was forced to chew them and swallow them." This man also testified that other people held in secret detention with him had been told that they too could be released if he were able, after his release, to raise enough money.

A student leader arrested in 1982 with a friend and detained for eight months under Decree 46-82 gave Amnesty International the following account of his treatment: "It all happened so quickly. Absolutely no warning was given. Three people in civilian clothes turned up, asking to talk to me, but when the people in the house where I was living saw that they were carrying rifles and machine-guns, they said that I didn't live there and that they didn't know me. ... These people identified themselves as members of the DIT ... they came into my room ... I was half-asleep, I barely heard one of them saying, 'OK, you son of a bitch, get up and don't move! ... Someone kicked me, and I woke up completely ... I could see they were pointing a rifle and a machine-gun at me. I tried to keep calm and asked for time to dress myself ... when I was ready they handcuffed me and took me out to a car without licence plates ... One guy said in a serious voice, 'Look, we've got another guerrilla, we've got you, and you're going to tell me everything. I don't want a single lie, or you die. And if anything happens to you, the same will happen to the person who came with you. If your hand gets broken, hers will too, and if you die, she dies. So you'd be better off to just tell me where the hideout is, where the arms are, where's the propaganda and who are your accomplices.'

"I couldn't speak and then they began to beat me. They tied my hands to my feet, they put an inner tube over my face and tightened it behind me till I couldn't get any air. I don't know how many times they did that, but it went on for four days, and they were kicking me in the stomach all the time ... until I defecated in my trousers. . .

"Suddenly one dawn they threw open the door, and beat me on the feet, and then told me to get up, that we were going for a little trip ... They took me out in a car with my eyes blindfolded ... then they took me to a room. They threatened me with death if I didn't sign some papers and if I didn't admit to what I was accused of. I refused to do this and the same thing went on for three days, beatings and blows.

"Then one day ... they came and said I was being consigned to the special tribunals. There we had no defence lawyer. They assigned someone just to make it look OK, the defendant wasn't allowed to speak for himself, because they threatened you with a longer sentence; it wasn't any use appealing because you had to accept whatever the official said, whatever accusation was made ... they even went so far as threatening defendants with pistols to make them sign these declarations. The sentences were handed down on the basis of confidential reports."

Another student arrested in 1982 under Decree 46-82 and tortured, also described his experiences to Amnesty International: "I was tortured mentally, physically and morally. The physical torture was in the form of blows that I received all over my body. They used different things for this, and I was given electric shock torture all over my body for about 30 seconds at a time. They also tied a cord around my neck to choke me. The moral torture was to treat me verbally like a thing that lacked all of the attributes and qualities that have made me a human. That is, they considered me like an irrational animal, undesirable from society's point of view. The psychological torture was all the threats they directed at me. They said if I didn't cooperate they would kill me.

"As a result of the first torture I lost consciousness completely for three days ... I could see, after I came to, that I had vomited huge amounts of blood, my left eye was completely red and it was bleeding. My ribs had been broken on the left side, it was impossible for me to move because I felt such terrible pain throughout my entire body. I couldn't eat anything because of the blows I had received to my stomach, I could only take water.

"It went on like that for days ... It also affected me very much to hear the terrible screams of other people that were being tortured. Many times I wished for death so I wouldn't have to go on suffering, but in the end I spent two months in that secret prison. After that I was transferred to the place where they held all those under the jurisdiction of the special tribunals.

"I was accused of more crimes, crimes that, according to the decree which had established the tribunals, were punishable by death. But as they could not prove the crimes of which they accused me, finally, nine months after I was arrested, I was freed."

Testimony of a Decree 46-82 detainee

A Protestant aid worker arrested in 1982, two days before Christmas, was interviewed by Amnesty International after his release on 31 August 1983.

He was seized in his home by heavily armed men and taken blindfold to a place which he could not identify, but which he thought must be outside the capital, because he could hear the wind whistling in the trees. When he refused to answer his captors' questions: "They started to beat me. There must have been around 10 of them, they beat me all over my body, but mainly in the stomach. They beat me with their fists and kicked me. Then they connected electric cable to me and gave me regular shocks at short intervals. The pain they caused me was so terrible that I can't describe it. As I was losing consciousness they tied a cord around my neck to strangle me." He passed out, and remained unconscious for two days. When he came round he realized that he had vomited a lot of blood and was in such pain he could not move. He was told that his brother had also been arrested and was taken to see him: "When I saw him I started to cry, but he was happy because they had told him that they had killed me, while he was listening to the screams of people being tortured." He was then tortured at two to three day intervals: "Many times I wished I would die quickly because I couldn't bear the suffering any more; I also thought about asking my torturers to please, when they killed me, at least leave my body where my family could find it. I was thinking of families who have had a relative kidnapped who never appears. They suffer so much they often say they'd be happy just to find the body so they could bury it."

He was eventually taken to the National Police Second Division prison hospital, where he was treated for internal bruising and bleeding. From there he was taken to be charged under Decree 46-82: "They had accused me of all sorts of crimes that I hadn't committed, like 'conspiracy', 'terrorist activities', 'possession of subversive propaganda' and 'illegal possession of arms'. They told me to sign the accusation and I had no choice." He was then taken to the Granja Pavón prison outside Guatemala City to await trial by special military tribunal: "Two days after they brought me to prison they called us to go to court, where they would take our declarations. Three officials took declarations from each of us. They asked us a series of questions — if it were true that we had committed all the crimes attributed to us. All our answers were negative because nothing they said was true. At the end of this procedure we had the right to engage a lawyer. If we didn't contract a lawyer they would assign one to us." After this he was no longer incommunicado and was allowed to see his family.

When his family visited him they told him of their efforts to trace him and his brother: "They had gone to all the detention centres, to the hospitals, to the fire station with photographs of us.[1] They went to all the places where bodies appear, to see if they recognized us.

---

[1] The firefighters collect bodies dumped on the streets of Guatemalan cities. A journalist interviewed by Amnesty International had been told by firemen from a large Guatemalan town that at one point during the Ríos Montt administration they had run out of body bags because there were so many bodies to collect.

One day they received a call from the countryside saying that we had appeared dead but when they arrived the bodies had already been buried. The keeper of the cemetery was sure it was us. They paid him to disinter the bodies. He'd said he was sure it was us just to get the money. They'd made all the preparations for our funeral. They went on like that, searching for two months, until the news that we were to appear before the special military tribunals."

About two months after he had made his declaration he was told he had been sentenced to 10 years and four months' imprisonment on charges of attempts against the security of the nation and illegal possession of arms. He appealed against his sentence. He was eventually released at the end of August 1983, the day before the special military tribunals were abolished.

The case of Michael Ernest and María Monteverde

On 8 March 1983 two foreign nationals who had been detained under Decree 46-82 were released after a sustained campaign by their families, legal counsel and foreign diplomatic intervention. They became the first people able to give first-hand information about the operating procedures of the special military tribunals. The two were also able to give information about others held under the decree with whom they had spoken while in detention or with whose cases they were familiar. Michael Glenn Ernest, a United States citizen, and María Magdalena Ascanio Monteverde Molenaar, a Spanish citizen, were arrested on 11 January 1983 on charges of having participated in two guerrilla raids 10 miles from San Lucas Tolimán, the town in Sololá where they were living. Buildings were burned down during both raids, which occurred on 6 and 9 January, and in one the owner of the Santo Tomas Perdido estate was killed. The authorities said that both Michael Ernest and María Monteverde had been identified by four witnesses who claimed they were involved in the incidents. Michael Ernest was also charged with the less serious offence of, during the raid, having threatened to kill four peasants unless they joined the guerrillas. Both denied the charges. María Monteverde obtained written testimony from witnesses who stated that she had been in San Lucas Tolimán when the raids took place. Michael Ernest produced his passport, which showed that he had been in Panama during the raids. He also had his return airplane ticket, as well as receipts for purchases he had made in Panama.

Amnesty International was able to interview Michael Ernest and María Monteverde shortly after their release and subsequently published a report on the circumstances of their arrest and imprisonment

110

and the handling of their case.[2]

Their own case was not typical of Decree 46-82 proceedings. Unlike others they had been given legal representation and their case had reached only the preliminary stages of procedures established by the decree before they were released. Despite the flimsy and inconsistent evidence against the two, the case was instructive. It showed the extent to which the authorities were prepared to proceed even when there was little or no evidence against 46-82 detainees. It also revealed inconsistencies in the conduct of Decree 46-82 cases, both in the time allowed in the various stages of proceedings and in the rights of the accused to legal representation.

The dangers facing lawyers willing to act for those held under Decree 46-82 were also highlighted. One of the lawyers representing Michael Ernest and María Monteverde reported that on 4 February a large black vehicle had parked near his home and hooded armed men had handcuffed him and searched his home. He believed they were members of G-2 (military intelligence unit), because of the way they acted and the weapons they carried — Israeli-manufactured Galil assault rifles.

In their interview with Amnesty International, Michael Ernest and María Monteverde stated that they believed they had been arrested because the government had to find someone to blame for the guerrilla raids.

They said that they were never formally told the exact charges against them or the legislation under which they were held, either by the security forces in whose custody they were held or by the tribunal before which they appeared. However, the crimes they were alleged to have committed were referred to at various stages. María Monteverde was told by a police officer that they were accused of subversion. During the first night of their arrest they were taken to the Retalhuleu military base where Michael Ernest was told they were being held on suspicion of "terrorism, subversion and insurgency". When they were later transferred to Guatemala City, both were told they were being held under *fuero especial*, special jurisdiction, but were given no further details.

The two were first allowed to see the consuls of their respective countries on 16 January, five days after their arrest, at which point lawyers were secured for them. They met their lawyers for the first time only a few minutes before the initial court proceedings on 20 January. At that point they were told they could contact lawyers whenever they wished, but when María Monteverde later asked to

---

[2] *Guatemala: proceedings under Decree Law 46-82 of July 1982*, AI Index: AMR 34/18/83

do so her request was refused on the grounds that under *fuero especial* she could be questioned without legal representation.

At the initial proceedings Michael Ernest and María Monteverde were taken before a panel of three. Two of the panel introduced themselves as lawyers, but María Monteverde's lawyer expressed doubt as to whether they were actually legally trained and considered that they were likely to have been military personnel. The third member of the panel functioned as a court reporter, putting questions to them from a prepared text and noting their responses. He seemed familiar with their case and asked direct questions such as: "Did you kill anyone? On how many occasions did you kill and burn property?" An interpreter translated for Michael Ernest.

On 24 January the two were put in separate identification parades. They stated that the parades appeared to have been manipulated in order to ensure their "identification" by supposed witnesses to the guerrilla raids. Both said that during the identification parades a soldier from the military base where they were held made gestures to single them out so that they could be "identified" by someone looking through a small door. María Monteverde said that a soldier had offered her a cigarette, but did not make the same offer to the other women in the parade. They believe that one of those brought to "identify" them in this way was a peasant who had witnessed the murder at Santo Tomas Perdido. He apparently stated that he had seen María Monteverde with a gun during the raid. It was at this point that she asked to see her lawyer and was refused.

A week later, on 31 January, Michael Ernest and María Monteverde were taken before television cameras for a press conference, apparently to prove that they were in good health. They were given no advance warning of the press conference and their lawyers were not present.

The couple's lawyers, their families who had travelled to Guatemala, a US Congressman from the State of Colorado (where both were resident), as well as US and Spanish Embassy officials, maintained throughout that they were innocent and pressed for their release. Their lawyers also drew attention to the fact that Decree 46-82 procedures had not been followed in their case, because after the first hearing on 20 January they should have been informed within eight days whether or not they were to be charged. However they were never formally charged.

The two were released on 8 March after 29 days in custody. An aide to General Ríos Montt told a US Congressional staff aide that they had been released because the tribunal found it had insufficient evidence to prosecute. However, the official government statement did not mention lack of evidence, and indicated that the tribunal had reserved the right to continue the investigation. Upon release Michael Ernest was told he was free to leave the country but that a "second phase" of proceedings could begin. María Monteverde was given no reason for her release. The papers she saw did not say that she was free, and she too believed that she was still under indictment, having been granted only "provisional liberty". Both left the country shortly after they were released.

The couple were able to confirm that at least three of those executed on 3 March had been tortured. Another woman held under *fuero especial*, whom María Monteverde met in the hospital where she was held, also claimed to have been tortured at various houses in Guatemala City. She stated that she had been blindfolded, tied up and kept naked for eight days during which she herself had been tortured and she had heard others being tortured but could not see them. She told María Monteverde that she had not been allowed to see her family, but had heard that they were trying to find her.

Conclusion

In April 1983 the Inter-American Commission on Human Rights (IACHR) found that Decree 46-82, in extending the offences carrying the death penalty, violated Guatemala's obligations as a party to the American Convention on Human Rights. Article 4(2) of the Convention states that the death penalty "shall not be extended to crimes to which it does not presently apply". On 8 September 1983 the Inter-American Court of Human Rights confirmed this finding.

After General Mejía Víctores overthrew the Ríos Montt administration in August 1983, Decree 46-82 was rescinded and the special military tribunals set up under it were abolished. Because the proceedings before those tribunals had been so arbitrary and had violated international norms for a fair trial, Amnesty International urged the Guatemalan Government to retry all such cases before regular courts. Under Decree 74-84 of July 1984, General Mejía Víctores officially pardoned all prisoners who were convicted of crimes by the special tribunals. Some 56 people were released under Decree 74-84 in July 1984.

To this day most Decree 46-82 detainees remain unaccounted for. On 12 April 1983, the Minister of Defence, General Mejía Víctores (who overthrew General Ríos Montt a few months later) announced that 458 people were then undergoing trial by special military tribunal. At the time he was directly responsible for the tribunals. However only 61 detainees were officially acknowledged to have been sentenced. They were named on a list issued by the Supreme Court on 7 September 1983. The number still missing is believed to be about 300.

CHAPTER IV

'Disappearances' during the administration of General Mejía Víctores

Queues of people waiting outside La Verbena Cemetery in Zone 7 of Guatemala City was a familiar sight when General Mejía Víctores was in power. They were waiting to see whether a missing relative or friend was among the many unidentified bodies which were brought there every night. Employees at funeral parlours in the city kept files of dozens of photographs of "disappeared" people, given to them by relatives who hoped they might be able to identify a missing person among the corpses.

"Disappearance" was not a new phenomenon. Thousands had vanished without trace since the 1960s.[1] However, after General Mejía Víctores came to power in a military coup in August 1983, "disappearances" in Guatemala once again became a major concern for Amnesty International. There were reports of scores of "disappearances" and killings carried out by heavily armed men in plain clothes. The testimony of witnesses, the choice of victims and the circumstances of both the abductions and the killings pointed consistently to official involvement.

The "disappeared" have come from all walks of life. They are politicians, university professors, students, trade unionists, lawyers, priests, lay preachers, businessmen, athletes, doctors, other health professionals, agricultural workers, journalists and Indian peasants. Many of the "disappeared" are children. Even hospital patients have been abducted from their beds, never to be seen again. Members of the armed forces have entered towns and villages in the countryside and captured groups of people, often whole families who have been taken away in army trucks and "disappeared".

No matter how someone "disappears", not knowing whether they are alive or dead causes untold suffering to their relatives who have to live with the uncertainty of wondering whether they will see their loved ones again and whether they are being held in some secret detention centre. And the "disappeared" are frequently the main breadwinners in the family. Relatives of the "disappeared" who have

---

[1] Appendix V gives a list of "disappearances" between 1981 and 1984 which were reported to Amnesty International.

tried to exert pressure on the government have found it difficult to achieve their aims. The Guatemalan courts have consistently proved to be ineffective in dealing with petitions of *habeas corpus* presented on behalf of the "disappeared" and although the police have sometimes claimed to be investigating their whereabouts they have rarely done so.

By the end of September 1983, less than a month after General Mejía Víctores came to power, the Guatemalan press had listed over 80 cases of "disappearance" since the August coup, attributing them to "heavily armed" men or "squads dressed in olive green", the coded references which the national news media had used for many years to suggest that the official security forces were responsible. That same month an editorial in the newspaper *La Hora* (The Hour) expressed the fear that Guatemala was returning to the large-scale "death squad" activities of the General Romeo Lucas García administration: "Guatemalans remember with horror the black days before March 1982 when the numbers of victims couldn't even be counted." Also in September, the Archdiocese of Guatemala issued a statement which expressed "deep concern at the resurgence of violence in Guatemala with bodies appearing daily, mutilated, showing signs of torture and bullet wounds."

Those who "disappeared" included trade unionists, lay religious workers, USAC staff, students and academics. Three people working on rural education programs funded by the US Agency for International Development (AID) "disappeared" in October 1983 after being arrested in Guatemala City by men in plain clothes. In November the authorities announced that their charred bodies had been recovered from a burnt-out car. Local police and firefighters maintained that they had died when their car crashed into a cliff and burst into flames. However, eye-witnesses said that the car had been pushed to the cliff, soaked with petrol and set alight. Colleagues said that the victims could not drive. The government, in announcing their deaths, implied that documents found in the car, which had somehow escaped the fire, had provided evidence that the victims had been involved in "suspicious" activities.

USAC—a long-term target

Students, lecturers and workers at the University of San Carlos in Guatemala City have been the target of human rights violations for many years.[2] The Guatemalan authorities have frequently described the university as a "centre of subversion". Many academics fled the

---

[2] See Appendix VI.

country after receiving death threats and many of those who remained "disappeared" or were killed.

On 12 August 1983, four days after the coup, the offices of the Engineering and Medical Students' Associations in Guatemala City were reported to have been raided and damaged following an anonymous telephone call telling them to stop participating in student activities. In September 1983 USAC Rector Dr Eduardo Meyer Maldonado said that some 13 members of the university had been murdered or abducted by "death squads" over the previous few weeks and publicly accused the government of responsibility. In November 1983 Dr Meyer, who had been threatened many times, told a Guatemalan newspaper that some 50 students had "disappeared" since he became Rector in July 1982.

Since then many other USAC staff and students have "disappeared" or been killed. By March 1984, 14 cases of the "disappearance" or killing of USAC staff, students and workers since the August coup had been reported to Amnesty International. For example, on 1 February 1984 unidentified armed men attacked and seriously wounded 29-year-old engineering student Sergio Vinicio Samayoa Morales, who was then taken to the Roosevelt Hospital. That night about 10 men broke into the intensive care unit where he was being treated and took him away. Five days later his body was found, riddled with bullets, just outside the capital on the road to Chinautla. He was the fifth member of his family to have "disappeared". His mother, Graciela Morales Herrera, who had been the treasurer of the USAC Economics Faculty for 27 years, was abducted on 11 September 1982 from her home in Guatemala City by men in plain clothes. Three of her children were kidnapped with her: two daughters, Gloria, aged 18, and 16-year-old Maritza, and her 20-year-old son, José. A *habeas corpus* writ was filed on their behalf, but there was no official comment on the case and there has since been no trace of them.

Between March and May seven members of the executive committee, almost the entire leadership, of the *Asociación de Estudiantes Universitarios* (AEU), Association of University Students, were abducted. Among them was sociology student Carlos Ernesto Cuevas Molina, son of the late Dr Rafael Cuevas Del Cid, former Rector of USAC.

Hugo de León Palacios, a primary school teacher and a student of law at USAC, was also abducted in March. He was on his way to the school when he was seized by four heavily armed men in plain clothes who beat him and forced him into a vehicle. Some of his primary school students saw him being abducted and shouted: "Don't take the teacher away, don't take the teacher away!" but to no avail.

He has not been seen or heard of since. Thirty-six years old when he was abducted, Hugo de León Palacios was married with two young daughters. *Habeas corpus* writs filed on his behalf have produced no response. The authorities deny any knowledge of his whereabouts.

Archeologist and university professor Carlos Enrique Ericastilla García was abducted on 7 May from his home in Guatemala City and left for dead near a football pitch. His body bore marks of torture. In June the AEU published a list of 22 USAC students who had been killed or had "disappeared" in preceding months.

In October the university Rector announced that he and several other members of the Supreme University Council had received death threats and the press reported that about 70 members of the university community had been killed or kidnapped since the beginning of the year. On 26 October Lic. Carlos de León Gudiel, a professor in the Economics Faculty, was shot dead by unknown men. The following day the Dean of the Faculty was shot dead on his way to his colleague's funeral.

In November 1984 a group calling itself *Universitarios Auténticos*, Authentic University Staff and Students, issued a communiqué in which it accused many university professors and students of being Marxists and involved in corruption and warned that the university authorities would be directly responsible for the consequences unless they brought this state of affairs to an end. Shortly afterwards, several USAC students and professors were killed. One of them was Héctor Estuardo Marroquín, a 23-year-old student, who was shot on 27 November on the university campus when government security forces opened fire on a number of students. He died in hospital the next day. On 28 November Carlos Alfredo de León, a student of agriculture, and Edgar Orlando Ramazzini Herrera, a student at the School of Communication Sciences, were found dead 20 kilometres south of the capital. Both had earlier been reported abducted. Another student, Noemi Eunice Pélaez, was found dead in Zone 12 of the capital on 30 November. On 3 December the bullet-riddled bodies of economics students Edson Figueroa Cruz and Leider Flores Pinto were thrown in front of the university from a moving vehicle. They had been abducted by armed men on 1 December. Two days later the tortured body of university professor Rudy Gustavo Figueroa Muñoz was found in Zone 21 of the capital. He had "disappeared" in mid-October after a strike by the *Sindicato de Trabajadores de la Universidad de San Carlos*, Union of Workers at San Carlos University, of which he was reportedly the founder.

The attacks on USAC continued in 1985. On 8 January security forces reportedly broke into part of the university premises and set fire to files and papers, as well as threatening staff who were present. Five days later an incendiary bomb exploded in the Department of Medicine, destroying machinery, office equipment and documents and damaging the building. In February the Guatemalan news media reported that members of the *Consejo Superior Universitario*, the university's governing body, had once again received death threats, by telephone and in anonymous notes.

Between January and August 1985 a further 10 USAC students were killed or "disappeared". Among them were Joaquín Rodas, Rafael Galindo and Ricardo Gramajo, all from Quetzaltenango, who "disappeared" on 2 March, after participating in demonstrations against decisions made by the Guatemalan Constituent Assembly about the regulation of higher education. On 27 March USAC economics professor Carlos Enrique Cabrera García was shot dead on his way to the university.

On 4 June Dr Edgar Leiva Santos, Director General of Administration at USAC and a member of the governing body, was machine-gunned to death in the university car park. He had represented USAC on a number of government-established bodies, including the *Comisión para la Paz* (Peace Commission).

Then, in September Amnesty International received reports that the military had temporarily occupied the USAC campus, and arrested scores of students in a move to quell protests over increases in bus fares.

Also in September, a USAC student "disappeared" in circumstances which pointed to the involvement of the security forces. Luis Fernando de la Roca Elías, a 25-year-old engineering student at USAC, was abducted in Guatemala City on 9 September. Three days later armed men in plain clothes searched the house where he lived with his 64-year-old mother. They neither identified themselves nor presented a search warrant, but told his mother that her son was being held at the second division of the National Police in Guatemala City.

The men returned to the house later that day with her son, whose clothes were stained with blood from a head wound. His mother thought he was behaving awkwardly, as if half asleep or under the influence of drugs. She asked the men who they were and they replied that they were friends of her son. On hearing this Luis Fernando de la Roca shouted to her that they were government agents.

The mother, her three-year-old granddaughter and her son were then driven in two different cars to the outskirts of the city. She said that when the cars stopped she could hear her son screaming in the other car as he was beaten. One of her captors turned on the radio to drown the screams. She says that she was then blindfolded, driven away and left near her home.

She had noted the numbers of licence plates on two of the cars used in the abduction. Under the procedure for filing *habeas corpus* writs this information was given to the Supreme Court who passed it to the *Departamento de Impuesto sobre Uso de Servicios y Actividades Comerciales*, Department of Tax on Commercial Services and Activities, of the Head Office of the Internal Revenue requesting the identity of the users of these licence plates. On 16 October the head office replied: ". . . according to the records kept for this purpose by the Division of Taxes on the Circulation of Vehicles, the licence plate P-253217 was assigned to the Justo Rufino Barrios Barracks and P-75177 was assigned to the Ministry of National Defence." The Justo Rufino Barrios Barracks is one of the places which Amnesty International has been told is used as a secret detention centre. Although the relevant authorities acknowledged that the two cars were registered by them, they claimed that both had subsequently been stolen.

On 13 January 1986, in an advertisement published in *La Hora* by the mother, she stated that the Supreme Court had declared the *habeas corpus* writ filed on behalf of her son inadmissable and considered that ". . . it is appropriate that the respective investigation be ordered, so as to establish who may be guilty, and because it refers to persons supposedly belonging to the army, the investigation shall be at the instruction of the Military Tribunals."

Luis Fernando de la Roca's case has been widely reported in the Guatemalan news media which has also published a number of advertisements paid for by the mother. Despite the writs of *habeas corpus* filed on her son's behalf the authorities have denied all knowledge of his detention and his whereabouts remain unknown.

Attacks on trade unionists

For 10 years and more trade unionists and their leaders have been victims of human rights violations. On 21 June 1980, trade unionism in Guatemala was dealt a heavy blow when 25 leaders of the *Central Nacional de Trabajadores* (CNT), National Workers Congress, were abducted as they met in the CNT headquarters in Guatemala City to plan the funeral of another CNT leader, Edgar René Aldana. He had been detained on 20 June 1980 and his body was found the following day bearing marks of torture and gunshot wounds. As the CNT leaders met, cars and a jeep crashed through the main door of the headquarters. About 60 men in civilian clothes then burst into the building and abducted the trade unionists. Each end of the street on which the building stood had been blocked. The raid took place only a block away from the National Police intelligence division headquarters and two blocks from its second division headquarters, yet no effort was made to apprehend the assailants. A foreign journalist who visited the CNT building two days later said he saw bloodstains on the floor and machine-gun cartridge cases on the stairs. The offices had been ransacked and the telephone wires cut, he said.

One trade union leader managed to escape by crawling out of a window onto the roof of the CNT headquarters and recognized the man commanding the kidnappers as the Chief of the Guatemala City Police Narcotics Squad. Several cars belonging to the kidnapped trade unionists were later recovered from the National Police garages. One government official, the Minister of Labour, assured people who wrote from abroad that the detained trade unionists had subsequently been released, but other officials denied that they had ever been detained. Despite the wealth of information available in the six years since their "disappearance" the authorities have not even made a cursory attempt to find out who abducted them. They remain missing. One of them, Irma Candelaria Pérez Osorio, was only 19 when she "disappeared".

In letters to Amnesty International, relatives of the trade unionists described the suffering caused by their "disappearence". The wife of one wrote: ". . . we were left completely helpless without any help of any kind. We have survived purely by a miracle since many of us have no education and therefore cannot find work. I have tried to find work but they won't give me any. We have nowhere to live and school expenses are harder to find each day."

On 24 August of the same year, another 17 CNT leaders were arrested by the National Police at the Finca Emaús, a trade union conference centre near the town of Escuintla. The tortured body of the centre's administrator, José Luis Peña, was found in September, but the trade union leaders have never been seen again.

Such attacks led many of Guatemala's remaining trade union leaders to seek safety abroad, resulting in the virtual dismemberment of the country's trade union movement. In 1984, however, Amnesty International noted a renewed effort to organize Guatemalan workers, which was followed in turn by a wave of "disappearances" and extrajudicial executions of the revived movement's leaders.

On 30 January 1984, Amancio Samuel Villatoro, a CNT leader and former Secretary General of the Adams Products trade union was abducted near his home in Guatemala City by armed men in civilian clothes, believed to be members of the security forces. The only information about what subsequently happened to him came from another trade unionist, Alvaro René Sosa Ramos, who escaped from detention and obtained asylum in a foreign embassy which took responsibility for his safety while he recovered in hospital from gunshot wounds and the effects of torture. (Several people were abducted from their hospital beds and murdered in 1984.) One of the few people known to have survived "disappearance" in Guatemala, he testified from exile that he had seen Amancio Villatoro in a secret detention centre in Guatemala City in March 1984. However, petitions of *habeas corpus* presented on behalf of Amancio Villatoro have produced no results and he too remains missing. Alvaro René Sosa testified that he had also recognized another trade unionist, Silvio Matricardi Salam, in a government detention centre. Silvio Matricardi was a former president of the national teachers' organization. His body was found, showing marks of torture, near Escuintla on 14 March.

In another incident, on 17 February 1984, Santiago López Aquilar, adviser to the *Federación Autónoma Sindical Guatemalteca* (FAS-GUA), Autonomous Guatemalan Trade Union Federation, was seized by armed men in Guatemala City. His bullet-riddled body, which also bore signs of torture, was found in the capital a few days later.

The occupation of the *Embotelladora Guatemalteca S.A.* (EGSA), Guatemala Bottlers Ltd., plant in Guatemala City was typical of renewed trade union activity in Guatemala in 1984. The plant was occupied in February 1984 in protest at suddenly announced plans to close it down. This was widely interpreted as an attempt to break the plant union which for many years had led the struggle to unionize Guatemalan workers. The EGSA plant, which bottled under franchise to Coca-Cola and a few smaller soft-drink firms, had been the focus of government attacks in the past. On a number of occasions during the 1970s and early 1980s, uniformed police and military units had entered the plant's premises and beaten and abducted workers. On other occasions, leaders of the EGSA union had "disappeared" or been killed at their homes, as they arrived at or left work, and as they did their rounds in delivery vans.

The occupation continued throughout 1984 and the plant became a gathering place for relatives of the "disappeared" who were trying to publicize the government's failure to ascertain their whereabouts. The army placed EGSA under constant surveillance and, in March, shot and killed one man and injured two others who they said had failed to stop at a road-block outside the plant.

A US trade union delegation, consisting of representatives of unions affiliated to the American Federation of Labor-Congress of Industrial Organizations (AFL-CIO), visited the occupied plant in March and also had talks with government representatives, including the Ministers of Foreign Affairs, Labour and the Interior. In the report of its discussions with the Guatemalan authorities, the delegation ". . . noted with concern the tendency to suggest that all trade unionists are subversives and the inference that all disappeared union leaders and advisors were targeted because of subversive activities. The delegation came away from these government meetings with the impression that the rationale of subversion is used to cover up attacks on the union movement. We were not confident that these attacks have ceased and were struck by the lingering danger surrounding the Coca-Cola workers and other trade unionists in Guatemala . . .

"The delegation believes that there is a systematic attempt to undermine free trade unionization using kidnapping and murder to intimidate workers and to instill fear of death for unionization activity. It appears that the international attention focused on the Coca-Cola plant limits the severity of attacks against these workers. The delegation, however, came away with a deep-seated concern that future reprisals will be taken against the union for their success in maintaining a strong union, an example for other unions in Guatemala."

During 1984 a number of trade unionists from other unions who supported the occupation of the EGSA plant subsequently "disappeared" or were murdered, apparently the victims of political killings. They included Edgar Fernando García, Minutes Secretary of *Sindicato de Trabajadores de Industria Centro Americana de Viorio* (STICAVSA), Union of Workers of the Central American Glass Industry, the trade union at the Cavisa glass factory, which manufactures bottles for the EGSA plant. As chief negotiator for the union, Edgar Fernando García was on the point of signing a new collective bargaining agreement with the Cavisa company when he was seized in Guatemala City in February 1984 and "disappeared". Witnesses state that his abductors were uniformed members of the National Police and the BROE. The authorities, however, have consistently denied that he was detained and numerous *habeas corpus* petitions presented to the courts on his behalf have produced no information on his whereabouts. A labour lawyer, Alfonso Alvarado Palencia, who was advising STICAVSA, had been abducted earlier, on 31 January, as he was leaving the factory.

Nineth Montenegro de García, wife of the missing trade unionist, wrote to the US Ambassador in Guatemala on 28 March: "I am a Guatemalan wife and mother who is today suffering as a result of one of the great scourges of our convulsed Guatemala: the kidnapping of my husband Edgar Fernando García, on 18 February of this year . . . (according to eyewitness accounts) when he was taken away by members of the BROE in a pale blue and white minibus . . . I have spoken to the highest military authorities, the Rector of the National University, international organizations, Guatemalan trade unions, the Red Cross and the APG [Guatemalan Press Association] and asked them to intercede on behalf of my husband, who is a trade union leader at the Cavisa factory. Edgar Fernando García is an honest, responsible and upright young man, who loves his family and is the father of a one-year-old baby girl." Nineth Montenegro de García is now the President of GAM.

Following Edgar Fernando García's "disappearance", five other members of the union's negotiating committee fled the country after being threatened. On 10 March 1984 the 16-year-old brother of one of the workers was kidnapped by armed men while on his way to school. He was released unharmed on 29 March and said that he had been held in a small room where hooded men repeatedly questioned him about his brothers and his father. The incident is widely believed to have been intended to intimidate the EGSA workers.

A year after the dispute began, on 1 February 1985, an agreement on working conditions and trade union rights was reached between the plant union and the new owners, a corporation of local businessmen. The plant was officially reopened on 1 March and production resumed. However the whereabouts of those trade unionists and their supporters who "disappeared" during the dispute remains unknown.

Julio Celso de León Flores, an executive member of the Christian Democratic Latin American Workers Federation, is another of the few "disappeared" to have been released alive. He was abducted on 11 September 1985 as he left his office in the centre of Guatemala City. Four heavily armed men seized him and threw him onto the floor of their Cherokee car, hitting him in the jaw and the base of the spine. Once he was in the car, his captors reported by radio that "We have the package; he's in one piece". According to an eye-witness several armed men had been watching his office on the day he was abducted.

In reaction to Julio Celso de León's abduction, the Deputy Secretary General of the Guatemalan Christian Democrat party stated that "acts of violence like these seriously compromise the country's return to constitutional life" and demanded that the government immediately clarify his whereabouts. However the authorities denied all knowledge of him.

Three days later, on 14 September, Julio Celso de León was dumped near the city centre by his captors. Following his release his brother held a press conference to thank trade unions and national and international organizations for the concern they had expressed about his seizure. Julio Celso de León told the press that he had been held by the army. He said he was kept handcuffed and blindfold, with his ears blocked, and that he had been given a sedative and made to drink something which made him feel dizzy. He said that he was submitted to hours of interrogation during which he was asked what kind of relationship he had with public employees and which trade unions he was advising. He also stated that he was threatened that he would be killed and that his wife and daughter would be kidnapped.

International expressions of concern about his abduction seem to have resulted in a change of attitude towards him. His captors told him that there had been "a lot of pressure from abroad" and inquired about his health, asking whether he needed any medicine. However before releasing him they warned him that they would be watching him and that he would be hearing from them.

El Gráfico reported on 14 September that National Police spokesman Colonel Mario Ramírez Ruiz, had promised to initiate an investigation into who was responsible.

A participant in Amnesty International's appeal on behalf of Julio Celso de León received the following reply from Guatemala's Ambassador to Spain: "As you say in your letter, Mr de León was indeed kidnapped by unidentified armed men in Guatemala City on 11 September . . . It would appear that during his kidnapping Mr de León suffered some maltreatment regarding which I do not yet have information. While Mr de León was disappeared, writs of *habeas corpus* were presented to the courts and received the appropriate attention, establishing that the trade union leader was not detained in any of the prisons or police stations in the capital. The government of Guatemala has emphatically condemned this unfortunate incident and is investigating it so as to to try and clarify it. This is another incident of violence and of human rights violations in my country, carried out by illegal extremist groups with the intention to obstruct or prevent the return to constitutionality . . ."

Political detainees among the 'disappeared'

People who were detained under Decree 46-82 of July 1982, during the administration of General Efraín Ríos Montt, must also be counted among the "disappeared". This decree established special military tribunals, which were empowered to impose the death sentence after summary proceedings. Some 15 people were executed after being sentenced by these tribunals.

Shortly after taking power, General Mejía Víctores announced that these military tribunals would be abolished on 1 September and those held under Decree 46-82 would be tried in the ordinary courts. On 7 September the Guatemalan Supreme Court published a list of 61 people who had been sentenced by the tribunals. However, government announcements made during the Ríos Montt administration indicated that many more had actually been detained under Decree 46-82. On 12 April 1983, for example, General Mejía Víctores, then Ríos Montt's Minister of Defence and therefore directly responsible for the operation of the special military tribunals, had announced that 458 people were at that time being tried by the tribunals. Similar figures were given at other times by officials. In addition foreign delegations of inquiry which visited Guatemala while Decree 46-82 was in force were able to visit at least one place where detainees were held under the decree and established that several hundred prisoners were being held there at any one time. However, neither the Ríos Montt nor the Mejía Víctores administration issued any information about the names, verdicts in cases or whereabouts of people arrested under the decree other than the list of 7 September.

Some 60 Decree 46-82 detainees were eventually released under a pardon granted by General Mejía Víctores through Decree 74-84 of 18 July 1984. However most of the latter were said to be ordinary criminals. Members of trade unions, *Comité de Unidad Campesina* (CUC), the Indian Peasant League, and other groups opposed to government policy who had been detained while Decree 46-82 was in force remain unaccounted for and are generally believed to number over 300. The administration of General Mejía Víctores denied that certain individuals had ever been detained even though their detention had been acknowledged by the previous administration.

There are reports that some of those who remain unaccounted for have been secretly detained in several places in Guatemala City, including the Justo Rufino Barrios military headquarters, and the former headquarters of the *Escuela Politécnica,* military school. Amnesty International fears that they and others may have been secretly and summarily executed. One such case is that of Ileana del Rosario Solares Castillo. She was originally reported to have been sentenced to 30 years' imprisonment by a special military tribunal, during the Ríos Montt administration, although the administration of General Mejía Víctores subsequently denied that she had been detained. A woman who said she herself was a Decree 46-82 detainee stated that she had seen Ileana del Rosario Solares in custody in August 1983. She gave this information in a letter which was reportedly smuggled out of the women's prison known as the *Centro de Orientación Feminina,* Women's Orientation Centre, where she said she was being held. The letter also gave information about two other women detained under Decree 46-82 who are now missing: "I, María Cruz López Rodríguez, aged 32, was on 22 November sentenced to 30 years' imprisonment. My 18-year-old sister Ana María and Luz Leticia Hernández were arrested along with me. We were all held in the same secret prison. I think it was the *Escuela Politécnica*. There we were shut up in *bartolinas* [small, dark, dungeon-like cells]. After a few days I learned that Ileana del Rosario Solares Castillo was also being held there. I saw her directly, face to face."

The letter went on to say that the whereabouts of the writer's sister and the other woman arrested with her were unknown. Their names do not appear on the list of Decree 46-82 detainees issued by the Supreme Court. According to her letter, María Cruz López was later taken to the headquarters of the second police division and then to Santa Teresa, before being confined in the women's prison. She stated that she learned that she had been tried and sentenced to 30 years in prison without once having seen a lawyer or appeared before her accusers.

One Decree 46-82 detainee, who had spent four months in detention, was pardoned and released in September 1983 under Decree 74-84 and was reportedly later abducted. Edy Amilcar Mérida Peralta, aged 27, graduated in science and literature from USAC and was employed by the Guatemalan Post and Telecommunications Service. He left his home in Guatemala City on 7 April 1984 to visit his mother, but never arrived. Two days later armed men went to his house to look for his wife and on finding she was not there told neighbours to tell her that she would find her husband in the police station. However petitions of *habeas corpus* presented on behalf of Edy Mérida have produced no results and he is still missing.

'Disappearances' in the countryside

Many people "disappeared" in the countryside during the administrations of General Lucas García and General Ríos Montt, whose counter-insurgency strategy was aimed at removing the civilian population from the areas where the security forces were fighting the guerrilla opposition. Many thousands of other non-combatant civilians were extrajudicially executed or forced to flee to other parts of the country or into exile. After General Mejía Víctores came to power there were indications that "disappearances" and killings in the countryside were taking place on a more selective basis than had been the case under his immediate predecessors. The total number of people who were killed or "disappeared" was therefore believed to be lower under the Mejía Víctores administration, but, according to information received by Amnesty International, such abuses continued.

For example, Amnesty Interntional received reports that over 80 men, many of them Indian peasants, had been detained by the Guatemalan army in villages near San Ildefonso Ixtahuacán, Huehuetenango, between 12 and 29 December 1983. According to these reports the men were taken to Army Base No. 19 in the town of Huehuetenango. Some of those detained were later brought back to their villages to identify others to the army. Sixty-two were later released after having been tortured in detention by being burned on the hands and feet. Further arrests in the area were reported in January and February and at least 23 men who were abducted at that time are still missing. The Guatemalan army has never acknowledged the detention of any of these men and has not responded to Amnesty International's inquiries about them.

Torture and secret detention centres

Amnesty International fears that most of those reported to have "disappeared" over the years were tortured while in secret detention and killed. Many bodies found throughout Guatemala bear marks of torture, but they are often so disfigured that it is difficult to identify them. This pattern continued under the administration of General Mejía Víctores. The cases of Santiago López Aquilar and Edgar Rolando Ramazzini, cited above, are two instances in which it was possible to identify the body of someone believed to have been abducted by the security forces.

One of the few known survivors of abduction and torture was trade unionist Alvaro René Sosa, whose case is also referred to above. Although he had been shot and wounded he was able to escape from his captors on 12 March 1984 and take refuge in a foreign embassy. He then went into exile and testified that he had escaped after being abducted and held for 52 hours by the *kaibiles* unit in, he believes, a private house in the capital city which was used as a detention centre. During this period he states that he was subjected to a variety of tortures, including being beaten while he was hung naked upside down, burned with cigarettes and subjected to electric shocks. He managed to escape when he was being driven round the capital to identify others whom the authorities wished to detain. He states that while in custody he saw other people being abducted on the streets of Guatemala City and that at the detention centre he heard others being tortured.

GAM also claim to have been reliably informed that several of those who had "disappeared" in early 1985 were being held in a secret torture centre in Guatemala City.

During successive administrations, Amnesty International has received many reports of the existence of secret detention centres in army barracks and private houses but no official body has ever undertaken a thorough investigation into these reports. There have also been reports of secret cells in at least one prison. On 3 July 1984, after four prisoners in Pavón Prison in Guatemala City were allegedly killed by prison guards and members of the security forces, the Director General of Prisons, Camilo Dedet Rosa, reportedly visited the prison and was told by detainees that 18 prisoners were held in secret cells in the basement. Camilo Dedet Rosa subsequently stated to the Guatemalan news media that he had immediately ordered their transfer to regular cells. He also publicly called for an investigation of other detention centres, in view of the discovery at Pavón Prison. The then President of the Guatemalan Supreme Court, Tomás Baudillo Navarro Batres, also urged that there be a rigorous investigation to determine whether there were clandestine cells in detention centres and suggested that their existence could mean that prisoners were held there until they were made to "disappear". However the prison authorities at Pavón later denied the existence of such cells.

Following the reports of secret cells at Pavón, the families of 76 "disappeared" people filed *habeas corpus* writs on behalf of their missing relatives. According to the Guatemalan news media the Supreme Court appointed judges on a temporary basis to investigate these "disappearances", several of whom reportedly visited Pavón Prison, but to Amnesty International's knowledge none of the 76 were found, nor was any information made public as to whether or not the investigating judges had verified the existence of clandestine cells in the prison.

CHAPTER V

Domestic efforts to investigate human rights abuses

Justice denied: the Guatemalan judicial system and human rights violations

Amnesty International has closely followed domestic efforts to investigate human rights violations. The organization has been particularly disturbed by the failure of the Guatemalan judicial system to investigate and punish these abuses.

The Amnesty International delegation which visited Guatemala in 1979 found that the collapse of the judicial system had partly resulted from the intimidation and repression of witnesses, lawyers representing relatives of the "disappeared" and victims of extrajudicial execution, and members of the judiciary themselves. That delegation collected information about the extrajudicial execution of 10 members of the legal profession between July 1978 and May 1979, attacks on or abductions of 10 judges, lawyers or law students, and the "disappearance" of another lawyer in the same period. Between 1 January 1980 and 31 October 1981 Amnesty International examined the cases of 50 members of the legal profession who were killed in circumstances suggesting official involvement.

In the succeeding years Amnesty International has received testimonies from lawyers detailing intimidation which included receiving death threats, solely because they had tried to act on behalf of trade unions attempting to gain legal recognition, families of the "disappeared" or those detained under Decree 46-82.

America Yolanda Urízar, a 42-year-old labour lawyer and adviser to the *Central Nacional de Trabajadores* (CNT), Guatemalan Workers' Congress, "disappeared" on 25 March 1983 after having been arrested near the Guatemalan border with Mexico. She had left Guatemala in 1980 reportedly as a result of receiving continuous death threats during the government of General Lucas García. On 23 March 1983 the government of General Ríos Montt had ended the "state of siege" and announced an amnesty which permitted political opponents in exile to return freely to Guatemala. On 25 March America Yolanda Urízar openly crossed the border. Several hours later she was reportedly abducted by heavily armed men in civilian clothes and driven off in an army jeep. The vehicle was later seen parked in the regional headquarters of the *Policía Militar Ambulante*, Mobile Military Police, in Santa Ana Berlín, in the department of Quezaltenango. The National Police denied that she had been taken into custody.

America Yolanda Urízar's husband and seven-year-old son had died in 1975 after the brakes failed on their car. It is believed that the vehicle had been tampered with and that she had been the intended victim. Her 16-year-old daughter, Yolanda de la Luz Aguilar Urízar, was arrested in October 1979 as she distributed leaflets protesting about the death of a trade union leader. She was tortured and raped in custody, before her release in November 1979.

America Yolanda Urízar's father, retired army colonel Augusto Urízar, actively tried to establish his daughter's whereabouts after she had "disappeared". On 13 July 1983 he collapsed and died after suffering a stroke. Sources in Guatemala have suggested that he suffered the stroke when old friends in the military told him that his daughter had been killed in custody.

Amnesty International's 1985 delegation received material from leading officials of the National Police suggesting that the intimidation of lawyers and judges was continuing. The material included documents prepared by the *Comisión para la Paz*, Peace Commission, formed in March 1984 under the coordination of the then Rector of USAC, Dr Eduardo Meyer Maldonado, and now defunct. One of the Commission's duties was to ensure that those fundamental rights and freedoms established in law should be enjoyed by all Guatemalans. The Peace Commission had criticized the acquittal or release of people who were clearly guilty solely because members of the judiciary feared for their own safety. The delegation was also told by relatives of the "diasappeared" that they had been unable to find lawyers willing to risk handling their cases.

In both 1983 and 1984 the Inter-American Commission on Human Rights (IACHR) of the Organization of American States (OAS) reports on human rights in Guatemala found that the judiciary had been stripped of its independence, autonomy and impartiality. The 1984 Commission report found that the judiciary had been particularly deficient in handling *habeas corpus* writs presented to the courts on behalf of people who had "disappeared" since the beginning of the year. The IACHR's 1985 report reiterated these concerns.

Amnesty International shares the IACHR's assessment that Guatemalan institutions, including the judiciary, have not carried out genuine investigations into reports of human rights violations. It appears that petitions of *habeas corpus* have been systematically blocked by the military authorities. Although, in a number of cases, the Guatemalan judiciary has requested permission to inspect detention centres where "disappeared" people are believed to be held, few such investigations have been permitted.

Between January and October 1984 over 800 writs of *habeas corpus* addressed to the Ministry of the Interior, the Ministry of Defence, the Treasury Police, the National Police and several military bases in the southwest, were presented to the courts by GAM and others. A further 600 or so writs were presented by the Mexico-based *Comisión de Derechos Humanos de Guatemala* (CDHG), Guatemala Human Rights Commission, some on behalf of people who had been missing since 1979. Most of the CDHG petitions referred to the "disappeared", but some were presented on behalf of people imprisoned under Decree 46-82.

Occasionally there have been reports of investigating judges visiting provincial prisons in an effort to find "disappeared" people on whose behalf writs of *habeas corpus* had been filed. However, Amnesty International is aware of only one case in which a *habeas corpus* writ has had positive results. According to press reports José María González was brought to court and released on parole after the CDHG presented a petition on his behalf in July 1984. The authorities acknowledged that he had been detained on 9 March 1984 and remanded on charges of activities against state security and trafficking in explosives.

In February 1984 the Head of Public Relations of the National Police responded to public protest about "disappearances" by declaring that 117 people feared by their families to have "disappeared" since March 1983 were, in fact, held by the DIT. He promised that in future the DIT would draw up a daily list of detainees indicating which courts they would be brought before. A list of 86 detainees was subsequently given to the Guatemalan press. However, none of the 117 "disappeared" were named on the list and most of those listed were ordinary criminals.

The Guatemalan Supreme Court responded to the publication of this list by stating that it had authorized arrest warrants for only some 40 of the 86 detainees. The *Colegio de Abogados*, Guatemalan Bar Association, sent an appeal to General Mejía Víctores requesting the following measures: a thorough investigation into the procedures followed by the police in the cases of the 117 "disappeared"; publication of the full list of everyone who had been arrested and subsequently detained in secret and their immediate commital for trial; that the police be ordered only to make arrests for which a warrant had been issued by a court (except in cases of *flagrante delicto*), that those arrested be brought promptly before a court; that the police refrain from unnecessary repression and ill-treatment of detainees; that the government take steps to control the police and prevent them from committing acts of violence so as to ensure that the state honoured its obligation to respect human rights.

In April 1984 the President of the Supreme Court, Ricardo Sagastume Vidaurre, was removed from office. At a press conference after his dismissal Ricardo Sagastume said he had been under pressure from the military authorities, the police, sectors of the public administration and public leaders, all of whom wished to obstruct the law for their own ends. He accused the military and the police of usurping the power of the courts by jailing or releasing people without legal authorization and often on the basis of whether or not they could extort money from the detainee in question. This is borne out by several testimonies received by Amnesty International stating that people secretly detained on political charges were able to secure their release only through payment of large sums of money to the police or judicial authorities. In one such instance relatives of a highly placed government official repeatedly extorted money from the parents of a young girl who had already died under torture in November 1983 while in secret detention. Her detention was never officially acknowledged.

During the ceremony at which he handed over to his successor, Ricardo Sagastume stated, in the presence of General Mejía Víctores, that while in office he had "found it necessary to call attention to abuses committed against the inhabitants of the Republic and against judicial authorities" and that "the greater part of these abuses had originated and continued to originate in police and military circles".

In response to Ricardo Sagastume's dismissal, the Guatemalan Bar Association declared that there had been an institutional crisis in the country for several years and this had "nullified the rights of its inhabitants to life, liberty, security and justice . . . There must be limits to arbitrary power", and "because such arbitrary acts went unpunished [and] given the evidence of the lack of independence of the judiciary, belief in justice, faith and the moral authority of the state had been shattered." The Guatemalan press reported that 14 magistrates and other court officials had resigned in support of Ricardo Sagastume.

On 31 August 1984, Tomás Baudillo Navarro Batres, who had succeeded Ricardo Sagastume as President of the Supreme Court, declared that the military authorities were continuing to obstruct *habeas corpus* writs. He also accused the judicial authorities of negligence in dealing with these writs.

Failure to prosecute police or military personnel

The failure of successive administrations to prosecute members of the police or armed forces for human rights violations illustrates a lack of political will to end these violations. Amnesty International knows of only one instance in recent years where proceedings were initiated in connection with human rights abuses committed by members of the armed forces against civilians. The victims in this case were Patricio Ortíz Maldonado, who worked for the Agency for International Development, and three of his companions. The four were detained and murdered by an army patrol in the department of Huehuetenango in February 1983. Given the fact that Patricio Ortíz was employed by a US-funded agency, a number of steps were taken by the US Government to press for an investigation into the case. As a result the lieutenant who had commanded the patrol was arrested in March 1983. At the time a number of observers concluded that this indicated a new commitment on the part of the authorities to alter the tactics the army used to deal with suspected "subversives". However, on 31 August 1983, General Mejía Víctores announced that the lieutenant had been released because there was no evidence to link him to the killings. Foreign journalists who investigated the case in depth for newspapers such as the *New York Times* reported that he had actually been released because junior officers threatened to revolt if he was punished for having carried out orders issued by the central army headquarters in Guatemala City.

Official claims that people believed to have "disappeared" or to have been killed had never been detained or that the matter was under investigation by the judiciary have often been found to have been inaccurate and distorted.

The 1984 report of the IACHR, for example, drew attention to the case of Dr Carlos Padilla Gálvez, who was abducted in August 1982 and taken to the Second Police Corps headquarters in Guatemala City. In September 1982 an IACHR delegation to the country raised the case with General Mejía Víctores, then Minister of Defence. According to the IACHR's report, he told the delegation that Carlos Padilla had not been detained by any of the security forces under his command, was not held in any government detention centre and had most likely been kidnapped by guerrillas. Two days later, the IACHR's delegation was invited for another interview with General Mejía Víctores. This time the delegation was told that in fact Carlos Padilla was at the Second Police Corps headquarters, having been taken there after he had willingly participated in his own arrest and had placed himself in incommunicado detention to protect his life, as opposition forces had threatened to kill him.

The IACHR then visited Carlos Padilla at the police headquarters and was told by him that he had neither arranged nor willingly participated in his own arrest but had been detained against his will.

He was eventually released on 28 October 1982. In a formal note to the IACHR on this case, the authorities stated that Carlos Padilla had been detained on 26 August and released on 28 October, after it had been established that he was not guilty of any crime. No reference was made to the prolonged arbitrary detention to which Carlos Padilla had been subjected nor to the fact that he had been held incommunicado and deprived of legal assistance and the protection of due process of law for the two months he was detained. Nor was the government's original denial of his detention mentioned. A number of cases reported to Amnesty International, in which eye-witness testimony or other evidence refuted the official version of events, are described elsewhere in this report.[1]

During Amnesty International's mission to Guatemala in 1985, representatives of the National Police presented the delegation with what were said to be lists of police officers who had been dismissed from duty, detained, and had proceedings instituted against them during 1984 and the first three months of 1985 for "human rights violations". However, Amnesty International found that not one of these officers had been disciplined for the torture, "disappearance" or extrajudicial execution of suspected political opponents of the government. Instead, most had been charged with ill-defined offences such as abuse of authority, or with crimes such as embezzlement, bribery and blackmail. One case presented to the Amnesty International delegation as proof of official commitment to improving respect for human rights involved a police officer who was dismissed and had proceedings instituted against him for having traded in illegal petrol coupons. Another had been committed to the courts for having tried to extort money in exchange for allowing a palm reader to continue her trade, while two others were facing arson charges arising from fires at a mushroom warehouse and processing plant. Such prosecutions are clearly not indicative of efforts by the Guatemalan police to ensure respect for human rights standards such as those set out in the UN Code of Conduct for Law Enforcement Officials, nor to protect the human rights of primary concern in Guatemala, notably those violated by the everyday practices of torture, "disappearance" and extrajudicial execution.

The cases of homicide cited in the National Police lists were found to relate largely to instances where the officers had either been drunk and opened fire on unknown people in the streets, or had attacked relatives after disputes. There were only two cases of police killings of civilians. One involved police officers who shot and killed two people, having mistaken them for others for whom they had an arrest

---

[1]   See particularly the case of the CNT leaders, Chapter IV.

warrant. On another occasion, police officers were charged with having killed two people arrested on suspicion of having participated in several armed criminal assaults. A significant aspect of the latter case was that the officers were also charged with "alteration of police records". The official notes on the case state that the officers had altered the documentation in order to suggest that the dead men were "subversives" and had thus attempted to "evade responsibility for their deaths". Amnesty International specifically asked the National Police legal adviser whether any of the cases listed referred to police action against political opponents of the government but their response did not address this question.

Whereas supporting documentation given to Amnesty International by the National Police — largely items from the Guatemalan press — made clear that in a number of cases those detained and committed to the courts were former police officers, the police lists did not make clear which were serving police officers at the time of arrest and which had already been dismissed or had left the force.

Articles also appeared in the Guatemalan press by journalists who had questioned the relevant judges following an earlier announcement by the National Police that proceedings had been instituted against some 400 police officers. These journalists could not find a single court official who had any knowledge of or information about these proceedings.

Plans to "clean up" the police have periodically been announced in the past, often following a change of government, but despite publicly announced changes in the composition, names or policies of Guatemala's various police units, the essential structures and policies of the police and the armed forces have remained unchanged since the early 1970s.

Attempts by Amnesty International's delegation to discuss such issues, or specific cases of extrajudicial execution or "disappearances" in which the National Police had been implicated, with the National Police commanders and their legal adviser were unproductive. The meetings took place in the presence of the news media, who appeared to have been invited by officials, and the National Police representatives read out prepared statements in response to questions which Amnesty International had not asked.

Amnesty International's delegation also wished to examine how the army investigated abuses of which its personnel had been accused by victims, witnesses, the press or others. The delegation questioned the head of the Civil Affairs Unit of the army; the commanders of Military Base No. 1 in Guatemala City; the Military Brigade *Mariscal Zavala*, also based in Guatemala City; the military base in Chimaltenango; the Head of the Military Academy in

Sacatepéquez; the Deputy Head of State and Chief of the Joint Chiefs of Staff and the Deputy Minister of Defence. It also asked the high-ranking government and military officials to whom it spoke how soldiers found guilty of human rights violations were disciplined. All simply stated that no investigations or disciplinary action had been necessary as such abuses had simply not occurred. The one exception was the commander at the military base at Patzún, who told the delegation that he had disciplined soldiers for "attacks on the civilian population".[2]

When faced with specific allegations of extrajudicial executions carried out by the security forces, some officials said they were totally unaware of the allegations despite the fact that these had been widely publicized. Some said that investigations were the preserve of another ministry and others stated that special units of the agency accused had investigated the reports and, as in all previous instances, had found that the deaths in question had either been accidental, the result of drug-related crime or attributable to the armed opposition. This bears out Amnesty International's observation that no one, whether government agent or civilian, has ever been charged with, tried for or convicted of involvement in extrajudicial executions.

The specific cases Amnesty International's delegation raised included those of two GAM leaders who died in March and April 1983; the meticulously documented attack on the village of San Francisco Nentón in July 1982 during which some 300 people died, including women, infants and old people; and allegations made by the press and other sources at the time of the delegation's visit that the army had killed a large number of unarmed civilians on the evening of 25 April 1985 near Las Canoas, San Martín Jilotepeque, Chimaltenango.

Similarly, officials repeatedly maintained that no evidence had ever been found which would implicate an agent of the security forces in any of the thousands of "disappearances" which have occurred in Guatemala in recent years. The cases raised included those of 107 people reported to Amnesty International to have "disappeared" since August 1983, named on a list which the delegation presented to a number of officials whom it met including the Attorney General of the Republic.[3]

Common explanations given by officials to whom the delegation spoke were either that people reported as "disappeared" had joined the guerrillas, or gone abroad for economic reasons, or left their wives for other women. Deputy Head of State General Rodolfo

---

[2] The circumstances in which he made this claim have been described in Chapter I.

[3] See Appendix VII.

Lobos Zamora gave a further explanation: the "lack of family feeling" and "fanaticism" of Guatemala's Indian people which, he said, meant that if Indians were killed in armed combat, families did not reclaim the bodies and the relatives were then incorrectly numbered among the "disappeared".

The delegation was given little concrete information about who had carried out the investigations said to have led to these conclusions, under what orders they operated or to whom they reported, and was unable to determine the composition or means of operation of any such "investigatory units".

In November 1984 General Mejía Víctores had announced the formation of a *Comisión Tripartita*, Tripartite Commission, composed of representatives from the Public Ministry and the Ministries of the Interior and Defence, to investigate "disappearances". Even officials described in the press as members of the Tripartite Commission and listed as such on the agenda of meetings drawn up for Amnesty International's delegation by the Ministry of Foreign Affairs did not agree about the commission's composition. One official named by the Ministry of Foreign Affairs as Chairman of the Commission told the delegation that he was not serving as the Commission's Chairman: the misunderstanding had arisen because he had allowed one of the Commission's meetings to take place in his office. Officials, including the President and the magistrates of the Supreme Court, whom the Commission might have been expected to approach in the course of its investigations, told the delegation that the Commission had never contacted them. High officials of the church confirmed the delegation's impression that the Commission had never actually functioned, describing it as "still-born". Shortly after the mission, Amnesty International learned that the Tripartite Commission had dissolved itself after reporting that it was unable to establish the whereabouts of any of the hundreds of people whose "disappearance" had been reported to it.

'Return them alive': the campaign to find the 'disappeared'[4]

Having failed to elicit any response from the authorities on their own, groups of relatives, friends and others have periodically joined together and formed committees in the hope that a concerted effort

---

[4] *"Vivos los llevaron. Vivos los queremos"* ("You took them away alive, we want them back alive"). This was originally the slogan of the Mothers of the Plaza de Mayo in Argentina in their campaign to find their missing relatives. It has since been taken up by relatives' committees throughout Latin America, including Guatemala.

might force the authorities to clarify the fate of the "disappeared". Many of these people have themselves become the victims of "disappearance" and extrajudicial execution. In 1980, for example, a number of people joined together to form a human rights committee, the first such citizens' committee since relatives of the "disappeared" banded together in the 1960s. However they disbanded when their leader, journalist Irma Flaquer, "disappeared" after being abducted in the centre of Guatemala City. Her son was killed during the incident. Shortly before her "disappearance", she had accused the government of complicity in "death squad" killings and had resigned as the committee's president on the grounds that it was "useless and suicidal" to work for human rights in Guatemala.

In the following years Amnesty International recorded massive reports of human rights violations in Guatemala, but noted that the two principle domestic groups working on human rights issues, the CDHG and the Justice and Peace Commission, were forced for security reasons to operate from Mexico City.

Without local human rights groups to turn to, relatives were ineffective in their efforts to locate "disappeared" family members and suffered in isolation even though there were tens of thousands of families in the same situation. The wife of a trade unionist who had "disappeared" in 1981 told Amnesty International that "We have to suffer so much sorrow, but we could not even express our feelings of injustice that someone can just suddenly 'disappear', just like that. We've had various groups over the years, but they have disappeared, and in the end it seems that each of us has had to live through on our own what has been lived through before . . ."

She spoke of the economic difficulties she faced. As her husband was not legally dead, no state or other benefit was available to her. She also described the painful choice she had had to make; how she had decided not to work openly for information about her husband so that she could keep her job and support her children, and not risk "disappearing" or being killed herself: "In my case, I really had to think about what I should do. If I were to join a committee, I had to take into account all of the things that can happen to you, you can possibly be killed or face other repression, or receive death threats. I had three children and a job, so I decided I'd better dedicate myself to my work. This is also extremely painful, because even if I am busy bringing up my children, which was what was left to me, I cannot forget my husband, the kind of man he was. He worked for a collective agreement at his plant, he marched more than 300 kilometres with the miners.[5] He was arrested and badly beaten up,

---

[5] She is referring to a march in 1978 which brought an estimated 100,000 people

138

and held in terrible conditions, but he carried on his trade union work. What is the future of a man who fights for justice in countries like Guatemala? The future is death. And what is the future of the families of men who fight for justice? A desperate economic situation, but in spite of this we have pride, the pride of having been the friends, the mothers and wives of brave men, nobody can take that away from us. The only thing we can count on to support our children is our will to carry on, and on our own labour, and if we support something, join a committee to try and locate our husbands, they take away our work, then what can we do? Really, I tell you sincerely, the situation in Guatemala is desperate."

Having outlined the difficulties faced by anyone who tried to inquire into the fate of the "disappeared", she went on to say: "But now there is a group that has the courage to carry on, to meet, for this feeling, this courage. But it seems as if it will need a miracle for this group not to be destroyed as so many others have been in our country." The group to which she was referring is GAM. GAM was formed in June 1984 by people dedicated to tracing their relatives, many of whom had been missing for up to five years. Since then the group has been meeting every week in Guatemala City and in March 1986 announced that it was working on 950 cases of "disappearance", symbolizing the many thousands which had occurred in Guatemala.

GAM works from Guatemala City, where it collects data on the "disappeared". People have come from all over the country, in some cases spending a week's wages to reach the capital, in order to register their "disappeared" relative with the group and provide a photograph of him or her. Since its formation, GAM has presented hundreds of *habeas corpus* writs on behalf of the "disappeared". It has also placed fortnightly advertisements in the press, appealing for information about people who have "disappeared", and drawing attention to "disappearances" in Guatemala. One advertisement depicted a number of children whose fathers had "disappeared" in Guatemala recently, and was headed: "Daddy, where are you?" Another advertisement, placed on behalf of a "disappeared" trade unionist, carried a photograph of his 18-month-old daughter and was headed: "To those who are holding my daddy". The advertisement continued: "Daddy, I love you. May God watch and protect you wherever you are. I know that you will come back. I only wish that it could be today that I would wake up and see you here."

In July 1984 GAM held a press conference at which they issued

---

into Guatemala City from all parts of the country, in support of the miners of Huehuetenango who were protesting about substandard working conditions in the mines there.

a threefold appeal to the Constituent Assembly, recently elected to draft a new constitution. First, GAM urged the Assembly to enforce the rights guaranteed to individuals in the Fundamental Statute which, in 1982, replaced Guatemala's suspended constitution.[6] Second, they called for the immediate formation of a permanent commission to investigate "disappearances" and to report on their preliminary findings within one month, and third, they appealed for the office of Human Rights Attorney to be created under the new constitution with responsibility for ensuring respect for the rights of Guatemala's citizens. GAM also called on the *Asociación de Periodistas de Guatemala* (APG), Guatemalan Journalists' Association, to help the families in their appeals to the government.

GAM has received support from political groups, trade unions, the Rector of USAC, the AEU and the *Conferencia de Religiosos de Guatemala* (CONFREGUA), Conference of the Guatemalan Clergy. In August 1984 the President of CONFREGUA, Father Jorge Turono, gave a sermon at a special mass for the "disappeared". He told the congregation: "We are all gathered together here: wives, mothers, brothers and sisters, priests, friends of so many 'disappeared', both civilian and military, in our country. We have cried a lot; we have known what it is to be broken-hearted; we have felt the solitude, the absence of so many husbands and wives, fathers and mothers, brothers and sisters, priests, monks and nuns who have been 'disappeared' by 'death squads', or, as our bishops say, 'by paramilitary groups and security forces themselves'. . ."

On 1 August 1984 General Mejía Víctores met GAM. GAM reports that at this meeting he assured them that an exhaustive investigation would be conducted into the cases they had brought to his attention and gave them information which led them to believe that 16 of those who had "disappeared" in the previous few months were in detention and would be released. They did not, however, receive official confirmation of this, and the 16 remain "disappeared" to this day.[7]

In September 1984 the group requested information about what

---

[6] The new Constitution came into force in January 1986 when the elected government of President Vinicio Cerezo Arévalo took office.

[7] Fourteen of the 16 "disappeared" (Amnesty International does not have the names of the other two) who GAM were led to believe were still alive and in detention are: Jorge Hiram Muralles García, Natael Isaías Fuentes Monzón, Edgar Fernando García, Sergio Saúl Linares Morales, Hugo de León Palacios, Carlos Ernesto Cuevas Molina, Otto René Estrada Illescas, Ruben Amilcar Farfán, Irma Marilú Hicho Ramos, Gustavo Adolfo Castañón Fuentes, Héctor Alirio Interiano Ortiz, Sergio Leonel Alvarado Arévalo, Víctor Hugo Quintanilla Ordóñez and Alma Libia Samayoa Ramírez.

progress had been made with the investigations. In response the Minister of the Interior, Gustavo López Sandoval, said at a press conference that "so far, the security forces have not obtained any positive results in the investigations that are being carried out to establish the situation of the 'disappeared'" and that the government had found "no trace" of the people.

Disappointed by what it saw as the government's failure to genuinely address its concerns, the group gradually turned to more public actions, including demonstrations in front of public offices. In October 1984 GAM organized a march to National Police headquarters, and then to the Metropolitan Cathedral, where a mass on behalf of the "disappeared" was held. The march — the first major demonstration of its kind in Guatemala since 1980 — attracted an estimated 80,000 to 100,000 people. In November GAM occupied the headquarters of the Constituent Assembly, saying that they were "tired of going in and out of the offices of top officials without obtaining any hope . . ." The President of the Assembly, Christian Democrat Lic. Roberto Carpio Nicolle, promised to intercede in order to secure GAM another audience with General Mejía Víctores.

GAM was again received by General Mejía Víctores, on 19 and 29 November. They presented him with an extensive list of all the people they believed to have "disappeared" and details of the location of secret detention centres, which they threatened to publish unless they received a satisfactory response from the authorities. On 29 November GAM reported that General Mejía Víctores had told them he would set up a commission to investigate "disappearances". This was the Tripartite Commission. According to GAM General Mejía Víctores also offered to arrange for them to visit any part of the country they wished so that they could verify the government's claim that secret detention centres did not exist.

Also in November GAM requested the extradition of former Minister of the Interior Donaldo Alvarez Ruiz, who they believed to be responsible for "disappearances" between 1978 and 1982. Donaldo Alvarez was then living in the USA. The official response was that the terms of the extradition treaty between the USA and Guatemala would not allow him to be extradited on such grounds.

In the same month Amnesty International received reports that members of GAM, particularly of its organizing committee, had received death threats and that peasants and Indians travelling from the countryside to attend GAM meetings were being harassed. GAM also reported that the Director of the National Police, Colonel Héctor Bol de la Cruz, had "suggested" to the national news media that they should cease to publish the group's notices and advertisements. GAM responded with a public declaration that: "Even though we know our lives are in danger, we will remain united, and as long as our loved ones don't appear, we will be the conscience of the people, crying out for human dignity to be respected."

A further meeting between GAM and General Mejía Víctores was scheduled for December, at which, GAM reported, the General had undertaken to inform them of the preliminary findings of the official investigation. As far as Amnesty International is aware, this meeting did not take place and in January 1985 GAM organized a series of demonstrations in protest at the lack of progress in the investigations. On 9 January, the group presented a petition to President Reagan's Special Envoy to Central America, Harry Schlaudemann, in which they stated: "Not one of those being held has been returned; on the contrary only two have appeared, but murdered and with cruel signs of torture, barely three days after we met the Chief of State."[8]

Then, in March and April 1985 respectively, two of the group's leaders, Héctor Gómez Calito and Rosario Godoy de Cuevas, were killed in circumstances which pointed strongly to government involvement.

Their deaths followed renewed public actions by GAM and apparently related attempts by the government to link the group to the armed opposition: in March, GAM had again occupied the Constituent Assembly buildings and announced that it intended to begin a hunger-strike in front of the Assembly unless deputies kept promises to the group to press for investigations into the fate of the "disappeared". Some days later, in a televised address at the Jutiapa military base, General Mejía Víctores declared that GAM was being used and financed by "subversives". Shortly afterwards, GAM leaders again received death threats.

Also in March, GAM announced through a series of letters to the international community that it intended to hold a large demonstration on 13 April, at which it would call on the government to acknowledge the detention of certain named individuals whom it believed to be alive. Days later, on 30 March, GAM spokesman Héctor Gómez Calito was seized by four armed men as he waited for a bus after attending a GAM meeting in Guatemala City. He was found dead the next morning on the road to Amatitlán where he lived. According to eye-witness testimony given to Amnesty International's delegation, his body had abrasions consistent with his having been tightly bound at the wrists and ankles and bore marks of mutilation and torture. His lip had been split, his teeth broken and the back of his head crushed. His abdomen appeared heavily

---

[8] They were referring to the cases of USAC students Edgar Orlando Ramazzini Herrera and Edson Figueroa Cruz (see Chapter IV).

bruised; burn marks around the back of his waist and on his clothes suggested that he may have been burnt with a blowtorch, either as he was being tortured, or in an attempt to destroy his body. The first person to see his body said she could not state with absolute certainty that his tongue had been cut out, but that it did appear to have been severed as she could see only little bits of skin in his mouth, which was full of coagulated blood. Photographs of his face as he lay in his coffin, examined by Amnesty International's delegation, showed facial wounds consistent with those described. According to eyewitnesses, members of the National Police had been looking for Héctor Gómez at his home only days before his death.

On 3 April, Héctor Gómez' tomb and the flowers and GAM banner which had been placed upon it were burned. An attempt had apparently been made to exhume the body, possibly to prevent any independent autopsy, but whoever was responsible had succeeded in digging only about six inches into the grave before they were discovered and fled.

Officials the delegation spoke to about the case gave contradictory explanations as to the manner of Héctor Gómez' death. One suggested that he must have been killed in an automobile accident while drunk; others that his body had been found in an area known to be frequented by thieves, who had probably beaten him up and killed him, or that he had been killed because of a personal grudge. The Chief Medical Examiner did admit to the delegation that abrasions on the wrists and ankles indicated that Héctor Gómez had been tightly bound, yet nonetheleess maintained that the other wounds — lesions on the entire body, cranial fractures, heavily damaged mouth and lips — were consistent with his having been run over in an automobile accident. The official death certificate, a copy of which was given to the delegation, stated only that death had been caused by an internal haemorrhage due to a ruptured liver. Following Amnesty International's visit to Guatemala, foreign journalists reported that the doctor who signed the death certificate had himself "disappeared".

The delegation also collected information and took statements about a series of abuses suffered by the Gómez family in the years preceding Héctor Gómez' death: Héctor Gómez had joined GAM in an effort to establish the whereabouts of a brother, René, who had "disappeared" in 1983. Another brother, Edison, had been killed in suspicious circumstances in 1981, shortly after joining a demonstration against rises in public transport fares. Another relative had twice "disappeared" for short periods in 1982 and 1984. She had been tortured and raped while held. The information about the death of Héctor Gómez and the previous abuses his family had suffered collected by the delegation suggested official complicity in each instance. Héctor Gómez' entire family later went into exile abroad after having received death threats from people they knew to be members of the security forces.

Amnesty International's delegation also collected evidence about death threats and other forms of intimidation and harassment directed at GAM leaders after Héctor Gómez' death. One GAM member showed the delegation the death threats she had received after she placed an advertisement in the press asking for information about her "disappeared" husband. The homes of several leading GAM members were surroundeed by heavily armed men in unmarked cars. One of them, Angel Reyes, was forced to flee into exile on 3 April, after heavily armed men tried to abduct him, first at his home and subsequently at his place of work.

On 4 April, the day after Héctor Gómez' grave had been desecrated, the National Police announced that another GAM leader, Vice-President and founder member Rosario Godoy de Cuevas, had been killed in a car accident. They said her body had been found in her upturned car at approximately 11.30pm in what they later described to the delegation as a "ravine at the side of a narrow dangerous curve", 15 kilometres outside Guatemala City on the old road to Amatitlán. The bodies of her two-year-old son, Augusto Rafael, and her brother, Mynor Godoy Aldana, were also in the car. The three had been missing since they left home at 11am. Rosario Godoy de Cuevas had read GAM's declaration at Héctor Gómez' funeral. Earlier she had gone with other GAM members to inspect the place where his body had been found and had noticed an unmarked Cherokee van with smoked glass windows, which are customarily used by the DIT, whose occupants appeared to be observing her and the others. (Other security agents were present at the morgue, where Héctor Gómez' body had been taken, and at his funeral, where they threatened some of the mourners.)

Rosario Godoy de Cuevas, like Héctor Gómez, had joined GAM in her search for a missing relative. Her husband, USAC sociology student and AEU leader, Carlos Ernesto Cuevas Molina, "disappeared" on 15 May 1984, in Guatemala City. Witnesses saw him shot and forced from his motorcycle into a car by four heavily armed men, believed to have been members of the security forces. Abducted with him was Otto René Estrada Illesca, an economics student at USAC. In the following days, four other members of the governing body of the AEU "disappeared", eliminating almost its entire leadership. Just before he was abducted, Carlos Ernesto Cuevas had also helped the AEU Executive Committee to organize a mass on behalf of the "disappeared" people of Guatemala.

In September 1984, Rosario Godoy de Cuevas had written to Amnesty International on behalf of her small son, who missed his father enormously, and "cried for him every day". She asked the organization to continue its work on behalf of Guatemala's "disappeared", so that their memories should not fade into oblivion and stated that she was convinced that her husband was still alive and in the hands of the DIT.

Only days before she died, in a letter to her husband's mother in Costa Rica, she wrote: "I just can't think of what else I can do. The days and nights pass so quickly and yet so slowly that I just want never to have to live through this nightmare. I look at Augusto Rafael and my desperation is worse, his little eyes keep crying out to me for peace, and a happy and stable home ... I only think of Carlos, and how I can get him out. That's all I can think of at the moment. Either they give me Carlos back alive, or they can take me too ... I shall never rest until I find him ..." Her letter also mentioned that local officials of the Ministry of the Interior had summoned the GAM leadership and told them to cease their activities. Otherwise, they were warned, they would be arrested and charged with "disturbing public order and threatening national security". She continued: "Believe me, all the threats we've received don't bother me, even when they've said they'd fill us full of lead if we keep pressing. But I'm going to continue." She told her mother-in-law that: "There's a rumour circulating widely that there's to be some surprise from the government, but the trouble is that we don't know if this means they are going to return some of the [missing] people, or eliminate us, the leadership of GAM." Her letter was dated 30 March, the very day on which Héctor Gómez was abducted. Five days later she herself was dead. Rosario Godoy de Cuevas, her little son and her brother died on Maundy Thursday, towards the end of Easter Week, which the Archbishop of Guatemala City, Mgr Próspero Peñados, described as "A Holy Week of blood, sorrow, fear and shame".

Amnesty International's delegation discussed her case with a number of officials. Here too, the organization identified a number of contradictions in the statements concerning the deaths made by different officials, as well as contradictions between these statements and the material evidence it collected while in Guatemala.

Members of the delegation inspected the point where Rosario Godoy de Cuevas' car had allegedly gone off the road. The gradient was slight, and could hardly be described as a "ravine". Nor did the point at which the three allegedly died merit the government's description of "narrow" or a particularly "dangerous" curve. The delegates also inspected the car, which showed only very slight damage, again making it difficult to accept without further evidence the National Police claim that the three had died in a car crash.

Journalists investigating the case could find no one in the area who remembered hearing the sound of an accident when the National Police said it had occurred. In addition, the time of the accident given by the police was some six hours later than the time given by the Chief Medical Examiner as the probable time of death. Nor is it clear how the National Police learned of the accident or how they were able to be on the spot so quickly after it had allegedly taken place. (The police said that the accident had occurred at approximately 10.30–11.00 at night and that they had recovered the bodies at 11.30pm.)

When interviewed by journalists, local police had stated that the place where the accident allegedly occurred was not known as a danger spot, and that they knew of no other fatal accidents occurring there. They did say, however, that the place had been used as a body dump in the past, and indeed Amnesty International's delegation saw a cross at the exact spot where Rosario Godoy de Cuevas' car was said to have left the road. The cross commemorated Arturo Carillo García, whose body had been dumped on that spot on 25 January 1985. Finally, neither the delegation nor any of the journalists or local residents whom it spoke to had been able to find anyone who had actually seen the bodies in the car. By the time independent witnesses were on the scene, the car was on the road (pulled back up after the accident according to the police), and the bodies had been taken to the morgue, where the family identified them.

The delegation also spoke to people who knew Rosario Godoy de Cuevas' plans on the day of her death. She left home at 11am to buy medicine for her young son at a nearby supermarket, saying that she would return immediately. As far as is known, she had no reason to visit Amatitlán that day, to use the old road to get there, or to have broken the pattern she had established after she began to receive death threats, which was to make sure that her family and friends knew exactly where she was going, and when she planned to return. She had also made an appointment to meet a foreign delegation in Guatemala City at midday, but she "disappeared" before she could keep it.

Those who saw the bodies of the three described injuries which were not consistent with the information given to the delegation as to the cause of death — neck and skull fractures — by the Chief Medical Examiner, and also appeared inconsistent with the claim that all had died in an automobile accident. Rosario Godoy de Cuevas' body showed slight discolouration in the abdominal region, for example. The preliminary forensic report prepared on Rosario Godoy de Cuevas on 4 April has been studied for Amnesty International by doctors and forensic pathologists, who report that it is insufficient as it fails to relate the pathological findings to antecedent events; that is, it does not state whether the injuries examined were non-accidental, nor their probable cause. Nor does it state, as is the responsibility of the forensic examiner, whether the injuries appear to confirm or refute the alleged cause of death.

The delegation also questioned officials about the procedures used to establish the time, place and manner of death; whether a crime had been committed; and if so, who had been responsible. It was assured that investigations were continuing into the deaths both of Rosario Godoy de Cuevas, her brother and son, and of Héctor Gómez. Indeed, some officials refused to discuss the cases on the grounds that they were still under investigation. When Amnesty International's delegation discussed the case with the Minister of the Interior, he stated that he was not empowered to compel the judiciary, the traffic police or the Medical Examiner's office to provide him with their findings concerning the state of bodies (and vehicles in the case of an apparent traffic accident); they would only make evidence available to other government officials or agencies if ordered to do so by a judge.

Simultaneously, however, the Guatemalan press carried articles which quoted this same Minister as saying that Rosario Godoy de Cuevas' death had been exhaustively investigated, and that it had been found to have occurred as a result of an automobile accident. The newspaper *Diario de Centroamérica* on 17 April 1985, for example, quoted the Minister as saying: "After analysis by the respective authorities, it can be said in all certainty that her death was the result of an unfortunate traffic accident." *La Razón* of 17–18 April quoted him in almost the same words. In response to such reports, Archbishop Próspero Peñados del Barrio of Guatemala City was widely quoted by the press and others as saying that he was not convinced that the deaths had been accidental and urging the government to continue its investigations.

The Chief Medical Examiner also told the delegation that he could provide no further information or offer any visual evidence about the state of the bodies when they were brought to the main morgue in Guatemala City. He said he had no photographic equipment and that, in any case, it was the police's responsibility to take photographs and fingerprints at the morgue. He told Amnesty International's delegation that the police were studying the available information about the deaths of Rosario Godoy de Cuevas and her relatives, and would present this to the examining magistrate. If the magistrate found cause to suspect foul play, a trained forensic examiner would then be called in to conduct a full forensic examination, and to offer an opinion as to the likely cause of death. He expected that the examining magistrate would decide within a month whether to order such inquiries.

Amnesty International asked to be kept informed about any developments or findings in the cases of Héctor Gómez and Rosario Godoy de Cuevas and the authorities agreed to do this. The organization has, however, received no such information in either case.

Amnesty International continues to receive reports that members of GAM and their relatives are being harassed and threatened by the security forces. In May armed members of the *Guardia de Hacienda*, Treasury Police, ransacked the home of a relative of a GAM leader, announcing that they were "looking for *Grupo de Apoyo Mútuo*'s arms". In another incident in May, GAM President Nineth Montenegro de García was reportedly followed by eight men in a jeep, who trained their weapons on her as she drove through Guatemala City.

Upon receiving reports of these incidents Amnesty International sent a telex to President Cerezo on 15 May 1986, from which the following is an extract:

"On a number of previous occasions, Amnesty International has expressed concern at evidence of the harassment, and the torture and extrajudicial execution of members of the GAM, apparently because of their efforts to establish the whereabouts of 'disappeared' family members. Such incidents included the deaths in April and May 1985 of GAM leaders Héctor Orlando Gómez Calito and Rosario Godoy de Cuevas, in circumstances suggesting official security force involvement. Amnesty International's concerns regarding human rights violations directed at the GAM and others were most recently summarized in a memorandum submitted to Your Excellency in December 1985, to which the organization has not yet received a response.

"Amnesty International continues to believe that in-depth investigations of past human rights violations, including those directed at members of the GAM, their relatives and supporters, are necessary to identify and modify the institutionalized structures and policies responsible for the gross instances of 'disappearance' and extrajudicial execution in Guatemala in recent years and so prevent their repetition.

"With respect to the new reports of harassment directed at GAM members and their relatives, and given the record of past abuses, including extrajudicial execution suffered by its leaders, Amnesty

International considers it imperative that Your Excellency's government urgently adopt measures to guarantee the physical integrity of the group's members so that they may continue their lawful activities aimed at locating their missing relatives. Amnesty International also urges that effective investigations be initiated to determine responsibility for these latest incidents, and that those found responsible for criminal acts be held accountable before the law."

Appendix I

Recommendations for the restoration of respect for human rights in Guatemala

In view of its long-term and continuing human rights concerns in Guatemala, Amnesty International submitted the following recommendations with its memorandum of December 1985 to both the outgoing government of General Mejía Víctores and the incoming elected government of President Cerezo Arévalo. The organization considers that these recommendations should be implemented to restore respect for human rights in Guatemala.

I Government responsibilities with respect to military, security and paramilitary units

1. There should be a prompt, impartial investigation of every allegation of abduction, torture or unlawful killing, as befits any serious crime. The method and findings of such inquiries should be made public in all cases. It is important that remedial measures be undertaken in cases where official wrongdoing is found, even if individual officials responsible cannot be identified. Where individual culprits can be identified, they should be brought to justice.

2. To effect this first, all-important recommendation, firm steps must be taken to ensure that investigation, prosecution and trial proceedings are carried out by impartial agencies independent of the security forces and of the executive power.

3. The government must ensure that all members of the regular military and security forces, including the civil defence patrols, not only are trained in, but abide by such internationally agreed standards as those set by the United Nations (UN) Code of Conduct for Law Enforcement Officials of December 1979 and by Article 3 common to the four Geneva Conventions on the Protection of Victims of War of August 1949 which regulates the conduct of armed forces in situations of conflict not of an international character.

4. The government must publicly campaign against the activities of the so-called "death squads", investigating and prosecuting the crimes they have committed.

II Arrest, detention and trial procedures

The relevant authorities must take steps to ensure that no one is arrested or detained on account of his or her non-violent political views and activities. Of vital importance is that the detention of captured persons be speedily acknowledged and that such persons be held in recognized detention centres only. These places of detention must conform to the UN Standard Minimum Rules for the Treatment of Prisoners (1955) and such people brought promptly before a judge and allowed access to family and legal counsel. Amnesty International understands that Guatemala's new constitution which is to come into force in January 1986, like the currently applicable *Estatuto Fundamental de Gobierno*, Fundamental Statute of Government, makes provisions along these lines. The organization urges most strongly that these provisions be strictly implemented.

III Judicial reform

1. The Guatemalan judiciary should be allowed to function in an independent manner and be given sufficient jurisdiction to enable it to bring to justice wrongdoers in the security forces.

2. At present Amnesty International understands that in remote rural areas, especially those in contention, those who exercise judicial functions are often untrained in the law, and are named by the local military commanders, who are also those against whom complaints of human rights violations are likely to be lodged. Amnesty International recommends strongly that this method of appointment of rural judicial officials cease.

3. Appropriate judicial agencies should be given the power to *subpoena* (that is, compel the production of) all records necessary for their investigations, including those of the military and security forces, as well as the medical and legal records maintained by forensic medical examiners and other relevant medical personnel.

4. The establishment of an independent National Bar Association charged with ensuring respect for the integrity of the judicial system should be facilitated.

5. Amnesty International has noted that Guatemala's new constitution provides for the establishment of a parliamentary human rights commission, and the appointment of a Human Rights Attorney. Amnesty International urges that both the Commission and the Attorney also be given appropriate powers of *subpoena* and that the mandate of these new entities should be to investigate all human rights violations reported to them, including those which occurred before they began to function.

6. Information should be made public concerning the working methods of the Tripartite Commission and the results of its inquiries into the hundreds of specific cases of "disappearance" which were presented to it for investigation. Amnesty International urges that investigation into the "disappearances" submitted to the Commission which the Commission reported it was unable to clarify should continue, and that it be made publicly known which government officials have responsibility for conducting these investigations, and for ensuring that they continue once the government has changed hands.

7. The government should also thoroughly review the present method of reporting and certifying violent deaths, particularly those resulting from actions taken by any person in an official capacity. The aim of such an inquiry should be to create procedures which will ensure that such deaths are reported to the authorities, who then impartially investigate the circumstances and causes of the deaths. All efforts should be made to identify the unidentified bodies

that are found throughout the country and frequently buried only as "xx", in order to determine time, place and manner of death and whether a criminal act has been committed.

IV Non-governmental human rights investigation and monitoring

1. In view of past abuses of people involved in human rights investigations, the government must make special efforts to protect those involved in the investigation of human rights violations: witnesses, family members, lawyers, journalists, and members of non-governmental organizations.

2. Amnesty International particularly recommends that members of the GAM and members of the Guatemalan human rights groups currently operating in exile who may elect to return to Guatemala be ensured the full protection of the law. Amnesty International also strongly urges that the results of the investigations thus far into the death of GAM leaders Héctor Gómez Calito and Rosario Godoy de Cuevas be made public. The time, manner and place of death of the two has not as yet been convincingly established and a number of contradictory official statements regarding their deaths have been issued. Amnesty International believes investigations should continue, and it should be made publicly known which government officials have the responsibility for these investigations and when the results of their inquiries can be expected.

3. Further with respect to human rights investigation and reporting, Amnesty International recommends that international delegations of inquiry be permitted to carry out inquiries in the country under circumstances that do not tend to inhibit free and confidential dialogue between such delegations and those they wish to meet and who may wish to meet them.

4. Data collected by human rights investigation groups, both domestic and international, should be fully investigated by the authorities, and prosecutions initiated against individuals suspected to have been implicated in human rights violations.

5. In accordance with Article 3 of the Geneva Conventions governing conflicts not of an international character, an impartial humanitarian body should be permitted to offer its services to the parties to the conflict.

V Compensation

Victims of torture and the families of victims of "disappearance" and extra-judicial executions should be given financial compensation by the authorities, as is required by such instruments of international law as the UN Declaration against Torture of 9 December 1975, Article 11, which stipulates that: "Where it is proved that an act of torture or other cruel, inhuman or degrading treatment or punishment has been committed by or at the instigation of a public official, the victim shall be afforded redress and compensation in accordance with national law."

VI Human rights education

Amnesty International considers that the human rights education program currently used to train Guatemala's military and police forces in their obligations under national and international law should be maintained and strengthened. Subjects taught in basic training should also be repeated at advanced level, and all materials directed at the public, as well as the military and police forces themselves, should reflect internationally agreed standards for the protection of human rights. Efforts to educate members of the military and police in their human rights obligations must be accompanied by genuine efforts to bring those who have not complied with the relevant standards to justice.

Appendix II

Letter from Thomas Hammarberg, Secretary General of Amnesty International, to President Vinicio Cerezo Arévalo

His Excellency President Vinicio Cerezo Arévalo
President of the Republic of Guatemala
National Palace
Guatemala City
GUATEMALA   25 June 1986

Your Excellency

As your Excellency will know, Amnesty International has been concerned for many years at reported human rights violations in Guatemala, including "disappearances" and extrajudicial executions on a gross scale over a period of more than two decades. Amnesty International therefore welcomed Your Excellency's declarations both prior to and following your election that you intended to promote respect for human rights in the country and has followed with great interest Your Excellency's efforts in this regard during your first months in office. A previous letter and memorandum submitted by Amnesty International to your Excellency in December 1985 suggested a number of measures which Amnesty International believes Your Excellency should take to assist in this respect. Amnesty International considers that many of the recommendations given there remain valid and would be pleased to have the opportunity to discuss them in more detail with Your Excellency or representatives of your government.

Your Excellency will note that in its December letter and memorandum Amnesty International urged that steps be taken to ensure that no one is arrested or detained on account of his or her non-violent political beliefs, that all political detentions be speedily acknowledged and that people so detained be held in recognized detention centres only and in conformity with the United Nations Standard Minimum Rules for the Treatment of Prisoners (1955). Further towards eliminating the formerly widespread practices of "disappearance" and extrajudicial execution, Amnesty International's memorandum urged that all members of the regular police and military forces, including the civil defence patrols, are not only trained in, but abide by, internationally agreed standards in the performance of their duties. Such standards include the United Nations Code of Conduct for Law Enforcement Officials of December 1979 and Article 3 common to the four Geneva Conventions on the Protection of Victims of War of August 1949 which regulates the conduct of armed forces in conflicts not of an international character.

In this regard Amnesty International has been interested to learn of the steps taken by Your Excellency with respect to the intelligence division of the National Police, the *Departamento de Investigaciones Técnicas* (DIT), Technical Investigations Department, a unit habitually implicated in reports of human rights violations including "disappearance" and extrajudicial execution under Your Excellency's immediate predecessors. According to Amnesty International's understanding, Your Excellency announced shortly after taking office in January 1986 that the DIT was to be disbanded and a new more professional criminal investigations unit established in its place.

Amnesty International would be interested to learn the state of proceedings in the case of the one DIT agent it understands has been charged (reportedly with possessing the gun of a murdered police officer) as well as the content of the training courses it understands are to be offered to former DIT agents who are to join the regular uniformed police.

Amnesty International would also be interested to learn what steps may have been taken to review the files of the new disbanded agency, to determine whether information was available there concerning illegal acts in which DIT agents were implicated during your predecessors' terms in office. Amnesty International believes that all allegations against the DIT, including those which the organization understands were filed after Your Excellency announced the disbanding of the organization, should be fully investigated.

Similarly, Amnesty International believes that investigations should be initiated into the alleged involvement of other Guatemalan police and military units in specific incidents of torture, "disappearance" and extrajudicial executions. The organization believes that it is essential to determine how these abuses were planned and carried out so that those structures and policies which permitted them to take place on a gross scale for so many years can be identified and modified, and further abuses prevented.

In this regard, Amnesty International believes that there is already enough information available concerning a number of such abuses to make it possible for further inquiries to establish those directly responsible and bring them to justice. I would like to draw Your

Excellency's specific attention to a number of incidents described in the enclosed memorandum, where evidence is given concerning the responsibility of specific agencies for human rights violations including "disappearance" and extrajudicial execution. They include:

The as yet unresolved "disappearance" of 25 leaders of the *Central Nacional de Trabajadores* (CNT), Guatemala Workers Congress, on 21 June 1980, and the further "disappearance" of 17 more trade union leaders from a trade union conference centre near the town of Escuintla in August of the same year. The centre's administrator was later found dead, but the unionists remain missing. In both cases, all evidence points to the responsibility of the National Police;

The abduction and torture in early 1984 of trade unionist Alvaro René Sosa Ramos, who later escaped from detention and testified abroad that the *kaibiles* (special counter-insurgency unit of the armed forces) had been responsible for his detention. While in their custody, Sosa Ramos stated that he also saw fellow trade unionists Amancio Samuel Villatoro, who is still missing, and Silvio Matricardi Salam, whose corpse, bearing marks of torture, was found near the city of Escuintla on 14 March 1984;

The abduction of trade unionist Edgar Fernando García in February 1984 in Guatemala City in the presence of witnesses by uniformed members of the National Police and its Special Operations Brigade, the *Brigada de Operaciones Especiales* (BROE);

The series of abuses, including arbitrary arrest, torture, "disappearance" and extrajudicial executions, which were reported between April 1984 and September 1985 in the department of Chimaltenango, particularly in and around the town of Patzún. For example, catechist Rafael Yos Muxtay "disappeared" after being seized by members of the armed forces in the presence of witnesses in the area of Patzún, Chimaltenango on 22 November 1985. In incident after incident, information is available to indicate the responsibility of the Guatemalan military, most specifically the detachment based at Patzún during that period, for the abuses in question;

The killings in March and April 1985 of GAM leaders Héctor Gómez Calito and Rosario Godoy de Cuevas. Here too, there is evidence to implicate official forces in their deaths, evidence which Amnesty International believes must be pursued;

The abduction, torture and subsequent "disappearance" of Luis Fernando de la Roca in September 1985 by heavily armed men in plain clothes whom Luis de la Roca identified as government agents when he was briefly brought back to his home. *Habeas corpus* writs filed by Luis de la Roca's mother elicited the information from the *Departamento de Impuesto sobre Uso de Servicios y Actividades*

Comerciales — Department of Tax on Commercial Services and Activities, that the licence plates of one of the cars used in his abduction had been issued to the Ministry of Defence; those of another were registered to the Justo Rufino Barrios military detachment in Guatemala City;

The arbitrary detention and subsequent murder of catechist Luis Che by soldiers based in the area of El Estor, Izábal on 23 October 1985;

The alleged arrest and subsequent "disappearance" of catechist Patrocinio Gertrudis Pérez Ramirez on 9 March 1986 by soldiers based in the area of his home, Buenos Aires, Morales, Izabal.

In addition to the abuses described in the memorandum, Amnesty International has information on numerous other past "disappearances" and extrajudicial executions, where substantial information already exists to suggest that official inquiries could establish responsibility for the events in question. Amnesty International would be pleased to provide this information to agencies of Your Excellency's government charged with ensuring respect for human rights in the country.

Amnesty International considers that the incidents described above as well as the thousands of other arbitrary detentions, "disappearances" and extrajudicial executions which took place in Guatemala in recent years were totally illegal and should not be exempt from legal proceedings. Amnesty International believes that governments have a responsibility for ensuring that courts or other investigative bodies are provided with the necessary powers for ensuring that the truth regarding past abuses can be publicly brought to light and those responsible brought to justice. Amnesty International is therefore opposed to the adoption of any procedures or legislation whose effect would be to obstruct the presentation of relevant evidence before the courts or to exempt from giving evidence before the courts any person whom the court might call upon to testify. In the opinion of Amnesty International such legislation would be incompatible with Resolution 34 of the UN Subcommission on Prevention of Discrimination and the Protection of Minorities which urges that states where "disappearances" have been denounced should abstain from promulgating laws which could impede the investigation of such abuses. Amnesty International has therefore been concerned about aspects of the general amnesty (Decree 08-86 of 13 January 1986), applied to all people responsible for or connected with political and common crimes committed between 23 March 1982 and 14 January 1986, one of the numerous decree laws promulgated in the final days of the retiring military government of General Oscar Humberto Mejía Víctores.

Amnesty International fears that by protecting members of the police and security forces (and civilians who worked with them), Decree Law 08-86 will make it impossible to establish the truth about the "disappearances" and extrajudicial executions. The organization is further concerned that the amnesty could also encourage further human rights violations by giving the perpetrators of past crimes a sense of immunity from prosecution.

In this regard, Amnesty International has noted that disturbing numbers of apparent extrajudicial executions and "disappearances" have continued to be reported since Your Excellency took office. A selection of such incidents where the evidence appears to be strongest as to possible official police or military responsibility is appended to this letter.[1] Amnesty International believes that they must be thoroughly and promptly investigated and their perpetrators brought to justice.

Further with respect to its concern that past abuses be investigated, Amnesty International has followed with great interest the various announcements made by Your Excellency since taking office as to possible investigation of the many thousands of "disappearances" which have occurred in Guatemala in recent years. Amnesty International believes such investigations would indicate compliance with Resolution 1983/23 of the UN Sub-Commission on Prevention of Discrimination and Protection of Minorities of 5 September 1983 which supports the right of the family to know the fate of their missing relative. It deeply regrets therefore that the latest effort to establish a body to investigate these past abuses, the combined commission announced in May 1986, is now reportedly cancelled.

Amnesty International urges that further consideration be given to the establishment of a body to carry out this important task. It has itself studied the experience of such commissions in a number of countries and has developed criteria concerning their composition, terms of reference and procedures, which it would be pleased to make available. In this regard, Amnesty International would be interested to learn of the priorities set by the human rights commission established by the new constitution for its own work, and its procedures for undertaking investigations and holding hearings. Has consideration been given to the role this commission might play in resolving the issue of past "disappearances"? In a similar vein, Amnesty International would also be interested to learn whether the new Human Rights Attorney, also provided for in the new constitution, has as yet been appointed?

Finally, Amnesty International would also be interested to learn

---

[1] reproduced as Appendix III.

what steps Your Excellency's government may have taken or intends to take to ensure the security of the leadership and members of the *Grupo de Apoyo Mutuo por el Aparecimiento con vida de Nuestros Hijos, Esposos, Padres y Hermanos* (GAM). As Your Excellency will know Amnesty International has been disturbed at recent reports of renewed threats directed at this group, which in the absence of official investigations of past "disappearances" had undertaken its own efforts to stimulate such inquiries. It appreciated the assurances from Lic. Julio Santos, Your Excellency's Secretary of Public Relations, in his message to Amnesty International of 20 May 1986 that these incidents were to be investigated and would be interested to learn of the results of these investigations.

In closing I would like to note that Amnesty International has been favourably impressed by certain recent legislative developments in Guatemala. It has been pleased to note, for example, that the new constitution and the new *amparo* and *habeas corpus* act (*Ley de Amparo, Exhibicion Personal de Constitucionalidad*) (Decree 1-86 of 8 January 1986) provide a number of positive changes in legal procedures, including abolition of the previously secret indictment (*sumario*) phase of judicial proceedings and that under Guatemala's new constitution the international conventions to which Guatemala is a party will henceforth explicitly prevail in principle over the country's own laws, including the constitution itself. In this regard Amnesty International would further urge that Your Excellency's government ratify other relevant international measures to which Guatemala is not yet a party, to further assist the institution of legal and procedural safeguards to prevent any future human rights violations. These should include: The UN International Covenant on Civil and Political Rights (1966) and its optional protocol, the UN International Covenant on Economic, Social and Cultural Rights (1966), the UN Convention against Torture and other Cruel, Inhuman or Degrading Treatment or Punishment of 10 November 1984 and the American Convention on Human Rights Article 45 [Competence of the Inter-American Commission of Human Rights].

Amnesty International would appreciate the opportunity to learn more about the measures taken thus far by Your Excellency's government with respect to the promotion and protection of human rights and regarding further steps envisaged. Amnesty International shares the desire expressed by the UN Human Rights Commission at its February session, that Your Excellency's government continue to take effective measures to ensure that human rights and fundamental freedoms are respected and would be honoured to have the opportunity to discuss with Your Excellency and other members of your government measures which it believes can assist in this process.

Appendix III

Human rights violations reported to have occurred since January 1986

The following cases are representative of human rights violations reported to have occurred since the Government of President Vinicio Cerezo took office:

On 29 January, Christian Democratic member of parliament Diego Velazco Brito reportedly denounced the killings of a number of peasants since President Cerezo took office (some sources give a figure as high as 19), and the wounding of one other when they were attacked by masked paramilitaries in the department of El Quiché. Among those killed was Diego Tay Agital, kidnapped and murdered in San Antonio Ilopango by four heavily armed men in civilian clothes on 16 January, and Antonio Cortez and Antonio Lobos, killed on 24 January in the same town.

Another deputy, Ramiro García, announced that Alfredo Sis, Secretary of the Christian Democratic Youth of San Miguel Chacaj, Baja Verapaz, his father and sister were killed by heavily armed men who forced their way into the Sis home. Neighbours blamed similar acts which had gone unpunished in the past on troops from the local military base.

Also on 29 January, Alfonso Jeronimo Pérez, local official in Jocatán, Chiquimula and member of the Christian Democratic party, was killed by armed civilians as he returned home. His assailants then cut off his hands, ears and head.

According to a statement made by Ana Leticia Portillo de Solis and reported by Guatemalan human rights groups, three armed men who identified themselves as members of the DIT arrived at the Solis home at 19th Avenue and 4th Street, Zone 18, Residenciales Atlantida, in the capital at 2.45am on 2 February. They forced their way into the house, pursued her husband Roberto Solis Sanabria into the bedroom of his youngest child where he had tried to escape from them, and shot and killed him.

José Mercedes Sotz Cote (also named as José Mercedez Soto), Secretary of Finances of the *Sindicato Central de Trabajadores Municipales* (SCTM), Central Municipal Workers Union, stated that he had been seized on a Guatemala City street on 7 February by heavily armed men who took him to a private home fitted out as a prison, where they held him for several hours while they tried to intimidate him into giving up his union activities.

Church sources reported that on 28 February Martin Miculax, 23, from Saquiyá, Patzún, Chimaltenango, was taken away by two soldiers who entered his home at 8pm and seized him in the presence of his wife. He had recently completed his military service.

Baltazar Quiacán Coché and Miguel Ulario, agricultural workers, were reportedly abducted by members of the armed forces between 11 and 13 April 1986 on the Finca San Basilio (San Basilio Estate), Rio Bravo municipality in the department of Suchitepéquez. They were abducted together with five other agricultural workers who were released on 16 April. The five reported they did not know where they had been held, and that they had been kept blindfolded, tied by their hands and feet and beaten. The military detachment at the San Basilio Estate was established on 15 January 1986, and military officials were subsequently reported to have intimidated and threatened inhabitants because of their supposed links with the armed opposition. A few days before the April detentions the local military authorities carried out a population census, reportedly asking detailed questions and placing particular emphasis on all males aged 18 and over.

On 15 April 1986 agricultural workers Francisco Coxun Chen and Emilio Perez Siana were reportedly detained by members of the Guatemalan security forces who broke into the parish house of Cobán, Alta Verapaz department, taking advantage of the priest's absence. Both had apparently been harassed for several days by their captors and had sought refuge in the parish house.

Enrique de Leon Asturias, Member of Congress affiliated with the Democratic Socialist Party (PSD), was kidnapped and held for three hours on 25 April by a group of men presumed to be government security force personnel. He stated that they beat him and "forced me to lie down on the seat and told me they had been watching me for two days and had become familiar with my political activities".

On 7 May Mauricio Cojulum Queme, President of the student body of the *Instituto Nacional de Varones del Occidente* (INVO), West-side National Institute for Young Men, was seized in Quetzaltenango. He was later released by his unidentified captors who reportedly warned him to leave the country.

On 15 May María Elena Rodas Orellana, aged 20, and a student at the Faculty of Engineering at the *Universidad de San Carlos* (USAC), University of San Carlos, "disappeared" in unknown circumstances on her way from Chimaltenango to university. Her whereabouts remain unknown and the authorities have denied responsibility for the detention.

Appendix IV

Massacres reported to have occurred in rural Guatemala between March and June 1982[1]

The following massacres were reported to have occurred between March and June 1982. In some cases the government attributed blame to opposition groups and this is noted where relevant, together with any differing versions of events.

It is also possible that some of these incidents overlap. Sometimes reports of killings did not give the exact date when they had occurred. On other occasions, killings which had occurred over a period of several days were reported by some sources as occurring in a group on one date. As only some of the killings which have occurred in Guatemala have been reported to Amnesty International, this should be regarded as only a partial list of the killings which occurred between March and June.

Finally, readers should note that Amnesty International cannot confirm in each instance the information given in reports, but has noted whatever conflicting information it has received.

March

24 March
: The villages of Sacataljí, Crumax, San Isidro and Samuc de Cobán, in the department of Alta Verapaz were all reportedly burned to the ground. Casualty figures are not clear.

24-27 March
: The villages of Las Pacayas, Cistram (or Cisirau), El Rancho Quixal and Chiyuc, in San Cristóbal Verapaz municipality, Alta Verapaz department, were bombed leaving 100 people dead.

26 March
: Nine peasant families, totalling 54 people, were killed and three peasants kidnapped by plainclothes soldiers who entered the village of Pacoj in the department of Chimaltenango.

31 March
: Fifteen peasants were shot dead and four burned to death in the village of Estancia de la Virgen, San Martín Jilotepeque municipality, Chimaltenango department, by heavily armed men who dragged them from their homes. Most of the huts in the village were burned to the ground. Peasant groups blamed the army for these killings.

30 March-
: Fifty-five people were killed in the village of Chinique,

1. This was first published as Appendix I of *Massive extrajudicial executions in rural areas under the government of General Efrain Ríos Montt*, an Amnesty International report of July 1982.

3 April	El Quiché department. The authorities described the killings as an encounter between guerrillas and a civil defence patrol.

April

2 April	Some 250 regular and paramilitary troops entered the village of El Adelanto, Concepción municipality, department of Sololá, kidnapping 10 women and killing them. They then set fire to their homes.
Circa 2 April	Armed men entered the village of Ximbaxuc, Chinique, Quiché, robbing, burning and killing 40 peasants, including men, women, the elderly and children.
Circa 3 April	Thirteen peasants were shot dead in the village of Nicabaj, Rabinal, department of Baja Verapaz. They were: Francisco Sis Osorio (aged 16); Felix Jerónimo Tecú (aged 60); Rosalío Jerónimo Tista (aged 32); Paulo Pangay (aged 30); Bernabé García (aged 70); Mario Valey (aged 17); Miguel A. Valey (aged 14); Juliana Osorio (aged 52); Fulgencia de Paz (aged 31); Julián Mendoza (aged 50); Silvestre Tecú (aged 57); Julián Jerónimo (aged 58); Arturo Jerónimo.
3-5 April	Twenty-nine peasants were burned alive in their homes in the villages of Chocorrales and Semejá I, Chichastenango, Quiché municipality, El Quiché department.
5 April	About 100 people were killed in the village of Mangal, and others in Chel, Juá and Amachel in northern Quiché. In one of the villages the army reportedly forced the entire population into the courthouse, raped the women, beheaded the men and battered the children to death against rocks in a nearby river. Thirty-five more people were reportedly killed on the same day on the Covadonga estate, Chajul municipality, in the department of El Quiché. Peasant groups accused the army of responsibility.
6 April	In the village of Palamá, San José Poaquíl, department of Chimaltenango, soldiers murdered a 100-year-old woman.
7 April	Soldiers killed at least three women after attacking the hamlet of Chirrenquiché, Cobán, Alta Verapaz. The following day soldiers returned to the hamlet and machine-gunned an entire family, including a one-year-old boy.
12 April	In the village of Santa Rosa Chujuyub, El Quiché, 12 people were massacred.
15 April	Soldiers returned to the village of El Adelanto, Concepción and machine-gunned or hacked to death with machetes 30 more people from the village, including 15 women, five men and nine children between the ages of six months and one year.

15 April	Peasant groups accused the army of attacking the village of Semejá I in Chichicastenango, tying 20 villagers to the poles of their houses and burning them alive. On the same day, in the village of Chocorrales, Santa Cruz, Quiché, an army patrol beheaded nine peasants, among them a nine-year-old girl, as the family was praying. Six of the dead were: Isaías Vicente Pérez; Vicente Pérez; Abelino Marroquín Xiquim; Víctor Tzoy Tiu; Mateo Tun; Juan Chio Itzay.
15 April	Peasants were killed in the village of Agua Caliente, San José Poaquíl municipality, Chimaltenango department. An army report stated that the peasants were killed by guerrillas who went from house to house asking for food and clothes and harassed some of the women, whereupon the villagers shot two guerrillas. Then the guerrillas shot the peasants. The army report stated that 14 peasants were killed; other sources reported that 23 died.
16 April	Thirty-five people were massacred in the village of Covadanga Barillas, Huehuetenango.
17 April	Fourteen peasants were killed and their homes burned in San José, Poaquíl, Chimaltenango.
Circa 17 April	An unknown number of peasants were killed in Agua Escondida, Chichicastenango, Quiché, and their homes burned.
17-22 April	Sixty-seven peasants were killed in the villages of Xasic, Choacama, Chitatul, Tabil and Cahjpal, in the department of El Quiché.
19 April	Thirteen people were murdered during the night in the villages of Tziquinay and San Martín Jilotepeque in the department of Chimaltenango.
20 April	Twenty peasants were killed in the village of Pojujel, Concepción municipality, Sololá department.
21 April	Eleven peasants were killed by hooded men who attacked the village of Agua Caliente, Comalapa, Chimaltenango, forcing the victims from their homes and killing them.
22 April	An entire family, including two children aged four and six, was murdered in the village of San Nicolás, Chiantla municipality in the department of Huehuetenango.
Circa 22 April	Thirty armed men entered the village of Macanché, Flores, in the Petén department, forced the inhabitants from their homes and shot them. The 15 peasants killed were: Natalio Alonso Castañeda (aged 80); Vilma Posadas Alonso (aged 22); Gonzalo Posadas Alonso (aged 12); Elías Posadas Alonso (aged seven); Julio A. Rodríguez López (aged 40); Macedonia Solís (aged 40); César Augusto Solís (aged 23); Adela Solís (aged 14); Antonio

Solís (aged nine); Elena Solís (aged six); Olivia Solís (aged 12); Marco Tulio Solís (aged three); Mario Mosadas (aged 24); Demetrio Ortega (aged 48); Gilberto Posadas Alonso (aged 24).

25 April In the village of Varituc, San Martín Jilotepeque municipality, department of Chimaltenango, 13 peasants were killed.

Circa 25 April Twelve peasants died in a bomb attack on the lorry in which they were travelling in Cantón Namaj, Santa Rosa Chujuyub, Quiché. Eight of the dead were: Gonzalo Quiñónes Sical (aged 45); Floridalma Quiñónes (aged56); Odeteh Quintana (aged 16); Blanca de León (aged 22); Mercedes Reyes; Celedonia Urízar; Santos Urízar; Víctor Urízar.

26 April The army was accused of killings in the hamlet of Chitnij, municipality of San Cristóbal Verapaz, department of Alta Verapaz (see 6 June). Twenty people were burned alive in their homes in the village of Chipiacul (or Chipun), Patzún, Chimaltenango. Survivors blamed the army. Those killed were: Bernardino Xínico Saquec (aged 47); Ventura Xínico (aged 35); Balbino Chuc Ajú (aged 23); Francisco Ajú (aged 16); Carlos Enrique Ajú (aged 25); Francisco Chonay Basibal (aged 43); Ricardo Ajú Sicajaú (aged 50); Alberto Ajú Sicajaú (aged 37); Pedro Marcelino Yaquí Mos (aged (44); Daniel Yaquí (aged 23); Alberto Yocón Chuc (aged 18); Sabino Ajú Sipac (aged 45); Teodoro Xínico (aged 17); Nicolás Baján (aged 26); Martín Xínico (aged 27); Nicolás Chonay (aged 74); Adrían Yaquí (aged 44); Merlinda Xínico (aged 17); Olivio Jocholá (aged 19); Basilio Ajcalón (aged 18).

26-27 April Thirty-two peasants were murdered in different communities in the departments of El Quiché and Chimaltenango. During the latter half of April, 27 people were strangled in the villages of Estancia de la Virgin, Tioxia, Chuatalún and Chicocón, San Martín Jilotepeque municipality, department of Chimaltenango.

May

2 May Several families were killed in the village of Chjocon.

3 May Fifteen peasants were murdered in Parramos, Chimaltenango, reportedly by the army. The army claimed they had been killed when troops clashed with guerrillas. An estimated 500 people had been killed over the last two months in the villages of Parraxtut, El Pajarito and Pichiquil. Some of these villages were deserted as all survivors had fled the area.

Circa 7 May A family of four were machine-gunned and hacked to death with machetes in San Pedro Jocopilas,

Quiché. Unidentified armed men kicked down the door while the family slept, dragged them from their beds and killed them. The victims were: Juana de Alecio; Santiago Alecio; Arnoldo Alecio; Candelario Alecio.

8 May
Fifteen peasants were burned alive in the village of Chamaxú, Huehuetenango department. They included: Fidelino Pérez; Valdemar Galicia R.; Rudy Galicia R.; Fidencio Galicia; Manuel Galicia Recinos; Antonio Galicia; Saúl Galicia; Byron Hernández; Miguel López; Emilio Alba; Arturo Galicia; Mateo Galicia; Margarito Galicia.

Six men, 15 women and 23 children were killed in the village of Saquilá II, Chichicastenango, El Quiché.

10 May
Twenty people were killed in the village of Salacuin, near Cobán, Alta Verapaz department. The authorities blamed the guerrillas.

14 May
Gildardo, Angel, Miguel, Antonio and Santiago López Velásquez — five brothers — were shot dead in the village of El Granadillo, Colotenango, Huehuetenango department. All were peasants.

14 May
Three women, Dolores Jon, Marcelina Gualin and Matilda Caal, and a 12-year-old girl, Marcelina Yac Jon were killed in the village of Najtilabaj (also given as Tilabán), San Cristóbal Verapaz, Alta Verapaz department. They were killed while asleep at home.

Three women and one man were found hacked to death with machetes and showing signs of torture, in San Ildefonso Ixtahuacán, Huehuetenango.

15 May
Three men were shot dead near Santa Cruz Barillas, Huehuetenango.

Eight peasants were killed in Cantón Semejá II, Chichicastenango, Quiché. They were identified as: Sebastián Canil Huescas (aged 45); María Huescas (aged 42); Manuel Canil Vargas (aged 25); María Cipriano Chun (aged 23); Sebastián Canil (aged 16); Manuela Canil (aged nine); Miguel Canil (aged eight); Tomás Canil (aged one).

Five peasants were killed at Los Brillantes, Sta. Cruz Mulúa, Retalhuleu: Angela Ventura (aged 55); Enríque Morales Ventura (aged 22); Ana Marcos Ventura (aged 16); Francisco Marcos V. (aged 14); Irma Judith Alvarez (aged 18).

17-18 May
Some 70 people were reportedly killed (including pregnant women and children) in San Juan Cotzal and Saquilá, Quiché department.

18 May
Twenty-five children between the ages of four months and 14 years, 15 women (some pregnant) and three men were killed in Saquilá II, Chichicastenango, Quiché

department, by armed men going from house to house. (Some of these killings may be the same as those reported above, on 17-18 May.)

18 May   Six men were killed in the village of Chillel, San Gaspar Chajul jurisdiction, El Quiché.

A secret cemetery was found in the village of Chuatalún, San Martín Jilotepeque municipality, Chimaltenango. It contained 84 bodies of men, women and children. Dogs and coyotes were devouring them.

19 May   Between 20 and 30 peasants were killed in the village of Sacualpa, Quiché department.

Circa 19 May   Fourteen peasants were machine-gunned and hacked to death by unknown men who attacked the village of Batzul, Chajul, Quiché.

Circa 20 May   Armed men attacked and killed families and burned their homes in Patzibal, Quiché. The 16 peasants killed were named as: Miguel Xen (aged 75); Martina Xen (aged seven months); Micaela Pansay (aged 48); Sebastián Xen; María Pol Pacajoy; Sebastián Chicoy (aged 11); Sebastián Calguá; Miguel Mejía (aged three); Micaela Pansay (aged eight); Tomás Canil (aged 10); Micaela Panjoj; José Xen (aged two); Tomasa Mejía (aged 30); Juana Esquilá (aged 45); Juana de Balán (aged 19); Juana Mejía (aged five).

21 May   Five bodies were found in Patzibal, seven in Matzul and one in Pocoil, municipality of Santo Tomás, Chichicastenango, Quiché department.

Circa 22 May   Three peasants were killed by armed, masked men in the village of Najtilabaj, San Cristóbal Verapaz, Alta Verapaz department. The victims were: Roberto Caal Mis; Virgilio Yuc Caal; Manuel Coc.

24 May   Ten people, including six children, were killed when some 30 armed men burst into a small leather factory near Santa Cruz del Quiché, El Quiché department.

Circa 25 May   In the village of Los Cerritos, Chiché, Quiché department, five peasants, including a five-year-old girl, were burned to death when armed men attacked them with machetes and set fire to their homes. The victims were: José Joaquín Morales; Julio Morales; Tomás Morales; Juan Manuel Morales; Tomasa Ignacio (aged five).

Circa 28 May   Four peasants were killed in Cantón Chocacruz, Sololá. Their bodies, taken to the hospital morgue, showed gunshot wounds and signs of torture. Three were identified: Jesús Lajuj; Pedro Morales; Inesario Morales.

June

Circa 5 June   The bodies of 10 peasant women were found near the village of Nahtiliabaj (also given as Najtilabaj), Alta Verapaz, showing torture marks and gunshot wounds.

The authorities and guerrillas accused each other of responsibility.

6 June The army was again blamed for massacres in Chitnij, municipality of San Cristóbal Verapaz. In all, 16 women and six children were reported killed in the hamlet on 26 April (see above) and in this incident.

7 June The bodies of 16 peasants were found in two places in northern Guatemala.

8 June Nine people, including three children and two elderly people, were burned to death on a road leading to San Pedro Carchá, Alta Verapaz department. Some 30 armed men in small cargo vehicles forced the victims out of their homes, placed them together, threw petrol over them and set them on fire, according to an eyewitness report.

11 June Fifteen peasants, including eight women and three children, were killed in the village of Las Pacayas, San Cristóbal Verapaz jurisdiction, Alta Verapaz department. The authorities stated that the guerrillas were responsible.

The following day, the army reportedly attacked a guerrilla camp in the area, killing eight guerrillas.

14 June Over 100 peasants were killed in the Nebaj area, Quiché department. The authorities blamed the guerrillas.

15 June According to an army statement 112 people were killed and 43 injured in the village of Chacalté, municipality of Chajul, El Quiché, by members of the *Ejército Guerrillero de Los Pobres* (EGP), the Guerrilla Army of the Poor. Other sources alleged that the army was responsible for the incident.

17 June Twenty peasants were killed in the village of San Marcos, Alta Verapaz department.

14-23 June Fourteen people were killed in Chinique, El Quiché, and an unknown number in Morales, Izabal.

Circa 22 June Eleven people were killed in Quiché department, including three in Chichicastenango by the name of Lastror Morales and the entire peasant family Pérez Guarcas from Cantón La Vega. The guerrillas and the authorities blamed each other for the killings.

Last week of June More than 80 peasants were killed in the villages of Las Pacayas, El Rancho and Najtilabaj, San Cristóbal Verapaz municipality, Alta Verapaz department, reportedly by the army and members of the civil defence patrols. Most of the victims were women and children. In the village of Pampacché, Alta Verapaz department, all the men were dragged out of their homes by some 300 soldiers. A few days later more than 70 tortured corpses were found near the village of Tactic, Alta Verapaz department.

Estimated number of killings: 2,186

The Guatemalan Government and the US Department of State later publicly challenged the statistics reported by Amnesty International. However, under the Freedom of Information Act, a human rights group in the USA later obtained copies of communications between the US Embassy in Guatemala and the Department of State which reveal that Amnesty International's statistics had been challenged solely on the basis of an explanation from the Guatemalan security forces about what had occurred in various incidents and not, as had been implied at the time, on independent investigation conducted by the US Embassy into the disputed incidents.

Appendix V

Guatemala: Compilation of Unresolved Cases of "Disappearance" 1981–1984

Note: in a number of cases listed below (not specified for security reasons) Amnesty International understands that witnesses did not make inquiries for fear of persecution, because they did not speak Spanish, or because they did not think it worthwhile to approach the authorities since they believed the official military or security forces had perpetrated the abuse in question.

Name & Place of "disappearance"	Age	Date	Profession	Unit named as responsible	Inquiries initiated with*	Response from Government	Other details
AJPOP, Trinidad (Tecpán, Chimaltenango dept.)	27	28.01.81	Market vendor	Taken by unknown men to military detachment of Tecpán	Municipal Police and local mayor		
ALVARADO AREVALO, Rolando Kaibil (Guatemala City)	27	17.12.81	Accountant/ USAC economics student and trade union leader	Plainclothes police	Head of State, Minister of the Interior, heads of police, Commander of Guard of Honour Brigade. All hospitals, morgues and detention centres	Commander of Guard of Honour Brigade promised to investigate but has not replied since	Reportedly first held in Salamá prison and later at the Mariscal Zavala barracks

Name & Place of "disappearance"	Age	Date	Profession	Unit named as responsible	Inquiries initiated with*	Response from Government	Other details
					searched. Requested but did not obtain audience with Head of State		
ALVARADO AREVALO, Sergio Leonel (Guatemala City)	20	19.05.84	USAC economics student/ radio and television technician/ worked for UNESCO	Members of G-2	Head of State, Minister of the Interior, heads of police and military. All hospitals, morgues and detention centres searched	Verbally informed that investigations would be conducted	Brother of Rolando Kaibil (above). Witnesses refused to indentify perpetrators for fear of reprisals
ALVARADO PALENCIA, Alfonso (Guatemala City)	44	31.01.84	Trade union leader	Plainclothes members of DIT	Head of State and Minister of the Interior		
ALVAREZ, Javier** (Caserío El Julec, Santa Ana, El Peten dept.)		18.11.?	Los Linces Battalion of Poptún Brigade				
ARGUETA TOMAS, José Léon (San Martín Jilotepeque, Chimaltenango dept.)	26	06.01.82	Farmer	Members of Civil Defence patrol	Visit to police stations, DIT and to military detachment of San Martín Jilotepeque		

Name & Place of "disappearance"	Age	Date	Profession	Unit named as responsible	Inquiries initiated with*	Response from Government	Other details
ARGUETA TOMAS, Pablo (San Martín Jilotepeque, Chimaltenango dept.)	24	01.06.82	Seminary student	Members of Civil Defence patrol	Visits to police stations, DIT and to military detachment of San Martín Jilotepeque		Brother of José León (see above)
AYALA SANDOVAL, Raul (*Caserío* El Julec, Santa Ana, El Peten dept.)		18.11.?		Los Linces Battalion of Poptún Brigade			
AYANEL ALVA, Juan (Chichicastenango, El Quiché dept.)		12.05.80	Trader	Military			
BAMACA LOPEZ, Leonardo Victor (Nuevo Progreso, San Marcos dept.)	19	29.10.83	Student				
BATZIBAL AJQUI, Pedro (Santa Elena)	15	29.08.82	Day labourer	Army			
BATZIBAL AJQUI, Tomás (Agua Escondida, Chichicastenango, El Quiché dept.)	27	15.08.81	Day labourer	Army			Brother of Pedro (see above)

Name & Place of "disappearance"	Age	Date	Profession	Unit named as responsible	Inquiries initiated with*	Response from Government	Other details
BEJARANO OSCAL, Gustavo Adolfo (Emaús meeting centre, Escuintla dept.)	32	24.08.80	Trade union leader	National Police and army	Judicial Police	6th Justice of the Peace agreed to carry out investigation but was shot dead two weeks later	"Disappeared" together with 11 other trade unionists and five members of the School of Trade Union Studies who were holding a seminar
BOCEL SAPIN, Carlos (Chicacao, Mazatenango, Suchitepéquez dept.)	36	31.03.84	Day labourer	Army			Entire village witnessed abduction
CABRERA URIZAR, Javier Erasmo (Finca Mocá, Santa Bárbara, Suchitepéquez dept.)		19.03.81					
CALEL LARES, Diego (Guatemala City)	15	06.11.81	Farmer and street vendor	Heavily armed men in plain clothes			
CALEL LARES, José (Chupól, El Quiché dept.)	24	06.09.80	Farmer and vendor				Brother of Diego (see above). Taken by van to military detachment of Chupól

Name & Place of "disappearance"	Age	Date	Profession	Unit named as responsible	Inquiries initiated with*	Response from Government	Other details
CALEL LARES, Tomás (Guatemala City)	17	06.11.81	Farmer and street vendor	Heavily armed men in plain clothes			Abducted together with his brother Diego (see above)
CALEL, Sebastian Joaquin (home, San Pablo Jocopilas, Suchitepéquez dept.)	22	24.09.82	Day labourer	Army	Head of State and Minister of the Interior		Approximately 50 heavily armed soldiers broke down the door of his house, accused him of being "subversive", burned him with a cigarette and took him with them "to the capital"
CALEL, Tomás Macario (Chugüexa Segundo, El Quiché dept.)	22	01.11.82	Farmer	Heavily armed men in plain clothes			Removed from his home in front of witness
CALEL TOL, Julia Margarita (Agua Escondida, Chichicastenango, El Quiché dept.)	6	?.?.83		Uniformed soldiers			Soldiers arrived at her home where she was asleep and from which her parents and brothers and sisters had fled, and took her away. Incident witnessed by her family from the place where they were hiding
CARIAS, Mario (Caserio El Julec, Santa Ana, Petén)		18.11.?		Los Linces Battalion, Poptún Brigade			Detained together with several others

Name & Place of "disappearance"	Age	Date	Profession	Unit named as responsible	Inquiries initiated with*	Response from Government	Other details
CARIAS SOLARES, César Giovanni (Colonia Bethania, Guatemala City)	16	21.09.83	Student	Security forces	Family immediately went to Supreme Court and asked for letter to be sent to National Police requesting information. Also sent memo to General Mejía; put advertisements in press; wrote to Ministry of the Interior, Bar Association, etc.	Request to the Supreme Court refused. No reply from others	Abducted, together with brother Herbert Orlando and two others, while out shopping. Reportedly held by National Police
CARIAS SOLARES, Herbert Orlando	13	21.09.83	Schoolboy/football player	" "	" "	" "	Same as for brother César Giovanni (see above)
CARILLO AJTZIP, Faustino (*Finca* Los Castaños, Chicacao, Suchitepéquez)	19	31.03.84	Farmworker and member of Civil Defence patrol	Army	Inquiries made of soldiers at *Finca* Los Castaños who said he was not there		Two of his fellow-civilian patrollers told family about his capture by the army who had called all the patrollers together at the *finca*
CASTAÑÓN FUENTES, Gustavo Adolfo (Zone 1, Guatemala City)	26	21.05.84	Accountant and economics student at the USAC	National police (DIT)	Numerous audiences requested; searches in hospitals and detention centres	Audiences refused; all results negative. Family told that investigation would be carried out	Member of the coordinating committee of the AEU. Abducted as he was on his way to the USAC Rector's office by a group of men travelling in three cars with smoked glass windows

Name & Place of "disappearance"	Age	Date	Profession	Unit named as responsible	Inquiries initiated with*	Response from Government	Other details
CERMEÑO REYES, José Julio (Santa Lucía Cotzumalguapa, Escuintla)	38	12.11.83	Driver/trade union leader	Security forces	Visits to all detention centres		Abducted by armed men in a car. Ex-leader of the CNT. Legal adviser for trade union at Pantaleón Sugar Mill
CHAN MAZARIEGOS, Esteban (Playa Grande, El Quiché dept.)		19.01.?	Farmer				Left home for work and was not seen again
CHAVEZ, Francisco (in front of the market, Mazatenango, Suchitepéquez dept.)	40	17.12.82	Farmer	Two plainclothes men			Shackled. The same night the same two men, in olive green uniform, came to search his house and asked where the arms were kept. Not finding anything they left, firing shots
CHICOL SIMON, Isaías (Parque Central, Comalapa, Chimaltenango)	16	10.01.82	Farmer	Army	Inquiries made at local army barracks, recruitment centres and the First Police Corps	Negative response	Taken away in front of witnesses

Name & Place of "disappearance"	Age	Date	Profession	Unit named as responsible	Inquiries initiated with*	Response from Government	Other details
CHIQUIRIN RAMIREZ, Marcelino (*Cantón* San Juan Cerritos, Santo Domingo, Suchitepéquez)	29	27.02.83	Farmer		Civilian and military authorities informed		Parents, children, wife, other relatives and neighbours witnessed abduction
CHIQUIRIN GUALIP, Vicenta (Sector Canales, Santo Domingo, Suchitepéquez)	32	17.01.81	Farmer	Men from a military detachment	Inquiries made at the military detachment to which she was taken		She was travelling in a van at the time of her capture. Her house was later searched; nothing was found
CHUMAJAY MENDOZA, Juan (*Finca* Milán, Chicacao, Suchitepéquez)	45	27.02.81	Farmer	Soldiers			A platoon of soldiers arrived and arrested him in his home. Several others from the same *finca* taken away the same day
COLAC, Macedonio (San Juan Comalapa, Chimaltenango)	27	02.07.82	Farmer	Army	No inquiries made		
COLINDRES ESTRADA, Mario Rolando (Amatitlán, Guatemala)	29	23.01.84	Worker (*obrero*)	10 unidentified armed men	Inquiries made of National Police and at other detention centres in capital		Armed men were driving a white panel van with smoked glass windows. Beat up victim, took him away with head-wound and tied up. Ransacked house

Name & Place of "disappearance"	Age	Date	Profession	Unit named as responsible	Inquiries initiated with*	Response from Government	Other details
CONOS LIX, Diego (San Andrés Semetabaj, Sololá)	32	15.04.82	Farmer	Soldiers	No inquiries made		A group of soldiers detained him as he was on his way to work
CONOZ XON, Tomás (Chichicastenango, El Quiché dept.)	44	11.07.82	Street vendor	Army	Inquiries made of army detachment in Los Encuentros and Guard of Honour Brigade in Chupol, Chichicastenango, El Quiché dept.		Detained in square in Chichicastenango while shopping
CORTEZ RIQUIAC, Tomás (Chupol, Chichicastenango, El Quiché dept.)	16	03.05.82	Street vendor	Army	Inquiries made in the "military zone"	"Military zone" said he had been released	
COY SOTZ, Salvador (San Juan Comalapa, Chimaltenango)	34	06.02.82	Farmer	Army	No inquiries made		
CURRUCHICHE CANA, Jacobo (San José Poaquil, Chimaltenango)	19	07.02.81	Farmer	Army	Inquiries made of military detachment in San José Poaquil		He was travelling in a pick-up truck in the square of San José Poaquil when he was asked by soldiers to accompany them to military detachment. Member of Evangelical Church

Name & Place of "disappearance"	Age	Date	Profession	Unit named as responsible	Inquiries initiated with*	Response from Government	Other details
DE LA PARRA MENDEZ, Francisco Rolando (Funerales Reforma, Guatemala City, Zone 1)	34	12.11.80	Mechanic	Security forces (believed to be the Judicial Police or G-2) — six men in plain clothes		Authorities denied the arrest	Detained together with others at his father's wake. Father had been shot dead in his home
DE LEON PALACIOS, Hugo (Guatemala City)	36	09.03.84	Primary school teacher and law student at the USAC	Four armed civilians	Many government officials and branches of the security forces (National Police, DIT, BROE)	The case is being investigated by the National Police	Abducted in street in front of his pupils
DEL CID SIAN, Angela Mirian (Arizona, Puerto de San José, Escuintla)	18	12.03.82	Seamstress	12 armed men	Inquiries made at local military base; two letters to the President		Abducted from her home; witnessed by neighbours
DOMINGUEZ IZAS, Edgar Leonel (Cantel, Quetzaltenango)	30	28.03.84	Doctor and surgeon at Cantel Private Sanatorium	Uniformed soldiers	Inquiries made of many government, military and police officials	Detention denied; said to be under investigation. Ambassador to USA said that it was "impossible to verify" the armed forces were responsible	As of May 1984, believed to be alive but badly tortured

Name & Place of "disappearance"	Age	Date	Profession	Unit named as responsible	Inquiries initiated with*	Response from Government	Other details
ESQUIT AJU, Lorenso (*Finca* El Retiro, San Martín Jilotepeque, Chimaltenango)	60	03.10.82	Farmer	Military patrol (60 men in army trucks)	Inquiries made via the GAM		Believed to have been taken to the military detachment at San Martín Jilotepeque
ESQUIT CHUTA, Margarito (*Caserío* La Buena Esperanza, San Martín Jilotepeque, Chimaltenango)	28	18.09.82	Farmer	Military patrol	Inquiries made via the GAM	A captain at a local military detachment said he would be sent to the capital	Captured while working in the fields
ESQUIT CHUTA, Victor (*Caserío* La Buena Esperanza, San Martín Jilotepeque, Chimaltenango)	25	18.09.82	Farmer and carpenter	Military patrol	Telegram to the Government		Summoned to the local school and taken away from there
ESQUIT GARCIA, Antonio (Paraje El Rincón, *Finca* La Merced, San Martín Jilotepeque, Chimaltenango)	47	05.08.82	Farmer	Military patrol	Inquiries made via the GAM		Abducted from his home and taken to the local military detachment

Name & Place of "disappearance"	Age	Date	Profession	Unit named as responsible	Inquiries initiated with*	Response from Government	Other details
ESTRADA, Regina (*Finca* La Merced, San Martín Jilotepeque, Chimaltenango)	17	14.08.82	Farmworker		Military detachment at San Martín Jilotepeque		Abducted with her sister-in-law. She was pregnant
FAJARDO, Edgar Eduardo (Santa Lucía Cotzumalguapa, Escuintla)	21	16.09.82	Mechanic		Letters to the authorities and visits to prisons		Went to visit *Finca* El Baúl with another man and a woman. None of them heard from again. Car found in San Antonio Suchitepéquez
FUENTES GOMEZ, Esteban Martín (*Aldea* San Ignacio, Nuevo Progreso, San Marcos)	39	19.03.83	Day labourer	Army	Mayor of Nuevo Progreso		Removed by force from his home
FUENTES MONZON, Natael Isaías (Zone 7, Guatemala City)	25	16.02.84	Worker at Peter Pan factory and USAC student	Security forces (four armed men)	Government authorities, including General Mejía V., Minister of the Interior and police	Minister of the Interior said case was being investigated	Left home at 6.30 am; 10 minutes later four armed men entered flat with keys and searched it. Taken away in yellow car
GARCIA, Edgar Fernando (Zone 11, Guatemala City)	26	18.02.84	Administrative worker and trade union leader at CAVISA	Uniformed members of BROE and National Police	Inquiries made of: Armed Forces Chief of Staff, Minister of the Interior, National Police, General Mejía Victores, etc.	Detention denied, investigations promised	Pushed into blue and white minibus in front of many people. Reportedly seen in secret detention by released prisoner

Name & Place of "disappearance"	Age	Date	Profession	Unit named as responsible	Inquiries initiated with*	Response from Government	Other details
GARCIA ESCOBAR, Lesvia Lucrecia (Zone 1, Guatemala City)	23	15.04.84	Textile technician (member of textile trade union)	Armed men	Police, hospitals, prisons		Pushed into Land Rover while on her way home from work at "Los Pollos"
GOMEZ CALITO, René Arnaldo (between Amatitlán, Guatemala, and south coast)	34	16.07.83	Tailor	Not known	Via the GAM		Left Amatitlán to visit the south coast and never returned. Brother of Héctor Gómez Calito, GAM leader, abducted and killed in March 1985
GOMEZ CARRETO, Efraín Pedro (Caserío San Miguel Pajapa, Pajapita, San Marcos)	19	27.01.84	Day labourer	8–10 armed civilians	All military detachments in the area and national authorities		Taken from his home together with his father, Segundo Gómez López (see below)
GOMEZ LOPEZ, Segundo (Caserío San Miguel Pajapa, Pajapita, San Marcos)	55	27.01.84	Day labourer	8–10 armed civilians	" "		Taken from his home together with his son, Efraín Pedro Gómez Carreto (see above)
GOMEZ PULA, Eulogio (San Jacinto, Chimaltenango)	19	26.02.82	Farmer	Army	San Martín Jilotepeque and Chimaltenango army bases; police	Detention denied; police said they would investigate	Was on his way to watch television in San Jacinto when he was intercepted and taken to San Martín Jilotepeque army base

Name & Place of "disappearance"	Age	Date	Profession	Unit named as responsible	Inquiries initiated with*	Response from Government	Other details
GONZALEZ, Federico Francisco (Santo Domingo, Suchitepéquez)	28	17.12.?	Farmworker	Military patrol	Military Zone headquarters	Detention denied	Abducted in the street in front of many eyewitnesses. Reportedly taken to the Military Zone headquarters
GONZALES AJQUI, Angel Rodolfo (Aldea Pacoral, Tecpán, Chimaltenango)	22	28.08.81	Agronomy student	Armed men			
GONZALEZ SUT, Salvador (Cantón Agua Escondida, Chichicastenango, El Quiché Dept.	12	29.03.82	Farmworker	Army			
GORRON HERNANDEZ, Juan (Cantón Santa Lucía, Santo Domingo, Suchitepéquez)	54	21.10.81	Farmworker	10 armed men, one with face hidden			Taken from his home. Neighbours and mother witnessed abduction

Name & Place of "disappearance"	Age	Date	Profession	Unit named as responsible	Inquiries initiated with*	Response from Government	Other details
GRAMAJO Y GRAMAJO, Miguel Angel (Quetzaltenango, Quetzaltenango Dept.)	17	13.04.83	Student	G-2 in plain clothes	Many government authorities	Gen. Lobos Zamora said letters were being sent from one military zone to another. (He was head of Zone 17 at the time)	Abducted together with his cousin, Walter Ramiro Gramajo Maldonado (see below), in presence of Carlos Rodrigo Méndez, who recognized the men as being from Zone 17 army base; he himself was abducted next day (see below). The three boys were reportedly seen in Military Zone No. 17 army base
GRAMAJO MALDONADO, Walter Ramiro (Quetzaltenango, Quetzaltenango Dept.)	17	13.04.83	Student	" "	" "	" "	See details as for Miguel Angel Gramajo y Gramajo
GRANADOS HERNANDEZ, Jorge Humberto (Zone 7, Guatemala City)	27	09.05.84	Baker	BROE	All police bodies, hospitals, press		"Disappeared" after leaving home. BROE agents later searched house, interrogated his wife and blindfolded his son. Took away money and photographs

Name & Place of "disappearance"	Age	Date	Profession	Unit named as responsible	Inquiries initiated with*	Response from Government	Other details
GRAVE, José, (Chicacao, Suchitepéquez)	44	13.05.81	Day labourer	12 soldiers from Chicacao	Chicacao army base		Soldiers removed him while he was chatting to some friends in street
GUARAN, Isaías (*Caserío* Jordan, Chimaltenango)	24	01.03.82	Farmworker	Soldiers from San Martín Jilotepeque army base	Military zones of San Martín Jilotepeque and Chimaltenango		Abducted from home, together with father, Pablo Guarán Acuta (see below) and brother (name not known); reportedly driven to military detachment at San Martín Jilotepeque
GUARAN ACUTA, Pablo (*Caserío* Jordan, Chimaltenango)	55	01.03.82	Farmworker	" "	" "		Same details as for Isaías Guarán (see above)
GUARCAS, Sebastian (*Cantón* Chepol, Chichicastenango, El Quiché dept.)	41	11.05.82	Small trader	Army	Military detachment at Chepol; National Police at Chepol		Taken from van he was driving together with others as they were en route to Chichicastenango, near military detachment of Chepol
GUARCAS AMBROCIO, Isabela (Tecpán, Chimaltenango)	18	04.03.82	Domestic servant	Two soldiers from Tecpán military detachment			Taken to Tecpán military detachment. Incident witnessed by her 10-year-old brother and others

Name & Place of "disappearance"	Age	Date	Profession	Unit named as responsible	Inquiries initiated with*	Response from Government	Other details
GUARCAS BATZIBAL, Florentina (Tecpán, Chimaltenango)	15	04.03.82	Domestic servant	Army			Soldiers asked for her by name and took her to military detachment at Tecpán. Witnessed by younger sister
GUARCAS TOL, Juan (Santa Cruz del Quiché, El Quiché dept.)	37	07.11.81	Small trader	Army	Quiché authorities		Member of the "*Iglesia de Dios*" (Church of God). Went to preach in *Cantón* Paquixic and was apprehended by army at the bus terminal in Santa Cruz, El Quiché dept.
GUERRA BALAM, Abraham (San Martín Jilotepeque, Chimaltenango)	26	26.11.81	Farmworker	Army	Military detachments at San Martín Jilotepeque and Chimaltenango; National Police		Taken from his mother-in-law's house together with brother-in-law
GUERRERO LOPEZ, Francisco (*Aldea* Tampó, Tactic, Alta Verapaz)	20	26.01.83	Student	Known military commissioners	Police in Tactic and Cobán; Cobán Military Base		Military commissioners went to house on 12.12.82, searched it and took away cousin of victim; threatened to remove others; returned on 26.01.83 and removed him

Name & Place of "disappearance"	Age	Date	Profession	Unit named as responsible	Inquiries initiated with*	Response from Government	Other details
HERNANDEZ AGUSTIN, Luz Leticia (Zone 4, Mixco, Guatemala City)	27	22.11.82	Accountant	BROE (names of officials known)	President Ríos Montt, Minister of the Interior, President of Supreme Court, head of National Police	No response	Detained together with María Cruz López Rodríguez, Ana María López Rodríguez (see below) and Gabriel Calate Temú. María Cruz López Rodríguez was later brought before a Special Military Tribunal, sentenced to 10 years but released when General Mejía came to power. She has publicly testified that all four were initially held in secret detention in what she believes was the old *Escuela Politécnica* in Guatemala City
HERNANDEZ FLORES, Sebastián (Playa Grande, Ixcán, El Quiché dept.)	46	02.02.82	Farmworker	Army			He was working on an engineering project at Playa Grande, but usually lived in *Cantón* Taracena, Santo Domingo, Suchitepéquez

Name & Place of "disappearance"	Age	Date	Profession	Unit named as responsible	Inquiries initiated with*	Response from Government	Other details
HERNANDEZ QUIROA, Oscar David (Zone 3, Guatemala City)	22	23.02.84	Electrician/ mechanic and volunteer firefighter	Armed men	Detention centres, police stations, hospitals		Was shot at and wounded by armed men in Zone 3 of the capital as he was walking along street. Other man escaped; captors later went to fire-station looking for him
HERNANDEZ MACARIO, Pablo (La Esperanza, Quetzaltenango)	35	10.11.82	Farmworker		Ministry of the Interior		
HERRARTE HERNANDEZ, Jorge Alberto (known as "Papeto") (Zone 1, Guatemala City)	31	15.05.83	Geological technician for US oil companies in Petén	DIT	Many government authorities	In Aug. 1983, Vice-Minister of Foreign Affairs denied detention but said investigations were being made	Taken from parents' house by armed civilians driving three cars. Reportedly seen alive in government custody. His car was also taken and was reportedly seen in the authorities' possession
HICHO RAMOS, Irma Marilú (USAC campus, Guatemala City)	23	21.05.84	Primary school teacher and USAC student (economics)	Security forces (four armed men)	Interviews with General Mejía and Minister of the Interior plus others	Detention denied	Member of the coordinating committee of the AEU. Bundled into a car by her captors

Name & Place of "disappearance"	Age	Date	Profession	Unit named as responsible	Inquiries initiated with*	Response from Government	Other details
INTERIANO ORTIZ, Héctor Alirio (USAC campus, Guatemala City)	28	21.05.84	Employee and economics student at the USAC	Armed men	General Mejía plus others	Detention denied	Abducted as he was leaving the USAC Research Institute. Ex-leader of the AEU
IQUILA, Tomás Salvador (Cantón Chicua 2do, Chichicastenango, El Quiché dept.)	18	05.03.82	Small businessman	Civilians believed to be from the army	Jutiapa military base and places in Huehuetenango		Made to get out of van in which he was travelling, and removed with other people. Abduction took place near Chepol military camp, Chichicastenango
IXCACO, Tomasa (Finca La Merced, Paraje El Rincón, San Martín Jilotepeque, Chimaltenango)	27	14.08.82	Weaver		Military detachment at San Martín Jilotepeque said that two women had been detained but had since been released		
IXCACO ATZ, Cornelio (Finca La Merced, San Martín Jilotepeque, Chimaltenango)	36	10.10.82	Farmworker	Civil Defence patrols	Inquiries made of local military detachment and local army commander		Abducted in presence of wife and neighbours
IXCACO XCAY, Agusto (Finca La Merced, San Martín Jilotepeque, Chimaltenango)	36	11.10.82	Farmworker	Civil Defence patrols	Inquiries made of local army commander and military detachment		Witnessed by family and neighbours

Name & Place of "disappearance"	Age	Date	Profession	Unit named as responsible	Inquiries initiated with*	Response from Government	Other details
IXCACO XCAY, Buena Ventura (male) (*Finca* La Merced, San Martín Jilotepeque, Chimaltenango)		10.10.82	Farmworker	Civil Defence patrols	Inquiries made of local army commander and military detachment		Abduction witnessed by family and neighbours
JOCOL SART, Luis (Parque Centroamérica, Quetzaltenango)	19	11.11.82	Peasant	Armed men in red car	National Police and Ministry of the Interior		
JUAREZ CANOJ, Enrique (*Cantón* Santísimo Trinidad, San Andrés Itzapa, Chimaltenango)		09.04.81	Tailor	Five masked men	Inquiries made in several places		The men had list of names. They stole dresses and material from his workshop. Some days before a military commissioner showed a list of names to several local people. It included names of other "disappeared" people
JUAREZ RAMIREZ, Francisco Javier (San Miguel Pajapa, Pajapita, San Marcos)	40	13.07.84	Farmworker and member of Civil Defence patrol	Armed men in uniforms with light blue shirts and navy-blue trousers	Military detachments at Santa Ana Berlín, La Ceiba, Catarina; Treasury Police at Tecun Umán		The men were driving a blue and white Toyota car said to belong to the military detachment at Santa Ana Berlín, Coatepeque

Name & Place of "disappearance"	Age	Date	Profession	Unit named as responsible	Inquiries initiated with*	Response from Government	Other details
JUAREZ TELON, Salvador (Guatemala City)	30	21.09.83	Architectural draughtsman		Various authorities including police stations		Left house at 4pm and did not return
JUAREZ VELASQUEZ, Eulogio Feliciano (*Caserío* San Miguel Pajapa, Pajapita, San Marcos)	65	13.07.84	Farmworker	Eight armed men in uniform (light blue shirts and navy-blue trousers)	Military authorities in Santa Ana Berlín and La Ceiba, Treasury Police at Tecún Umán and others		Taken from home together with son, Javier Francisco Juarez Ramírez. Captors were driving blue and white Toyota car said to belong to military detachment at Santa Ana Berlín, Coatepeque
LEMUS GARCIA, Axel Raúl (Zone 1, Guatemala City)	19	03.06.82	Student at *Escuela Normal* and student leader	Mobile Police and/or DIT	Many authorities including President Ríos Montt and wife, Minister of the Interior, Deputy Minister of Defence (General Mejía Víctores), Minister of Education, National Police, army officials, etc, Guatemalan Red Cross, Archbishop of Guatemala	Denied detention; said investigation would be conducted. However, police seem to have initially acknowledged he was being held for investigation	Captured together with another student in front of many witnesses. Reported in press, including photograph of him being captured (*Prensa Libre*, 10 June 1982). Mother warned in 1979 that he should stop his student activities

Name & Place of "disappearance"	Age	Date	Profession	Unit named as responsible	Inquiries initiated with*	Response from Government	Other details
LLACXON CHENEN, Fausto (Mazatenango, Suchitepéquez)	21	04.10.81	Farmworker	Armed men	Military and police installations		
LOPEZ, Jacobo (*Aldea* Tampó, Tactic, Alta Verapaz)		26.01.83	Health worker	Military commissioners (names known)	Police in Tactic and military base in Cobán		
LOPEZ CHAMALE, Carlos Alfredo (Zone 3, Guatemala City)	18	28.01.82	Student	Two armed men in Subaru car	National Police, Judicial Police, Interpol		
LOPEZ MONTAÑEZ, Persi Horlando (Retalhuleu, Retalhuleu Dept.)		19.06.83					Pushed into a "command vehicle" by unknown men opposite San Nicolás Market
LOPEZ QUEJ, Rodolfo (*Aldea* Tampó, Tactic, Alta Verapaz)		26.01.83	Worker at INDECA	Military commissioners (names known)	Police and army		Abducted together with Jacobo López (see above). Had been warned by a military commissioner (named) that they would be kidnapped

Name & Place of "disappearance"	Age	Date	Profession	Unit named as responsible	Inquiries initiated with*	Response from Government	Other details
LOPEZ RODAS, Lauro (San Miguel Pajapa, San Marcos)	26	29.04.84	Farmworker and member of civil patrol	Armed men in plain clothes	Military bases at Santa Ana Berlín and La Ceiba		Abducted together with father, Vicente López Simero (see below), from their home
LOPEZ RODRIGUEZ, Ana Maria (Zone 4, Mixco, Guatemala City)	18	22.11.82	Domestic servant	BROE (names of officials known)			Same details as for Luz Leticia Hernández Agustín (see above)
LOPEZ SIMERO, Vincente (San Miguel Pajapa, San Marcos)	50	29.04.84	Farmworker and member of civil patrol	Armed men in plain clothes	Military bases at Santa Ana Berlín and La Ceiba		Abducted together with son, Lauro López Rodas (see above), from their home
LOPEZ SIMON, Benigno (Cofradía de la Virgen Maria [Brotherhood of the Virgin Mary], San José Poaquil, Chimaltenango)	30	08.09.84	Farmworker	Local mayor and military commander (names known)	Inquiries made at military detachment at San José Poaquil	Detention denied	Mayor and commander entered the place, burned some things and threatened to kill everyone. Took him away with his brother Gabriel (see below) and the statue of the Virgin, which they returned next day
LOPEZ SIMON, Gabriel (see above)	32	"	Farmworker and second-in-command to military commissioner	" "	" "	" "	

Name & Place of "disappearance"	Age	Date	Profession	Unit named as responsible	Inquiries initiated with*	Response from Government	Other details
LORENZO, Salvador (*Cantón* Chepol, Chichicastenango, Quiché)	23	25.08.81	Street vendor	Army	Military bases in Huehuetenango, Jutiapa, Retalhuleu, etc	Said that he had been taken to Guatemala City	He was on his way to play football in Chepol, together with brother Tomás (see below), when they were stopped at army checkpoint
LORENZO XOM, Tomás (*Cantón* Chepol. Chichicastenango, Quiché)	17	25.08.81	"	"	" "	" "	Same details as for his brother Salvador Lorenzo (see above)
LUCAS QUINO, Juan (San José Poaquil, Chimaltenango)	24	02.08.84	Municipal Treasurer	Local mayor and army lieutenant from San José Poaquil (names known — same ones who captured Benigno and Gabriel López Simón, see above)	Military detachment at San José Poaquil; local mayor	Wife told to go and ask in Chimaltenango. Mayor called lieutenant who put her in jail for 15 hours, fined her and threatened to kill her if she went on making inquiries	Taken from his home

Name & Place of "disappearance"	Age	Date	Profession	Unit named as responsible	Inquiries initiated with*	Response from Government	Other details
MARTINEZ, Reymundo (*Caserío* El Julec, Santa Ana, Petén)		18.11.?		Linces Batallion of Poptún Brigade			Detained with several others; one man killed
MARTINEZ, Rodrigo (*Caserío* El Julec, Santa Ana, Petén)		,,		,, ,,			,, ,,
MAYORGA MOLINA, Luis (Santa Lucía Cotzumalguapa, Escuintla)	24	16.09.82	Carpenter		Looked for in several places		Same details as for Edgar Eduardo Fajardo (see above)
MEJIA LORENZO, Simeón (San Martín Jilotepeque, Chimaltenango)	25	20.12.81	Farmworker / truck driver	Judicial Police in plain clothes	Via the GAM		He drove trucks from San Martín to the capital. Captors were waiting for him when he arrived in San Martín
MEJIA XON, Tomás (Place not known)	19	25.01.81	Shoeshiner				He went to work in the capital and never returned
MEJIA YAT, Domingo (*Finca* Milán, Mazatenango, Suchitepéquez)	25	27.02.81	Day labourer	Army			Soldiers who guarded the *finca* came asking for him and took him away

Name & Place of "disappearance"	Age	Date	Profession	Unit named as responsible	Inquiries initiated with*	Response from Government	Other details
MENDEZ, Carlos Rodrigo (Road to Olintepeque, Quetzaltenango)	16	14.04.83	Student	Army	Quetzaltenango military base		He had witnessed the abduction of Miguel Angel Gramajo y Gramajo and cousin (see above). Next day he himself was abducted by same men. A note was received from him saying he was at Quetzaltenango military base. Recipient of the note was later sought by hooded men
MENDEZ DE SANTIZO, Luz Hayde (Haydée) (Colonia San Francisco, Zone 19, Guatemala City)	36	08.03.84	Housewife	Army (G-2)	Neighbours rang 4th National Police Station to report disturbance in the area	Police said it was an army operation (men themselves said they were government agents)	Armed men went to house and stayed there for eight hours. Believed to be waiting for husband, professor at the USAC who did not turn up
MIRANDA AGUILAR, Edelfino Israel (Aldea San Ignacio, Nuevo Progreso, San Marcos)	28	19.03.83	Day labourer	Army	Local authorities in Nuevo Progreso		Taken away at 4am

Name & Place of "disappearance"	Age	Date	Profession	Unit named as responsible	Inquiries initiated with*	Response from Government	Other details
MIZA CALI, Agusto (San José Poaquil, Chimaltenango)		25.06.84	Farmworker	Soldiers from San José Poaquil military detachment	Military detachment at San José Poaquil	Detention denied	The army called people together in front of town hall and took him away
MORALES, Arnulfo Gabriel (San José Poaquil, Chimaltenango)	35	01.08.84	Bricklayer and carpenter	Military detachment at San José Poaquil (name of commander known)			Was summoned to local army base at San José Poaquil by commander to do some urgent work and never came back. Local mayor also believed to have been involved
MORALES, Maynor Rigoberto (Zone 19, Guatemala City)	18	04.10.84	Video student	DIT			Abducted from home together with father, Rigoberto Morales Garrido (see below), and removed in car with smoked glass windows
MORALES, Rufino (Aldea El Molino, San Martín Jilotepeque, Chimaltenango)	15	07.09.82	Farmworker	Army			Relatives saw him being taken away
MORALES AMBROCIO, Tomasa (Place not known)	22	29.03.82	Domestic servant	Army			Taken from home by army travelling in three trucks

Name & Place of "disappearance"	Age	Date	Profession	Unit named as responsible	Inquiries initiated with*	Response from Government	Other details
MORALES CALEL, Manuel (*Cantón* Agua Escondida, Chichicastenango, Quiché)	49	29.03.81	Farmworker	100 soldiers			Abduction witnessed by relatives
MORALES CASTILLO, Juan Carlos (Zone 1, Guatemala City)	23	27.04.84	Student of business administration and employee of SIECA	Armed men in plainclothes			Taken from home together with wife, Carmen Morales de Morales, and maid, María Rosalía Xiloj, (see below)
MORALES DE MORALES, Carmen (Zone 1, Guatemala City)		27.04.84		" "			Same details as for Juan Carlos Morales Castillo (see above)
MORALES GARRIDO, Rigoberto (Zone 19, Guatemala City)	45	04.10.84	Surveyor	DIT			Same details as for his son, Maynor R. Morales (see above)
MORALES PAREDES, Marcelino (*Aldea* El Molino, San Martín Jilotepeque, Chimaltenango)	32	07.09.?	Farmworker	Army	Various military detachments		Many neighbours saw him being taken away handcuffed by the army as he was on his way to work

Name & Place of "disappearance"	Age	Date	Profession	Unit named as responsible	Inquiries initiated with*	Response from Government	Other details
MORALES SUT, Tomás (*Cantón* Agua Escondida, Chichicastenango, Quiché)	15	01.11.81	Day labourer	Judicial Police			
MORALES XAPPORT, Andrés (San Martín Jilotepeque, Chimaltenango)	30	04.03.82	Farmworker/ peasant	Military commissioner (name known)			Told to go to oratory by military commissioner in order to go on patrol. Never returned
MURALLES GARCIA, Jorge Hiram (Barrio Monterrey, Retalhuleu)	29	03.01.84	Teacher	DIT	General Mejía V., Minister of the Interior and others	Detention denied; said that investigations were being made	About 21 armed men abducted him from his home in the presence of his family
ORDON, Carlos (San Martín Jilotepeque, Chimaltenango)	27	28.11.81	Farmworker	Soldiers	Inquiries made at police stations and army bases in San Martín Jilotepeque and Chimaltenango	Detention denied	Detained by a group of soldiers in San Martín Market; witnessed by many people. His brother, Emilio Ordón, had been abducted two days earlier (see below)

Name & Place of "disappearance"	Age	Date	Profession	Unit named as responsible	Inquiries initiated with*	Response from Government	Other details
ORDON, Emilio (San Martín Jilotepeque, Chimaltenango)	26	26.11.81	Farmworker	Soldiers	Police station and army base in Chimaltenango	Detention denied	Taken from his home in presence of his mother. Brother Carlos abducted two days later (see above). Other brother Genaro abducted in 1980 (see below). Father of all three murdered in 1980
ORDON, Genaro (San Martín Jilotepeque, Chimaltenango)	19	24.05.80	Farmworker		Inquiries made at police stations and army bases		Precise details of circumstances of abduction are not known. Brothers Carlos and Emilio abducted in 1981 (see above)
ORDOÑEZ, Rodrigo (Santa Ana, Petén)	27	13.06.84	Football player		Authorities in Petén		Went out to get birth certificate for his baby son at Santa Ana, Petén town hall and never returned
ORDOÑEZ VICENTE, José Alfredo (*Finca* Palmira, Colombo Costa Cuca, Quetzaltenango)	23	16.08.80		Army			

Name & Place of "disappearance"	Age	Date	Profession	Unit named as responsible	Inquiries initiated with*	Response from Government	Other details
ORELLANA, Gertrudes (*Caserío* El Julec, Santa Ana, Petén)		18.11.?		Los Linces Battalion, Poptún Brigade			Detained with several others; one man killed
OSORIO MENDOZA, Jacinto (*Finca* Milán, Chicacao, Suchitepéquez)	36	27.02.81	Farmworker	Army	No inquiries made		Taken away in front of family. Soldiers stayed to guard the *finca* and ate in their house
PAR IXCOL, Juan Buenaventura (*Comunidad Agraria*, San Pablo Jocopilas, Suchitepéquez)	23	24.09.82	Day labourer	Army	National Police and Military Police in Mazatenango	Detention denied	Abducted from home in presence of witnesses. Threatened to take them also if they tried to stop them taking him
PARABAL JURACAN, Tomás (*Aldea* Zacaleu, Tecpán, Chimaltenango)	18	15.08.81	Farmworker	Army	No inquiries made		Plainclothes army officers detained him as he was walking through village. Believed to have been taken to capital
PEREZ ALVARADO, José Adán (*Caserío* El Julec, Santa Ana, Petén)		18.11.?		Los Linces Battalion, Poptún Brigade			Detained with several others; one man killed
PEREZ TZEJ, José Petronilo (Mazatenango, Suchitepéquez)	64	20.12.82	Farmworker	Men in plain clothes	National Police and No. 13 army base in Mazatenango		Went to Mazatenango to do some shopping and did not return

Name & Place of "disappearance"	Age	Date	Profession	Unit named as responsible	Inquiries initiated with*	Response from Government	Other details
PEREZ VILLASEÑOR, Rosa Estela (Zone 10, Guatemala City)	32	03.05.83	Secretary at Centre for Folklore Studies at the USAC	Four men armed with machine-guns	Inquiries made of government authorities, at hospitals and morgues, of press etc. and Human Rights Commission of Constituent Assembly	Vice-Minister of the Interior at time, Haroldo Cabrera Enríquez, told relatives that many others had "disappeared" and all they could do was to "ask God"	On her way to Café Zurich when she was pushed into a car in front of witnesses. At first believed to be held under Decree Law 46-82
PINEDA MARTINEZ, Amilcar (Caserío El Julec, Santa Ana, Petén)		25.11.?		Los Linces Battalion, Poptún Brigade			Detained with two brothers, Fernando and Avelino (see below), and Adán Fabián Sagastume (see below). Other brother, Clemente, left dead at door of house
PINEDA MARTINEZ, Avelino		25.11.?		" "			Details same as for Amilcar Pineda Martínez (see above)
PINEDA MARTINEZ, Fernando		25.11.?		" "			" "

Name & Place of "disappearance"	Age	Date	Profession	Unit named as responsible	Inquiries initiated with*	Response from Government	Other details
POPOL SIQUINAJAY, Inocente (San Andrés Itzapa, Chimaltenango)	22	28.08.83	Day labourer	Military commissioners (names known)	Appeals to President Ríos Montt and others via the GAM		Taken to local prison at first and next day transferred to Military Zone No. 3. Not involved in politics; motive believed to be revenge (reasons not known)
QUIEJ, Enrique Ceferino (*Finca* el Pensamiento, Chubá, Quetzaltenango)		14.07.80	Farmworker/ postal worker	Army	Military base at Colomba Costa Cuca		Captured at 5am as he was taking post from Palmira to Colomba
RABINAL CHAN, José Inés (Tecpán, Chimaltenango)	60	15.01.82	Commercial transport worker	Armed civilians	Local authorities and via the GAM		His two children saw him being abducted
RABINAL TUCUBAL, Mario (*Aldea* Zacaleu, Tecpán, Chimaltenango)	34	28.12.81	Driver	Two men in plain clothes plus soldiers	Inquiries made directly of authorities and via the GAM		Arrested in the presence of witnesses

Name & Place of "disappearance"	Age	Date	Profession	Unit named as responsible	Inquiries initiated with*	Response from Government	Other details
RAMIREZ GALVEZ, Carlos Guillermo (Zone 21, Guatemala City)	20	14.02.84	Student at Technical Training Institute (INTECAP), practising at Roosevelt Hospital	DIT	Letter to President Mejía asking for his intervention		Captors arrived at house in two cars, surrounded it and banged on doors and windows with guns. Tied him up and tortured him with electric shocks in front of witnesses. Men planted fragmentation bombs in his clothes and pretended they had found them
RAMOS, Telesforo Isidro (Ixcán, Playa Grande, Quiché)	34	22.01.82	Farmworker				Left home to go to work and never came back
RIVAS MARTINEZ, Oscar Rolando (Zone 11, Guatemala City)	33	16.02.82	Doctor and surgeon; professor at the USAC		DIT, National Police		Left home in minibus to go to pick up results of laboratory test at Cancer Hospital. "Disappeared" together with vehicle

Name & Place of "disappearance"	Age	Date	Profession	Unit named as responsible	Inquiries initiated with*	Response from Government	Other details
RODAS ALVAREZ, Gustavo (Raxruja, Cobán, Alta Verapaz)	30	21.06.81	Driver	Three men in a jeep	Fray Bartolomé De Las Casas Police Station in Cobán; Detective Corps, Guatemala City		He was sleeping in his truck when the men arrived and offered to sell him some corn. Two of them got in truck with him and said they would show him where it was. Set off towards Sebol, where the truck was found burned out
ROQUEL TUYUC, Gabriel (Cantón 1°, San Juan Comalapa, Chimaltenango)	30	10.01.82	Farmworker	Army	Several letters and telegrams taken to National Palace personally	Negative	Abducted from his home in presence of family and neighbours
SAENZ CALITO, Edgar Enrique (Zone 1, Guatemala City)	34	09.06.81	Agronomist	Comando 6 or G-2	Appeals to President Lucas, which the latter passed on to Minister of the Interior Alvarez Ruiz, who passed them on to Director General of National Police		He was arrested by 2nd National Police Corps but absolved by courts of charges. On being released, in the company of relatives he was abducted one block from the police station. Brother was in Pavón Prison at the time, accused of guerrilla activities

Name & Place of "disappearance"	Age	Date	Profession	Unit named as responsible	Inquiries initiated with*	Response from Government	Other details
SAGASTUME, Adán Fabián (*Caserío* El Julec, Santa Ana, Petén)		25.11.?		Los Linces Battalion, Poptún Brigade			Detained with the Pineda Martínez brothers (see above)
SALANIC CHIGUIL, Manuel Ismael (Zone 12, Guatemala City)	18	13.02.84	Student at Instituto Rafael Aqueche	Uniformed BROE plus others in plain clothes	Ministry of the Interior; National Police; DIT; President Mejía; Tripartite Commission	Detention denied; Tripartite Commission said they would investigate	20 armed men broke into house in middle of night, threatened family and took him away. Also took documents and other belongings.
SALAZAR, Rafael (*Finca* La Merced, San Martín Jilotepeque, Chimaltenango)	38	10.10.82	Farmworker	Civil Defence patrol	Military detachment in San Martín Jilotepeque	Detention denied	Abducted from his plot of land in front of relatives and taken to San Martín Jilotepeque military detachment
SANDOVAL, Eulalio (*Caserío* El Julec, Santa Ana, Petén)		18.11.?		Los Linces Battalion, Poptún Brigade			Detained with several others; one man killed

Name & Place of "disappearance"	Age	Date	Profession	Unit named as responsible	Inquiries initiated with*	Response from Government	Other details
SANDOVAL, Luis (*Caserío* El Julec, Santa Ana, Petén)		18.11.?		" "			Same details as for Eulalio Sandoval (see above)
SENTE CALEL, Manuel (Chichicastenango, Quiché)	24	03.12.81	Street vendor	Armed men	Police	No response	Men pushed him into car while he was out selling
SHON CATIZ, Pedro [=Chupol?], (Chopol [=Chupol?], Chichicastenango, Quiché)	28	18.05.82	Street vendor	Army			Was on his way to Chichicastenango in truck when he was forced to get out
SICAY PAVO, Antonio (*Finca* Soledad, La Concha, Chicacao, Suchitepéquez)	28	11.10.82	Day labourer	Army	Authorities in Mazatenango and Quetzaltenango		Soldiers burst into his home and took him away by force, saying if he had done nothing he would be back but if he had he would not return
SIRIN, Juan (*Finca* Urizabal, Santo Domingo, Suchitepéquez)	57	09.07.83	Day labourer	Army	Mazatenango Military Zone barracks	Colonel at barracks at first denied he was being held but later said he was. Told them to go and talk to another colonel	Abducted from the *finca* where he lived and worked
SIRIN CALI, Juan (San José Poaquil, Chimaltenango)	32	05.03.82	Day labourer	Army			Abducted from home in front of family

Name & Place of "disappearance"	Age	Date	Profession	Unit named as responsible	Inquiries initiated with*	Response from Government	Other details
SOLARES CASTILLO, Ileana del Rosario (Zone 11, Guatemala City)	24	25.09.82	Accountant	Security forces (G-2)	Many authorities of the Ríos Montt and Mejía administrations	Detention denied although family claim it was tacitly acknowledged by the Ríos Montt administration	Detained while driving her car. Reportedly seen in secret detention by "public employee". Also seen by ex-prisoner, María Cruz López Rodríguez, who was tried under Decree Law 46-82 while she was held in what she believed to be the old *Escuela Politécnica* in capital. Was in poor health at time of arrest
SOLOMAN, Mariana (*Finca* El Recuerdo, San Miguel Pochuta, Pochuta Chimaltenango)	30	17.02.83	Housewife	Armed men in plain clothes	Military detachment at Chimaltenango, National Police, Military Reserves	Detention denied	Abducted from her home in presence of husband and children. Her brother, Santos, had been abducted four days earlier (see below)
SOLOMAN, Santos (*Caserío* La Unión, San Miguel Pochuta, Chimaltenango)	21	13.02.83	Day labourer	" "	" "	" "	Abducted from his home in the presence of his mother. Had previously been detained and held in Patulul military detachment. Sister Mariana detained four days later (see above)

Name & Place of "disappearance"	Age	Date	Profession	Unit named as responsible	Inquiries initiated with*	Response from Government	Other details
SUT BOCAL, Juan (Zone 4, Guatemala City)	52	22.05.82	Day labourer	Judicial Police			Went to capital to sell produce and was detained at the bus terminus in Zone 4
SUT BOZEL, Tomás (Km. 106, *Cantón* Agua Escondida, Chichicastenango, Quiché)	26	17.02.82	Haberdasher	Soldiers			A group of of about 50 soldiers arrived with five tanks and two trucks and took him away in presence of wife, then burned their house down and wife and children had to flee to the mountains
SUT GUARCAS, Juan (San Juan Comalapa, Chimaltenango)	47	05.07.82	Shop owner	Security forces			Was abducted from his shop
SUTUY ACQUIJAY, Celestino (*Aldea* El Molino, San Martín Jilotepeque, Chimaltenango)	37	07.09.82	Farmworker	Army			Abducted in presence of mother and many others together with three others
SUTUY ACQUIJAY, Rafael (Place not known)	24	04.10.82	Farmworker	Military commissioner (name known)			Abducted in the presence of witnesses from home and taken to nearby village

Name & Place of "disappearance"	Age	Date	Profession	Unit named as responsible	Inquiries initiated with*	Response from Government	Other details
TCHAJ SAJCATUN, Clemente (Parque Central, Comalapa, Chimaltenango)	17	08.04.82	Farmworker	Army	Military bases, National Police, prisons, Congress, President	Told by army official he may have been taken to the local military headquarters	Abducted on Maundy Thursday from a park in the presence of parents
TOJ, Paulino (Tactic, Alta Verapaz)	58	25.09.83	Farmworker	Military commissioner from Tactic (name known)	Authorities in Tactic, Pululá, Cobán and Salamá		He had been ordered to participate in the civilian patrols and had refused to do so
TOL AJQUEY, Custodio (? Tecpán, Chimaltenango?)		28.01.82	Day labourer and street vendor	Army	Local authorities including military commissioner		Detained on market-day as he was selling his produce. Seen in local military detachment
TOL CHABALAN, José (Main Square, Tecpán, Chimaltenango)	25	28.01.82	Farmworker	Armed civilians	Military detachment in Tecpán	Detention denied	Abducted and taken to military detachment at Tecpán. Witnessed by father
TOL LARES, Diego (Tecpán, Chimaltenango)	40	21.01.82	Day labourer and member of cooperative	Army			Put in lorry and taken away in presence of wife
TOL RABINAL, Santiago (Main Square, Tecpán, Chimaltenango)	33	28.01.82	Day labourer and street vendor	Army	Local authorities and comisionado militar (military commissioner)		Detained while selling produce in Tecpán square. Seen in local military detachment by others. Detained together with Custodio Tol Ajquey and José Tol Chabalan (see above)

Name & Place of "disappearance"	Age	Date	Profession	Unit named as responsible	Inquiries initiated with*	Response from Government	Other details
TUCUBAL SALAZAR, Eladio (*Aldea* Pacorral, Tecpán, Chimaltenango)	29	20.08.81	Primary school teacher	Judicial Police	Police, local authorities, President Ríos Montt		Abducted from home at night; captors also robbed family
VASQUY LOPEZ, Marino Alejandro (*Aldea* San Ignacio, Nuevo Progreso, San Marcos)	25	19.03.83	Farmworker	Army	Village mayor and other local authorities		Taken from home in front of his mother and grandmother
VELASQUEZ BAUTISTA, Oscar Leonel (Colonia Santa Marta, Zone 19, Guatemala City)	34	31.10.83	Mechanic	Eight armed men	Various authorities	Detention denied	Detained near his home and taken there. Captors also took things from house. Returned three days later and removed more things
VELASQUEZ OSORIO, Diego (*Cantón* Concepción, Chimán, Chicacao, Suchitepéquez)	30	28.02.82	Driver	A group of armed men, some in plain clothes and some in olive green uniforms	Inquiries made in Mazatenango, Quetzaltenango, Pavón Prison, etc.		On his way to visit another village when he was intercepted and taken onto a coffee plantation. Told he was held at *Finca* Medellín, Chicacao

Name & Place of "disappearance"	Age	Date	Profession	Unit named as responsible	Inquiries initiated with*	Response from Government	Other details
VELASQUEZ SOTO, Jorge Alfonso (Zone 1, Guatemala City)	28	28.11.83	Solderer	Army	Various authorities	Negative	Abducted by eight armed men who beat him up and removed him in direction of Justo Rufino Barrios military barracks. On 1 December they took him to his home and ransacked it before taking him away again
VICENTE, Felipe Matías (*Finca* El Pensamiento, Colomba Costa Cuca, Quetzaltenango)	30	16.08.80	Farmworker	Army			
XAGIL HERNANDEZ, Cristóbal (Paraje Chipila, Estancia La Virgen, San Martín Jilotepeque, Chimaltenango)	35	28.12.81	Farmworker	Army	Military detachment at San Martín Jilotepeque	Dention denied	Stopped at a military checkpoint while driving his truck
XILOJ, María Rosalía (Zone 1, Guatemala City)		27.04.84	Domestic servant	Armed men in plain clothes			Abducted together with Juan Carlos Morales Castillo and his wife (see above)

Name & Place of "disappearance"	Age	Date	Profession	Unit named as responsible	Inquiries initiated with*	Response from Government	Other details
XOM CALEL, Manuel (Panimaché, Chichicastenango, Quiché)	17	11.03.81	Farmworker	Army			Abducted together with brother Miguel (see below) during a military operation
XOM CALEL, Miguel (Panimaché, Chichicastenango, Quiché)	19	11.03.81	Farmworker	Army			Abducted together with brother Manuel (see above)
XUM IXCOL, Juan (Chicacao, Suchitepéquez)	27	26.04.82	Driver and mechanic	Army	Various authorities	Detention denied	Abducted in front of many witnesses. Reportedly handed over to army command at *Finca* Corona
ZAMORA MEDA, César Felicito (*Aldea* "El Jocotillo", Villa Canales, Guatemala dept.)	15	31.12.84	School student	Army (G-2 or DIT)	Telegrams to President Mejía; appeals via the press, prisons and many other authorities		Abducted together with brothers Oscar Noé and Rafael Libardo as they were returning from their father's *finca* in *aldea* El Jocotillo, together with a 17-year-old friend, Edwin Rogelio Cu Mérida. A witness managed to escape

Name & Place of "disappearance"	Age	Date	Profession	Unit named as responsible	Inquiries initiated with*	Response from Government	Other details
ZAMORA MEDA, Oscar Noé (*Aldea* "El Jocotillo", Villa Canales, Guatemala dept.)	13	31.12.84	School student	" "	" "		Abducted together with brothers César (see above) and Rafael (see below)
ZAMORA MEDA, Rafael Libardo (*Aldea* "El Jocotillo", Villa Canales, Guatemala dept.)	18	31.12.84	Student	" "	" "		Abducted together with brothers César and Oscar (see above)
ZAMORA SANTOS, Gustavo Adolfo (Santa Ana, Petén)	25	24.08.83	Farmworker	Military commissioner from Santa Ana, Petén (name known) together with a group of armed masked men	Many authorities, including President Mejía		Abducted from home together with brothers José Lizandro and Rolando Arnulfo. Reportedly taken to Poptún military base
ZAMORA SANTOS, José Lizandro	23	24.08.83	"	" "	" "		See Gustavo Adolfo Zamora Santos above
ZAMORA SANTOS, Rolando Arnulfo	31	24.08.83	"	" "	" "		" "

Appendix VI

I Partial list of staff and students at the university of San Carlos (USAC) reported to Amnesty International as having been the victims of 'disappearance' or extrajudicial execution under the administrations of General Romeo Lucas García (July 1978 to March 1982) and General Efrain Ríos Montt (March 1982 to August 1983)

1. **Herdelbert Gerónimo Leal Feddek,** ex-professor of psychology at the USAC, "disappeared" on 5 August 1983 in Guatemala City.
2. **Ana Lucrecia Orellana Stormont,** lecturer in psychology at the Faculty of Medicine at the USAC, "disappeared" in Guatemala City on 6 June 1983. Unconfirmed reports suggest that she is in secret detention in the Matamoros Barracks in Guatemala City.
3. **Edgar Raúl Rivas Rodríguez,** ex-lecturer at the USAC, "disappeared" in Guatemala City on 6 June 1983.
4. **Dr Ernesto Joaquín Gutiérrez Castellanos,** former supervisor of the *Ejercicio Profesional Supervisado,* a program run by the USAC for sending medical and dental students to rural areas to gain practical experience before graduating, "disappeared" in Guatemala City on 3 May 1983.
5. **Rosa Estela Pérez Villaseñor,** secretary at the *Centro de Estudios Folklóricos,* Centre for Folklore Studies, at the USAC and member of the *Asociación de Secretarias de Guatemala,* Guatemalan Secretaries' Association, "disappeared" in Guatemala City on 3 May 1983.
6. **Rolando Enrique Medina,** professor of history at the USAC, "disappeared" in Guatemala City on 28 September 1982.
7. **Graciela Morales Herrera,** Treasurer of the Faculty of Economics at the USAC for 27 years, and her three children, Gloria, Maritza and José Samayoa Morales, "disappeared" in Guatemala City on 11 September 1982. (Her remaining son was killed in February 1984—see Part II, No.7.)
8. **Guillermo Toralla Loarca,** lecturer at the Humanities Faculty at the USAC, "disappeared" in Guatemala City on 22 May 1982.
9. **Dr Octavio Cajas Sosa,** Director of Epidemiology at the Faculty of Medicine at the USAC, "disappeared" on 2 March 1982. His body was identified by his family in an unmarked grave in La Verbena Cemetery, Guatemala City on 25 April 1982.
10. **Dr Emil Bustamente,** doctor of veterinary sciences and director of the regional centres of the USAC, "disappeared" between Santa Catarina Pinula and Guatemala City on 13 February 1982.
11. **Mario Roberto Bendfeldt Zachrisson,** professor at the Faculty of Architecture of the USAC, "disappeared" in Guatemala City on 1 September 1981. In April 1983 the then Guatemalan Ambassador in Washington, Jorge Luis Zelaya Coronado, told Amnesty International that, "from information unofficially revealed by an official in the previous adminis-

tration, it could be concluded that the architect Bendfeldt Zachrisson died shortly after his "disappearance". This information is known by the Bendfeldt family in Guatemala." No further details were given about how his death occurred and Amnesty International does not consider this to be a satisfactory explanation of what happened to him.

12. **Oscar Bonilla, Carlos Amancio Ortiz and Carlos Enrique Tuch,** all lecturers in the Faculty of Law at the USAC, were shot dead on 7 May 1981.

13. **Jorge Romero Imeri,** Dean of the School of Political Science at the USAC, "disappeared" on 14 March 1981 in Guatemala City. His body was identified by his wife on 11 June 1981 after being exhumed from a grave in Mazatenango where it had been buried after being found floating in the Siguacán River.

14. **Jorge Palacio Motta,** professor of law at the USAC, was shot dead in Guatemala City on 4 March 1981.

15. **Guillermo Alfonso Monzón Paz,** professor of law at the USAC, was shot dead in Guatemala City on 27 February 1981.

16. **José Gerardo Reyes Alvarez,** lecturer at the USAC, was shot dead in Guatemala City on 26 February 1981.

17. **Mario Arnoldo Castro Pérez,** former President of the Association of Law Students at the USAC, was shot dead in Guatemala City on 25 February 1981.

In all the above cases Amnesty International believes that there is evidence to suggest that the Guatemalan military or security forces, or paramilitary groups acting in conjunction with them, were responsible for the reported human rights abuses.

II Partial list of staff and students at the University of San Carlos (USAC) reported to Amnesty International as having been the victims of 'disappearance' or extrajudicial execution under the administration of General Oscar Humberto Mejía Víctores (August 1983 to March 1984)

1. **Dr Gustavo Adolfo Meza Soberanis,** aged 26, a surgeon and doctor with his own clinic in Cobán, Alta Verapaz, who graduated from the USAC in 1982, "disappeared" in Zone 12 of Guatemala City on 7 September 1983. Next day his sister:

2. **Mayra Janneth Meza Soberanis,** aged 23, a psychology student at the USAC, was abducted in the same part of the city. In both cases the assailants were armed and driving vans with smoked glass windows. *Habeas corpus* petitions presented by the family achieved nothing. She was later released and then abducted again on 25 January 1985, and found dead the next day with her throat cut.

3. **Marco Antonio Quiñonez Flores,** aged 33, a law student in the Faculty of Juridical and Social Sciences at the USAC, was abducted from his home in Amatitlán in the early hours of 8 September 1983 by six to eight

armed men. He was taken away in his own car, wearing only his pyjamas. The car was found later that day on the road to Escuintla. His present whereabouts are not known. At the time of his "disappearance" he was about to sit his final law examinations.

4. **Luis René Juárez Villela (or Valladares)**, Director of the *Instituto América*, American Institute, in Guatemala City and ex-lecturer in the Schools of History and Communication Sciences at the USAC, "disappeared" on 9 September 1983 in Guatemala City. His present whereabouts are not known.

5. **Dr Benjamín Rolando Orantes Zelada**, a veterinary surgeon who had connections with the USAC, was found shot dead in a market near the airport in Guatemala City on 12 November 1983.

6. **Leonel Carrillo Reeves**, Dean of the School of Chemical Sciences and Pharmacy and ex-Rector of the USAC, was shot dead by unknown men on 25 November 1983 as he got out of his car on the university campus.

7. **Sergio Vinicio Samayoa Morales**, aged 29, an engineering student at the USAC who also worked for a coffee firm, was attacked and wounded near his office by unidentified armed men on 1 February 1984 and taken to the Roosevelt Hospital in the capital. That night about 10 armed men broke into the intensive care unit where he was being treated and took him away. His bullet-ridden body was found on 6 February on the road to Chinautla just outside the capital. He was the only remaining son of Graciela Morales Herrera (see No.7, Part I).

8. **Natael Isaías Fuentes Monzón**, aged 26, a student in the Faculty of Juridical and Social Sciences, "disappeared" in early February 1984 in Guatemala City.

9. **Alfredo Fernando Aguilar**, aged 25, a journalism student at the School of Communication Sciences at the USAC, "disappeared" in Guatemala City on 3 February 1984.

10. **Jorge David Calvo Drago**, aged 29, a political science student at the USAC and a member of the *Asociación de Estudiantes de Ciencias Políticas*, Association of Students of Political Sciences, was seized by heavily armed men from his home in the centre of Guatemala City on 14 February 1984. The previous day his father, Jorge Roberto Calvo Barajas, had been seized from his car in the centre of the city. As far as Amnesty International knows they are both still missing.

11. **Victor Hugo Quintanilla Ordoñez**, lawyer and legal adviser to a trade union federation, and his wife:

12. **Alma Lidia (or Libia) Samayoa Ramírez**, a doctor of dentistry, were abducted by armed men in Guatemala City on 19 February 1984. Both were members of the *Consejo Superior*, governing body of the USAC, between 1979 and 1982.

13. **Sergio Saúl Linares Morales**, aged 31, a civil engineer at the *Instituto de Fomento Municipal*, Municipal Institute of Public Works, lecturer at the Engineering Faculty at the USAC and member of the *Consejo Superior*, governing body of the USAC, was seized by armed men on 23 February 1984 in Guatemala City. His home was raided by armed men and some property removed.

14. **Luis Rodrigo Fernández,** an economic science student at the USAC, was abducted from the Roosevelt Hospital in Guatemala City at the end of February 1984. He had been admitted to the hospital six days before with bullet wounds. The Minister of the Interior said that there would be an investigation into why the orders that had been previously given to increase security at the hospital had not been carried out.

In all the above cases Amnesty International believes that there is evidence to suggest that the Guatemalan military or security forces, or paramilitary groups acting in conjunction with them, were responsible for the reported human rights abuses.

Appendix VII

Partial list of 'disappearances' reported to Amnesty International from August 1983 to November 1984

The following list details 107 representative cases of the several hundred "disappearances" which reportedly occurred between August 1983 when General Mejía Víctores came to power and November 1984. Writs of *habeas corpus* were filed in most of these cases but the authorities did not acknowledge the detention of any of those listed. This list was first published as an appendix to "'Disappearances' in Guatemala under the Government of General Oscar Humberto Mejía Víctores (August 1983–January 1985)" (AI Index AMR 34/01/85).

NAME	AGE	PROFESSION	DATE	DETAILS
Jorge Alberto Rosal Paz	28	Agronomist	12 August 1983	Reportedly taken away between Teculután and Zacapa by men in army uniform in an army jeep.
Gustavo Adolfo Zamora Santos	25	Farmer	24 August 1983	These brothers were taken from their home in Santa Ana, Nueva Flores, Petén by armed men in the presence of their mother, wives and children.
José Lizandro Zamora Santos	23	Farmer	24 August 1983	
Rolando Arnulfo Zamora Santos	32	Farmer	24 August 1983	
José Saturnino Pajarito Usen		Lutheran development worker	27 August 1983	Taken from office in Chimaltenango, with three others, by men in army uniform. Reportedly seen in local army base but authorities deny holding him.
Gustavo Adolfo Meza Soberanis	26	Surgeon and doctor	7 September 1983	Abducted by armed men in Zone 12, Guatemala City. He ran his own clinic in Cobán, Alta Verapaz.

NAME	AGE	PROFESSION	DATE	DETAILS
Mayra Janneth Meza Soberanis	23	Psychology student at USAC	8 September 1983	Abducted by armed men in the same area of the city as her brother Gustavo. (Later released but again abducted by armed men, on 25 January 1985, and found dead the next day on open land in Zone 11 with her throat cut.)
Marco Antonio Quiñonez Flores	33	Law student at the USAC	8 September 1983	Taken from his home in Colonia Lupita, Amatitlán in his pyjamas by armed men in his own car. Car later found on the outskirts of Escuintla.
Guadalupe Lara Pérez	28	Catechist/truck driver	8 September 1983	Abducted in Santa Lucía Cotzumalguapa, Escuintla from his truck by armed men and taken away in a white van.
Román Reyes Elias	37	Catechist	8 September 1983	Abducted from his home in Miriam, Santa Lucía Cotzumalguapa, Escuintla in his underclothes and driven away in a light blue van.
Julián Back Quiej	50	Catechist/farmer	14 September 1983	Abducted by armed men in El Rosario, Santa Lucía Cotzumalguapa, Escuintla in the presence of local priest and taken away in white van. Three days later he was taken away by his captors to the house of another catechist, who managed to escape.
Luis Jesús López Monzón	18		15 September 1983	Detained by uniformed police in a Guatemala City bus station in the presence of his brother and sister.

NAME	AGE	PROFESSION	DATE	DETAILS
César Giovanni Carias Solares	16	Student	21 September 1983	Abducted in Guatemala City at 7pm while out shopping. César and Herber Carias are brothers. Gustavo Dávila's mother reportedly received a secret message from her son saying that all four were being held by BROE at the National Police headquarters.
Herbert Orlando Carias Solares	13	Student	21 September 1983	
Gustavo Adolfo Dávila Valdez	20	Salesperson	21 September 1983	
Mario Rolando Pérez Canastuj	18	Salesperson	21 September 1983	
Socora España	38	Peasant	28 September 1983	Husband and wife. Taken away by uniformed soldiers in La Unión, El Petén.
Juan Gutiérrez	42	Peasant	28 September 1983	
Valentín Alvarado		Peasant	29 September 1983	All members of the same family. They were abducted from their homes in Chiquirines, Ocós, San Marcos by armed men.
Pablo Carreto		Peasant	29 September 1983	
Pedro Gómez Gómez		Peasant	29 September 1983	
Alberto Paz		Peasant	29 September 1983	
Jorge Paz		Peasant	29 September 1983	
Bartolomé Sales Marroquín		Peasant	29 September 1983	
Guillermo Alberto Boy Gallego	29	Farmer	27 October 1983	Abducted with four others from a house in Zone 11, Guatemala City by armed men. One of the vehicles used by the captors was reportedly seen in the DIT.
Oscar L. Velásquez Bautista	34	Mechanic	31 October 1983	Taken from home in Guatemala City by men in plain clothes who said they were from the authorities. He is a member of the Elim Church.
Cecilio Tejax Coj	36	Day labourer and trade unionist	6 November 1983	He was taken from a bus in Santa Lucía Cotzumalguapa, Escuintla in front of his wife and children by armed men who drove him away in a car with the number plates back to front. He was secretary of the union at the Finca Santa Rosa, Sumatán, Chimaltenango, where he worked.

NAME	AGE	PROFESSION	DATE	DETAILS
José Julio Cermeño Reyes	38	Trade union leader	12 November 1983	Precise circumstances not known but believed to have been abducted in Guatemala City by members of the security forces. He is legal adviser to the trade union at the Pantaleón Sugar Mill (see José López and Miguel Gómez).
Herminio Edelfo Ramos Pérez	24	Linguist working for US AID	mid-November 1983	Dragged from his home in Los Corrales, Quetzaltenango by seven armed men.
Ramiro Estrada López	37	Farmer	24 November 1983	All three were taken from their homes at Finca Palmera Xolhuitz, El Palmar, Quetzaltenango in the middle of the night by soldiers.
Salvador Ramírez Gramajo		Farmer	24 November 1983	
Filadelfo Ruano López	41	Farmer	24 November 1983	
José Luis López Bran	37	Electrician and trade unionist	27 November 1983	Both set off for Guatemala City to do their Christmas shopping but were stopped on the main road near the Pantaleón Sugar Mill, Escuintla, where they worked, by members of the security forces in plain clothes. They were both leaders of the trade union at the sugar mill.
Miguel Angel Gómez		Trade unionist	27 November 1983	
Jorge Alfonso Velásquez Soto	28	Solderer	28 November 1983	Detained by armed men who said they were members of the security forces in Zone 1, Guatemala City. On 1 December the same men brought Velásquez handcuffed to his home, ransacked the house and then took him away again.

NAME	AGE	PROFESSION	DATE	DETAILS
José Antonio Méndez Jiménez		Peasant	December 1983	These 10 men were detained in Huehuetenango department, the first in Ixtahuacán, the following four in La Cumbre, San Ildefonso Ixtahuacán and the remaining five in Polaja, San Ildefonso Ixtahuacán. They were all reportedly detained by the army and taken to Army Base No. 19 in Huehuetenango City. Others arrested with them were later released and reported that the 10 had been tortured. However, their arrest has never been acknowledged.
José Garcia Morales		Peasant	23 December 1983	
José Jiménez Ortiz		Peasant	23 December 1983	
Marcos Morales Felipe		Peasant	23 December 1983	
Antonio Sales Pérez		Peasant	23 December 1983	
Alonzo Lainez G.		Peasant	24 December 1983	
Pedro López R.		Peasant	24 December 1983	
Alonzo Maldonado L.		Peasant	24 December 1983	
Marcos Maldonado L.		Peasant	24 December 1983	
Miguel Ordoñes		Peasant	24 December 1983	
Alma Lucrecia Osorio Bobadilla	26	Student at the USAC	31 December 1983	Detained in Guatemala City by uniformed members of BROE who, a few days later, brought her back to her home, handcuffed and in a bad physical state, searched the house and then took her away again. They have nevertheless denied holding her.
Jorge Hiram Muralles García	29	Teacher	3 January 1984	Armed men in plain clothes burst into his home in Retalhuleu in the early morning and took him away half-dressed and handcuffed. The abduction was witnessed by several members of his family and by neighbours.
Darío Inocente Roldán Gómez	44	Farmer and manager of a cooperative savings bank	3 January 1984	Taken from his home in Retalhuleu by about 20 armed men who said they were from the Judicial Police and took him away in an official vehicle.
César Augusto Dávila Estrada	26	Ex-leader of trade union federation CNUS	3 January 1984	Abducted in the street in Guatemala City by BROE, who that night took him handcuffed to his home and proceeded to remove the entire contents in a truck.

NAME	AGE	PROFESSION	DATE	DETAILS
Tomás Baltazar		Peasant	3 January 1984	These eight men were all reportedly detained by the army in the department of Huehuetenango, the first two in Xoxlac, Barillas and the other six in Pojom, San Mateo Ixtatán. They are believed to be held at Ixquisis Army Base near Sachán, San Juan Ixcoy, Huehuetenango.
Pedro		Peasant	3 January 1984	
Francisco Mateo		Peasant	6 January 1984	
León Mateo		Peasant	6 January 1984	
Mateo Francisco		Peasant	12 January 1984	
Gaspar Mateo		Peasant	12 January 1984	
Francisco Pablo		Peasant	12 January 1984	
Francisco Miguel		Peasant	6 February 1984	
Juan García Godínez		Peasant	circa 15 January 1984	These five were reportedly arrested by the army around 15 January 1984, all in Huehuetenango department, the first three from Talajcheu, Cuate, San Juan Atitán, the fourth from Cojtón, San Juan Atitán and the fifth from Ixquilam, Cuata, San Juan Atitán. Their present whereabouts are not known but it is believed that they may have been taken to Army Base No. 19 in Huehuetenango City.
Diego García		Peasant	circa 15 January 1984	
José García		Peasant	circa 15 January 1984	
Rafael Rubén Domingo		Peasant/catechist	circa 15 January 1984	
Juan Domingo		Peasant	circa 15 January 1984	
Octavio René Guzmán Castañeda		Teacher	17 January 1984	Abducted by armed men from a health centre in Zone 19, Guatemala City.
Alejandro Del Cid Hernández		Trade unionist	26 January 1984	Both men, who are trade union leaders at the Mirandilla Sugar Mill in Escuintla, were removed by armed men from their homes.
José Guillermo García		Trade unionist	26 January 1984	
Jorge Mauricio Gatica Paz	27	Student	27 January 1984	Abducted by armed men in a shopping centre in Zone 11, Guatemala City. Reportedly seen alive in detention in April 1984. His brother Alan Gatica died on 10 February 1984 in mysterious circumstances while searching for him.

NAME	AGE	PROFESSION	DATE	DETAILS
Amancio Samuel Villatoro	47	Trade unionist	30 January 1984	Abducted as he was leaving his place of work in Zone 19, Guatemala City. The same day armed men went to his home and removed money and property. He was reportedly seen alive in a secret detention centre in the third week of March 1984 by escaped prisoner Alvaro René Sosa Ramos. Villatoro is ex-Secretary General of the union at the Adams' Products factory.
Alfonso Alvarado Palencia	44	Trade unionist and trade union adviser	31 January 1984	Abducted by armed men believed to have been members of DIT near Roosevelt Hospital, Guatemala City after attending a meeting with the union at CAVISA glass factory.
Alfredo Fernando Aguilar Tzoc	25	Journalism student at the USAC	3 February 1984	Precise circumstances not known but believed to have been abducted in Guatemala City by members of the security forces.
Carlos Guillermo Ramírez Galvez	19	Student at Technical Training Institute (INTECAP)	14 February 1984	Abducted by eight armed men from his home in Zone 21, Guatemala City in the presence of his family in the early hours of the morning. Allegedly tortured in front of parents and young brothers and sisters.
Natael Isaías Fuentes Monzón	25	Student at USAC and employee at the Peter Pan factory	16 February 1984	Abducted in Guatemala City by armed men as he set off to work. Ten minutes later four armed men entered his house with his keys and took away all of his belongings. Unconfirmed reports indicate he is alive and in a secret detention centre.

...civilians who drove them away in a blue car.

NAME	AGE	PROFESSION	DATE	DETAILS
Silverio Sacarín Sajbin Chiquín Manuel Sacarín	25	Tailor/catechist Tailor/catechist	26 July 1984 26 July 1984	These brothers were abducted in Guatemala City by armed men in a white pick-up van together with 23-year-old tailor and catechist Rosario Teni, who was pushed out of the vehicle later that day and shot dead in the street. Another catechist from Quiché, Cruz Santiago Vicente, was shot dead also on the same day.
Luciano Velásquez		Cigarette seller and catechist	26 August 1984	From Chajbal, Quiché. Abducted by armed civilians in Guatemala City.
Edgar Fernando García	25	Worker and trade union leader at the CAVISA glass factory (also trained teacher and ex-USAC student)	18 February 1984	Abducted in Zone 11, Guatemala City by members of BROE and the National Police and taken away in a white and light blue minibus. Unconfirmed reports indicate that he is alive and in a secret detention centre.
Victor Hugo Quintanilla Ordoñez	32	Law student and economics lecturer at the USAC	19 February 1984	Abducted at 8.30am by armed men in Zone 11, Guatemala City. From 1979 to 1982 both husband and wife were members of the *Consejo Superior*, Executive Council, of the USAC.
Alma Libia Samayoa Ramírez	29	Dentist and lecturer at the USAC	19 February 1984	
Sergio Saúl Linares Morales	31	Civil engineer and lecturer at the USAC (computer specialist)	23 February 1984	Abducted in Guatemala City by armed men as he was leaving work at the *Instituto de Fomento Municipal*, Municipal Institute of Public Works, to go to the USAC. The same day, uniformed police and men in plain clothes went to his home and, after breaking down the door, searched the house in the presence of his wife and his mother, who was beaten. Unconfirmed reports indicate he is alive and in a secret detention centre.
Luis Rodrigo Fernández		Economics student at USAC	late February 1984	Abducted by armed men from his sickbed in the Roosevelt Hospital, Guatemala City, to which he had been admitted six days earlier with bullet wounds.

NAME	AGE	PROFESSION	DATE	DETAILS
Luz Hayde (Haydée) Mendez de Santizo	36	Housewife	8 March 1984	Abducted from her home in Zone 19, Guatemala City by armed men who went there looking for her husband, USAC professor Marco Antonio Santizo Velásquez, who was not there. Neighbours who inquired at the Fourth National Police Station were told that the armed men were from the authorities and that they were conducting an investigation. Army intelligence (G-2) believed to be responsible.
Hugo de León Palacios	36	Teacher and law student at the USAC	9 March 1984	Abducted in Guatemala City as he was going to the school where he worked in the company of 30 of his young pupils, by four armed men who beat him up and took him away in a white car.
Edgar Leonel Domínguez Izas	30	Doctor	28 March 1984	Abducted by uniformed soldiers 15 minutes after leaving the private clinic at which he worked in Cantel, Quetzaltenango. The car in which he was taken away was later found abandoned. Unconfirmed reports indicate that he is alive and has been badly tortured in a secret detention centre.
Edgar Gerardo Rivera Arévalo	22	Student of journalism at the USAC	23 March 1984	Abducted by armed men after leaving his home in Zone 7, Guatemala City.
Alejandro Hernández González	27	Trade unionist and office worker	13 May 1984	Left home in Guatemala City at noon to meet some friends and never returned. He is

NAME	AGE	PROFESSION	DATE	DETAILS
Héctor Alirio Interiano Ortiz	28	Economics student and employee at the USAC	21 May 1984	Abducted by armed men as he was leaving work at the University Research Institute in Guatemala City. In 1978 he was leader of the *Asociación de Estudiantes Universitarios* (AEU), Association of University Students.
Gustavo Adolfo Castañon Fuentes	26	Accountant and economics student at the USAC	21 May 1984	Abducted by armed men near the university, Guatemala City.
Yolanda Consuelo Rodríguez Arteaga	54		July 1984	Both mother and daughter were removed by uniformed soldiers from a bus between Coatepeque and Retalhuleu while they were travelling from Quetzaltenango, where they lived, to Guatemala City.
Dina Patricia Cardoza Rodríguez	26		July 1984	
Eulogio Feliciano Juárez	65		13 July 1984	Father and son abducted together from their home in *Caserío* San Miguel Pajapa,

Amnesty International at work

The working methods of Amnesty International are based on the principle of international responsibility for the protection of human rights. The movement tries to take action wherever and whenever there are violations of those human rights falling within its mandate. Since it was founded, Amnesty International groups have intervened on behalf of more than 25,000 prisoners in over a hundred countries with widely differing ideologies.

A unique aspect of the work of Amnesty International groups—placing the emphasis on the need for *international* human rights work—is the fact that each group works on behalf of prisoners held in countries other than its own. At least two prisoner cases are assigned to each group; the cases are balanced geographically and politically to ensure impartiality.

There are now 3,341 local Amnesty International groups throughout the world. There are sections in 43 countries (in Africa, Asia, the Americas, Europe and the Middle East) and individual members, subscribers and supporters in more than 120 other countries. Members do not work on cases in their own countries. No section, group or member is expected to provide information on their own country and no section, group or member has any responsibility for action taken or statements issued by the international organization concerning their own country.

Continuous research

The movement attaches the highest importance to balanced and accurate reporting of facts. All its activities depend on meticulous research into allegations of human rights violations. The International Secretariat in London (with a staff of 175, comprising 30 nationalities) has a Research Department which collects and analyses information from a wide variety of sources. These include hundreds of newspapers and journals, government bulletins, transcriptions of radio broadcasts, reports from lawyers and humanitarian organizations, as well as letters from prisoners and their families. Amnesty International also sends fact-finding missions for on-the-spot investigations and to observe trials, meet prisoners and interview government officials. Amnesty International takes full responsibility for its published reports and if proved wrong on any point is prepared to issue a correction.

Once the relevant facts are established, information is sent to sections and groups for action. The members then start the work of trying to protect the individuals whose human rights are reported to have been violated. They send letters to government ministers and

234

embassies. They organize public meetings, arrange special publicity events, such as vigils at appropriate government offices or embassies, and try to interest newspapers in the cases they have taken up. They ask their friends and colleagues to help in the effort. They collect signatures for international petitions and raise money to send relief, such as medicine, food and clothing, to the prisoners and their families.

A permanent campaign

In addition to case work on behalf of individual prisoners, Amnesty International members campaign for the abolition of torture and the death penalty. This includes trying to prevent torture and executions when people have been taken to known torture centres or sentenced to death. Volunteers in dozens of countries can be alerted in such cases, and within hours hundreds of telegrams and other appeals can be on their way to the government, prison or detention centre.

Symbol of
Amnesty International

Amnesty International condemns as a matter of principle the torture and execution of prisoners by *anyone*, including opposition groups. Governments have the responsibility of dealing with such abuses, acting in conformity with international standards for the protection of human rights.

In its efforts to mobilize world public opinion, Amnesty International neither supports nor opposes economic or cultural boycotts. It *does* take a stand against the international transfer of military, police or security equipment and expertise likely to be used by recipient governments to detain prisoners of conscience and to inflict torture and carry out executions.

Amnesty International does not grade governments or countries according to their record on human rights. Not only does repression in various countries prevent the free flow of information about human rights abuses, but the techniques of repression and their impact vary widely. Instead of attempting comparisons, Amnesty International concentrates on trying to end the specific violations of human rights in each case.

Policy and funds

Amnesty International is a democratically run movement. Every two years major policy decisions are taken by an International Council comprising representatives from all the sections. They elect an International Executive Committee to carry out their decisions and supervise the day-to-day running of the International Secretariat.

The organization is financed by its members throughout the world, by individual subscriptions and donations. Members pay fees and conduct fund-raising campaigns—they organize concerts and art auctions and are often to be seen on fund-raising drives at street corners in their neighbourhoods.

Its rules about accepting donations are strict and ensure that any funds received by any part of the organization do not compromise it in any way, affect its integrity, make it dependent on any donor, or limit its freedom of activity.

The organization's accounts are audited annually and are published with its annual report.

Amnesty International has formal relations with the United Nations (ECOSOC), UNESCO, the Council of Europe, the Organization of African Unity and the Organization of American States.